A Reference Grammar of Dutch

A Reference Grammar of Dutch is aimed at English-speaking students of Dutch at beginner/intermediate level. It is designed to be practical and user-friendly: grammatical information is presented in short entries arranged in alphabetical order, allowing students to gain easy access to specific points of grammar or problematic points of vocabulary as they encounter them in practice. Each grammatical rule is illustrated by simple, everyday Dutch examples of the kind likely to be encountered and used by the learner. Specialised linguistic terminology is kept to a minimum, with a glossary of essential terms provided, and charts and tables are included to help the student focus on the main points. Each entry is linked to a set of exercises which are graded according to complexity, and there is a key to the exercises at the back of the book. A comprehensive index is also provided.

Carol Fehringer is Lecturer in German Linguistics and Dutch at the University of Newcastle upon Tyne. She has published articles on theoretical morphology and German and English dialects in a number of journals.

A Reference Grammar of
Dutch

with Exercises and Key

CAROL FEHRINGER
University of Newcastle upon Tyne

ANTONIO GARCIA FUERTE

CAMBRIDGE
UNIVERSITY PRESS

PUBLISHED BY THE PRESS SYNDICATE OF THE UNIVERSITY OF CAMBRIDGE
The Pitt Building, Trumpington Street, Cambridge CB2 1RP, United Kingdom

CAMBRIDGE UNIVERSITY PRESS
The Edinburgh Building, Cambridge, CB2 2RU, United Kingdom
40 West 20th Street, New York, NY 10011–4211, USA
477 Williamstown Road, Port Melbourne, VIC 3207, Australia
Ruiz de Alarcón 13, 28014 Madrid, Spain
Dock House, The Waterfront, Cape Town 8001, South Africa

First published 1999
Reprinted 2002, 2003

Printed in the United Kingdom at the University Press, Cambridge

Typeset in 10/12pt Monotype Baskerville and 9/12pt Frutiger   [SE]

A catalogue record for this book is available from the British Library

Library of Congress cataloguing in publication data

Fehringer, Carol
    A reference grammar of Dutch: with exercises and key / Carol
    Fehringer.
        p.   cm.
      ISBN 0 521 64253 1
        1. Dutch language – Grammar.   2. Dutch language – Textbooks for
    foreign speakers – English.   3. Dutch language – Grammar – Problems,
    exercises, etc.   I. Title.
    PF112.F44   1999
    439.31′82421 – dc21   98-11647 CIP

ISBN 0 521 64253 1 hardback
ISBN 0 521 64521 2 paperback

Contents

Foreword

The purpose and style of this book

The purpose of this book is to provide an accessible reference grammar of the Dutch language for English-speaking students of Dutch and to help consolidate their knowledge through practical exercises on a whole range of grammatical topics. It is intended both for beginners and for students at an intermediate level. In addition, advanced learners wishing to revise particular grammatical points may also benefit from this book. As the grammar is designed for practical use, linguistic terminology is kept to a minimum and only traditional grammatical terms are used. The book is divided into two main parts: Part 1: a reference grammar of Dutch; Part 2: a set of exercises relating to the grammatical problems dealt with in Part 1.

Part 1   Dutch reference grammar

The reference grammar is specifically designed to be practical and user-friendly. Grammatical points are explained in short separate entries arranged in alphabetical order. This allows the student to gain quick and easy access to a particular grammatical problem and to concentrate entirely on that problem without being confused by other related issues. In this way, the layout of the reference grammar is more like that of a dictionary than that of a traditional grammar.[1] In addition, for students preferring a 'basic-to-complex' progression, a didactic guide has been included at the beginning of the book which sets out the most important grammatical topics for a beginner (or intermediate student) to learn and suggests a possible order in which these should be tackled.

Although most of the points covered are grammatical, some entries deal with specific questions of vocabulary which cause difficulties when translating Dutch into English or vice versa. Each point is explained as concisely as possible and illustrated by the use of simple, everyday Dutch examples of the kind likely to be encountered and used by the learner. Some of the larger sections contain charts and tables to help the student focus on the main points in question. Unpredictable exceptions to rules and more complicated issues, which may be of interest to intermediate or more advanced learners, are dealt with at the end of each section and introduced by the symbol ▱▱ . At the end of the reference grammar there is a comprehensive index containing references to the entries and to more specific grammatical problems covered in the reference grammar.

Part 2   Exercises

Each entry is linked to an exercise or set of exercises specifically designed to practise a particular grammatical problem. In sections with more than one exercise, the first one

---

1 Compare M. Swan, *Practical English Usage* (Oxford: Oxford University Press, 1995) which has a similar layout

(**A**) concentrates on the recognition and understanding of particular Dutch forms. Students are required to explain the use of a specific form or construction and/or translate Dutch words and sentences into English. The second exercise (**B**) focuses on the application of the rules learned in the reference grammar. This involves filling in gaps, giving the correct forms of individual Dutch words, reformulating Dutch sentences etc. Exercise (**C**) consists of a free composition in which students are required to write short texts in Dutch.[2] There may also be a dialogue at the end of the section which serves as a basis for a reformulation or gap-fill exercise.

In the larger sections, each exercise is graded according to complexity. Exercises marked **1** are designed for beginners to intermediate students and deal with the straight-forward application of rules. Those marked **2** are aimed at intermediate to advanced students and include more complex constructions and exceptions to rules.

The exercise section is followed by a key to the exercises and an alphabetical list of common irregular verbs.[3]

---

2 Note that the instructions are deliberately general so that teachers can adapt (C) to the requirements of their students.

3 I also recommend the following Dutch grammars for English-speaking students: B. C. Donaldson, *Dutch: A Comprehensive Grammar* (London and New York: Routledge, 1997); W. Z. Shetter, *Dutch: An Essential Grammar* (London and New York: Routledge, 1994) and the accompanying exercise book by J. Delap and E. Stronks, *Beginning Dutch Workbook* (Groningen: Wolters-Noordhoff, 1993). Advanced students and teachers of Dutch may also wish to consult the following grammars written in the Dutch language: A. F. Florijn et al., *De regels van het Nederlands. Grammatica voor anderstaligen* (Groningen: Wolters-Noordhoff, 1994); A. M. Fontein and A. Pescher-ter Meer, *Nederlandse grammatica voor anderstaligen* (Utrecht: Nederlands Centrum Buitenlanders, 1993).

Acknowledgements

I would like to thank those teachers and colleagues in the German Department of the University of Manchester who first encouraged my interest in the Dutch language, in particular Professor Martin Durrell, Dr Kersti Börjars and Ms Irene Juurlink. My thanks are also due to friends and colleagues in the Department of German Studies, University of Newcastle upon Tyne, for their support during the writing of this book. I am particularly grateful to Dr Jonathan West for his many helpful comments and to Mr Mark Whitaker for his (much needed!) advice on word-processing techniques. In addition, I acknowledge with gratitude my debt to the Dutch Harting students Ms Annika Op 't Zandt, Ms Erica Kramer and Mr Ritske Zuidema, upon whose native-speaker intuition I have frequently called, and am especially grateful to Mr Theo van Lenthe in Groningen for his thorough reading of the manuscript and many useful suggestions. My thanks are also due to Dr Roel Vismans, Dr John Palmer, Gerdi Quist and Erna Eagar, whose comments and suggestions have been extremely helpful. Finally, I would like to thank my husband Gerhard not only for his sound practical advice but also for his moral support and encouragement which have been invaluable to me.

Grammatical terms

ABSTRACT NOUN A noun referring to an idea rather than to something concrete which one can see or touch, e.g. E. **beauty**, **honour**, D. **vrijheid**.

ACCENT In writing, a mark such as ´ or ` placed over a letter to indicate stress or differentiate one word from another, e.g. D. *één*.

ADJECTIVE A word used to describe a noun or pronoun, e.g. E. *a **pretty** woman, she is **clever***, D. *een **mooie** vrouw*.

ADVERB A word used to describe a verb or an adjective, e.g. E. *he speaks **quickly**, he is **surprisingly** good*, D. *hij spreekt **snel***.

AGENT The person or thing that carries out the action described by the verb, e.g. E. ***the boy** played tennis, I was arrested by **the police***, D. ***ik** schreef een brief*.

ARTICLE A word, such as *a* or *the* used before a noun (see DEFINITE ARTICLE and INDEFINITE ARTICLE).

AUXILIARY VERB A verb, such as *have* or *be*, which is used with other verbs to make different tenses, e.g. E. *I **have** worked*, D. *ik **heb** gewerkt, ik **ben** gegaan*.

BARE INFINITIVE In Dutch, the infinitive without *om* or *te*, e.g. D. *ik moet **gaan***.

CLAUSE The part of the sentence containing the finite verb (usually with a subject), e.g. E. *[John came round*₍Clause 1₎*] and [I made some tea*₍Clause 2₎*]*, D. *[de student werkt hard*₍Clause 1₎*] maar [hij krijgt steeds slechte cijfers*₍Clause 2₎*]*.

COLLECTIVE NOUN A singular noun which is used to refer to a whole group of people or things, e.g. E. *a **herd** (of cattle), the **police***, D. *de **familie***.

COMPARATIVE The form of the adjective used when comparing one person or thing to another, e.g. E. *John is **taller** than Peter*, D. *Jan is **groter** dan Piet*.

COMPOUND (WORD) A word made up of two or more other words which can also occur independently, e.g. E. *post + man = **postman***, D. *appel + boom = **appelboom***.

CONDITIONAL A tense used to refer to hypothetical situations in the future, e.g. E. *I **would go***, D. *ik **zou gaan***.

CONDITIONAL PERFECT A tense used to refer to hypothetical situations in the past, e.g. E. *I **would have done** it*, D. *ik **zou** het **gedaan hebben** / ik **had** het **gedaan***.

CONJUNCTION A word, such as **and**, **but**, **because**, **while** etc., which links clauses together, e.g. E. *John studies French **and** his friend studies German*, D. *ik studeer Duits **maar** ik vind het moeilijk*.

CONSONANT A speech sound, such as **p**, **t**, **g**, **d**, **s**, **f**, **l** etc. which is not a vowel or diphthong.

CO-ORDINATING CONJUNCTION A conjunction, such as D. **en**, **maar**, **want** etc., which does not affect word order (contrast SUBORDINATING CONJUNCTION).

DEFINITE ARTICLE A word (i.e. *the* in English) placed before a noun to make it definite or specific, e.g. E. *the man*, D. *de man, **het** huis* (contrast INDEFINITE ARTICLE).

DEMONSTRATIVE PRONOUN A word, such as *this, that, these* etc., which points out a specific person or thing, differentiating it from other similar members of its class, e.g. E. ***this** person*, D. ***deze** man, **dat** huis*.

DIMINUTIVE A word with a special ending used chiefly to indicate smallness, although it may also be used to express endearment or contempt, e.g. E. *pig**let**, dad**dy***, D. *kind**je***.

DIPHTHONG Two different vowel sounds occurring within the same syllable, e.g. E. *ai* in *wait*, *ou* in *house*, D. *ij* in *mijn*, *ui* in *huis*.

DIRECT OBJECT The direct recipient of the action described by the verb, e.g. E. *I read **the book**, I saw **my friend***, D. *hij schreef **een brief*** (contrast INDIRECT OBJECT).

FINITE VERB The part of the verb which may change its form to show person, number and tense. It usually occurs with a subject, e.g. E. *John **lives** abroad, he **went** to work*, D. *ik **ga** als jullie **gaan*** (contrast INFINITIVE).

FIRST PERSON The grammatical category of pronouns or verbs used by the speaker/writer to refer to himself/herself either alone or with others, e.g. E. ***I am**, **we are***, D. ***ik ben**, **wij zijn*** (contrast SECOND PERSON, THIRD PERSON).

FUTURE PERFECT A tense used to refer to completed actions in the future, e.g. E. *I **will have done** it by next week*, D. *ik **zal** het **gedaan hebben***.

FUTURE TENSE A tense used usually to refer to future time, e.g. E. *I **will do** it soon*, D. *ik **zal** het **doen***, or to express an assumption, e.g. E. *he **will be** there by now*.

GENDER (GRAMMATICAL GENDER) In Dutch, the use of special grammatical forms (e.g. different definite articles) to differentiate common gender nouns (i.e. old masculines and feminines) from neuter nouns, e.g. D. ***de** man, **de** vrouw, **het** kind*.

IMPERATIVE The form of the verb used to give an order or command, e.g. E. ***come** here!*, D. ***ga** weg!*

INDEFINITE ARTICLE A word (i.e. *a* in English) used to indicate that the following noun is not specific, e.g. E. ***a** man*, D. ***een** man* (contrast DEFINITE ARTICLE).

INDEFINITE PRONOUN A word, such as *some, somebody, any, every* etc., which refers to things that are not specific, e.g. E. ***some** people like jazz*, D. ***veel** studenten hebben geen geld*.

INDIRECT OBJECT (Usually a person.) The recipient of the direct object, e.g. E. *I gave the book to **the teacher**, I introduced my friend to **my parents***, D. *hij schreef een brief aan **zijn vriendin*** (contrast DIRECT OBJECT).

INFINITIVE The part of the verb which is always given in dictionaries and does not change its form to show person, number and tense, e.g. E. *to work, to go, to come*, D. *werk**en**, gaa**n**, kom**en***.

INSEPARABLE VERBS A set of Dutch verbs with the prefixes *be-, her-, ont-, ver-, ge-* and *er-*. These prefixes are never separated from the verb, e.g. D. *ik **be**grijp het, ik heb het **ver**taald* (contrast SEPARABLE VERBS).

INTRANSITIVE VERB A verb not taking a direct object, e.g. E. *he **died***, D. *ik **lachte*** (contrast TRANSITIVE VERB).

IRREGULAR Not following the normal rules, e.g. E. not ✗ *I teached* but *I **taught***, D. *ik **ging**, hij **zong*** (not ✗ *ik gaade*, ✗ *hij zingde*).

MAIN CLAUSE In Dutch, a clause which does not begin with a subordinating conjunction, e.g. D. ***ik heb gehoord** dat hij ziek is* (contrast SUBORDINATE CLAUSE).

MANNER An expression of manner describes *how* something happens, e.g. E. *he came **quickly**, I arrived **in a bad mood***, D. *hij gaat **met de trein***.

MODAL VERBS A set of verbs used, together with the infinitive form of other verbs, to express a range of moods such as volition, obligation, ability etc., e.g. E. *I **want** to go, he **can** do it*, D. *ik **wil** gaan, ik **moet** het doen*.

NOUN A word used to name a person, thing or concept. In English and Dutch, it may occur after an article and may be either singular or plural, e.g. E. *a **man**, the **boys**, **happiness***. D. *een **hond**, het **huis**, de **kinderen***.

NUMBER A term used to refer to the grammatical categories of singular and plural (see SINGULAR and PLURAL).

OBJECT (Obj.) (See DIRECT OBJECT and INDIRECT OBJECT.)

PARTICIPLE (See PRESENT PARTICIPLE and PAST PARTICIPLE.)

PASSIVE A grammatical construction used to shift the emphasis from the **agent** of the verb (i.e. the doer) to the **recipient** of the action described by the verb, e.g. E. ***I was praised by the teacher*** (as opposed to *the teacher praised me*). Often, the agent is left unspecified, e.g. ***the thief was arrested***, D. ***het wordt nooit gedaan***.

PAST PARTICIPLE The part of the verb used in the perfect, pluperfect and passive which does not change its form to show person and number, e.g. E. *they have **done** it, it was **written** yesterday*, D. *ik heb hard **gewerkt**, wij hebben niets **gezegd***.

PAST TENSE (SIMPLE PAST) A tense used to refer to past events, e.g. E. *I work**ed**, he **went***, D. *hij werk**te**, hij **ging***.

PERFECT TENSE A tense used to refer to actions in the past which are still relevant to the present, e.g. *I **have cleaned** the kitchen (and it is still clean)*, D. *ik **heb** de hele dag **gewerkt**, ik **ben** nooit in Amsterdam **geweest*** (contrast PLUPERFECT TENSE).

PERSON (See FIRST PERSON, SECOND PERSON and THIRD PERSON.)

PERSONAL PRONOUN A pronoun referring to one or more persons, e.g. E. ***I, you, he, they, me, him, them***, D. ***ik, jij, hij, wij, mij, hem, ons*** etc., or to inanimate objects, e.g. ***it, they, them***, D. ***het, hij, hem, ze*** etc.

PLUPERFECT TENSE A tense used to refer to events in the past which are no longer relevant to the present, e.g. *I **had cleaned** the kitchen (but it is now dirty again)*, D. *ik **had** de hele dag **gewerkt**, ik **was** nooit in Amsterdam **geweest*** (contrast PERFECT TENSE).

PLURAL (pl.) The grammatical form used to refer to more than one person, thing or concept, e.g. E. *the table**s**, **we were***, D. *twee mann**en**, **wij** werk**en*** (contrast SINGULAR).

POSSESSIVE PRONOUN A pronoun used to denote possession, e.g. E. ***my*** *house*, ***your*** *cat*, ***his*** *dog*, E. ***mijn*** *man*, ***jouw*** *vriend*, ***hun*** *kinderen*.

PREFIX Something that is attached to the beginning of a word, e.g. E. ***un**happy*, D. ***uit**gaan*.

PREPOSITION A word, such as *in, on, over, under* etc. used before a noun or pronoun to relate it to other words in the sentence, e.g. E. *the book is **on** the table, he went **with** his wife*, D. *zijn auto stond **voor** het huis*.

PREPOSITIONAL PREFIX A preposition attached to the beginning of a word, e.g. D. ***op**bellen, **uit**gaan, **voor**komen*.

PRESENT PARTICIPLE In English, the form of the verb ending in '-ing' which is used in a number of different grammatical constructions, e.g. *I am **working**, he was still **sleeping***. Dutch present participles end in *-d(e)* and are used as adjectives and adverbs, e.g. D. *het **huilende** kind*.

PRESENT TENSE A tense used primarily to refer to present time, general time and habitual actions e.g. E. *John **feels** ill, the world **is** round, they **meet** once a week*, D. *Jan **werkt** te hard, de kinderen **blijven** thuis*.

PROGRESSIVE FORMS In English, verbal constructions using *to be* plus a present participle, e.g. *I **am going**, he **was reading**, **have** you **been crying**?*

PRONOUN A word, such as *I, he, it, they, this, that, who* etc., used to refer to a noun (see DEMONSTRATIVE PRONOUN, INDEFINITE PRONOUN, PERSONAL PRONOUN, POSSESSIVE PRONOUN, RELATIVE PRONOUN).

REFLEXIVE VERB A verb whose object refers back to its subject, e.g. *I* [Subj.] *wash **myself*** [Obj.]. The objects of reflexive verbs are known as **reflexive pronouns**, e.g. E. ***myself, yourself, himself, themselves*** etc., D. ***me, je, zich*** etc.

RELATIVE CLAUSE A clause beginning with a relative pronoun, e.g. E. *the girl **who came to dinner***, D. *de man **die met mijn vrouw werkt***.

RELATIVE PRONOUN A pronoun that refers back to a noun already mentioned in the sentence, e.g. E. *the man **who** lost his job, the problem **which** must be solved*, D. *de vrouw **die** om de hoek woont, het huis **dat** verkocht wordt.*

SECOND PERSON The grammatical category of pronouns or verbs used by the speaker/writer to refer to the person(s) whom s/he is addressing, e.g. E. ***you are***, D. ***jij bent, u bent, jullie zijn*** (contrast FIRST PERSON, THIRD PERSON).

SENTENCE A group of words containing one or more clauses. In writing, it begins with a capital letter and ends with a full stop, e.g. E. ***That man works with my wife***. D. ***Die man werkt met mijn vrouw maar zij vindt hem niet aardig.***

SEPARABLE VERBS A set of Dutch verbs with prepositional prefixes such as *aan-, in-, uit-, door-, om-, op-* etc. These prefixes are separated from the verb in certain grammatical constructions, e.g. D. *ik **belde** hem **op**, hij is **aan**gekomen* (contrast INSEPARABLE VERBS).

SINGULAR (sg.) The grammatical form used to refer to one person, thing or concept, e.g. E. ***a table, I was***, D. ***een man, hij** werkt* (contrast PLURAL).

STEM (See VERB STEM.)

STRESS In speaking, emphasis placed on a particular syllable of a word, e.g. E. ***fa**ther, pre**tend***, D. ***moe**der, **ta**fel.*

STRONG VERB A verb that forms its past tense and past participle by changing a vowel, e.g. E. ***sing – sang – sung***, D. ***rijden – reed – gereden***.

SUBJECT (subj.) A noun or pronoun which carries out the action described by the verb, e.g. E. ***the dog** chases the cat*, D. ***hij** leest het boek*. The subject may also experience the state described by the verb, e.g. E. ***he** feels unwell*, D. ***die man** is heel dik.*

SUBORDINATE CLAUSE In Dutch, a clause beginning with a subordinating conjunction, e.g. D. *ik ben niet naar de bioscoop gegaan **omdat ik geen geld had***.

SUBORDINATING CONJUNCTION In Dutch, a conjunction, such as ***als, dat, omdat, terwijl*** etc., which sends the finite verb to the end of the following clause, e.g. D. *ik weet **dat** hij geen geld heeft.*

SUPERLATIVE The form of the adjective used to denote an extreme or unsurpassed level, e.g. E. *the **biggest** house, I am the **cleverest***, D. *de **intelligentste** man.*

SYLLABLE That part of a word which usually contains a vowel, e.g. E. ***man***, D. ***vrouw*** consist of one syllable, E. ***woman***, D. ***moeder*** consist of two and E. ***computer***, D. ***opbellen*** consist of three.

TENSE A category of the verb, such as present tense, past tense, future tense etc., which expresses relations of time.

THIRD PERSON The grammatical category of pronouns or verbs used by the speaker/writer to refer not to himself/herself nor to the addressee but to some third party or something else, e.g. E. ***he is, they are***, D. ***het is, zij zijn*** (contrast FIRST PERSON, SECOND PERSON).

TRANSITIVE VERB A verb taking a direct object, e.g. E. *he **kicked** the cat, I **found** some money*, D. *ik **stuur** twee brieven.*

VERB A word which indicates the performance or occurrence of an action or the existence of a condition. In English and Dutch, it usually occurs with a subject and may change its form to show person, number and tense, e.g. E. *he **works**, I **felt** unwell*, D. *het **groeit**, wij **waren** ziek.*

VERB STEM In Dutch, the infinitive minus *-en*, with the appropriate spelling changes, e.g. D. ***werk, woon, zit, leef*** (infinitives *werken, wonen, zitten, leven*).

VOICELESS (of a consonant) Produced without vibration of the vocal chords. Some voiceless consonants in English and Dutch are ***p, t, k, f, s, ch***.

VOWEL The speech sounds ***a, e, i, o, u*** (and ***y*** at the end of words), e.g. E. *b**e**d, b**a**by*, D. *b**a**d, b**oo**m.*

How to use this book

The reference grammar

When first looking for a particular grammatical topic it is advisable to refer to the alphabetical index at the end of the book. If there is more than one section number listed for a particular topic, the number given in bold highlights the section which deals with that topic in the most detail. Students are advised to refer to that section first. As they become more familiar with the book, students will soon recognise which (more general) grammatical topics comprise a whole section, and the alphabetical listing of these will allow for quick and easy access without the need for an index.

Most sections are divided into numbered subsections with bold headings. These usually deal with the main rules of Dutch grammar which beginners and intermediate students should learn. Exceptions to rules, less common forms and observations on style and usage which may be of more interest to advanced learners are usually given in the paragraphs marked ◿◿◿ at the end of the section or, alternatively, in footnotes.

Exercises

Each section of the reference grammar corresponds to a set of exercises which enable students to work on the topic covered in that particular section. They are organised according to type and level.

Type A	Recognition and understanding of Dutch forms
B	Application of rules
C	Free composition
Level 1	Beginners to intermediate
2	Intermediate to advanced

The answers to the exercises are given in the key at the end of the whole exercise section.

EXAMPLE If you want information on the past tense, do the following

ACTION TO TAKE	WHAT YOU WILL FIND
STEP 1 → Go to Index, look under 'p'	Past tense: 27.1, **47**, 50 ◿◿◿ ◿◿◿
STEP 2 → Go to Section **47** of the reference grammar	**47 Past tense**
	47.1 ...
	47.2 ...
STEP 3 → • Read **47.1** and **47.2** for formation of past tense	etc.
• Read **47.3** for usage	
• Read ◿◿◿ if interested in further information	

If you also want to do exercises on the **past tense**, do the following

ACTION TO TAKE	WHAT YOU WILL FIND
STEP 1 → Go to **47 past tense** in the exercises section	**47 Past tense** **A1** . . . **2** . . . **B1** . . . **2** . . . **C1** . . . **2** . . . etc.
STEP 2 → Choose exercises appropriate to your level	
STEP 3 → Go to Key to check answers	**47 A1** . . . etc. (answers)

Didactic guide for beginners

The grammatical topics dealt with in this book have been arranged alphabetically for quick and easy access. However, some students, particularly beginners, may also feel the need for a 'didactic guide' suggesting which topics they should tackle first in order to attain at least a basic level of Dutch. In this way, the learner can gradually build up his/her knowledge of Dutch grammar on a 'basic-to-complex' basis, in addition to focusing on specific topics when needed. The charts below set out the main areas of Dutch grammar covered in this book and suggest a possible order in which to tackle each one, beginning with those needed to produce simple sentences in Dutch and then moving on to more complex forms and constructions.

A   Sounds and letters

Grammatical topic	Section(s)
Pronunciation	58
Spelling	65
Punctuation – capital letters	11
commas	13
apostrophes	7

B   How to form a simple sentence in Dutch

Grammatical topic	Section(s)
Present tense: I **WORK**, HE **WORKS** etc.	55
Forms of *zijn* 'to be'	33.1(c)
Forms of *hebben* 'to have'	33.1(b)
Personal pronouns – subject: I, YOU, HE etc.	49.1 (Table 24)
object: ME, HIM, US etc.	49.1 (Table 25)
difficulties	49.2, 49.3
Direct and indirect objects: I see THE MAN	45
I give it TO THE MAN	
Word order in simple sentences	78.1(a)
Conjunctions not affecting word order: AND, BUT etc.	17.1

C   Questions and commands

Grammatical topic	Section(s)
Question words: WHO?, WHAT?, WHERE? etc.	60
Word order in 'yes–no' questions	78.1(c, i)
Imperative: COME here!	28

D   Some basic parts of sentences (1)

Grammatical topic	Section(s)
Nouns – gender	25
plurals	42
Possessives: MY, YOUR, HIS, JOHN'S etc.	51, 52
Demonstratives: THIS, THAT etc.	19
Adjectives – adjective endings	2
Adverbs: QUICKLY, NICELY etc.	5
Prepositions: ON, IN, OUT, WITH etc.	53

E   How to negate a sentence

Grammatical topic	Section(s)
Use of *niet* 'not'	41
Geen 'no/not any' before nouns	24

F   Some basic parts of sentences (2)

Grammatical topic	Section(s)
Articles: A, THE (use of)	8
Comparatives: BIGGER etc.	14
Superlatives: BIGGEST etc.	67
Functions of *er*	21

G   The use of other tenses and verbal constructions

Grammatical topic	Section(s)
Modal verbs with infinitives: e.g. I **WANT** TO WORK	40
Future tense: I **WILL** WORK	23.1, 23.2
Conditional: I **WOULD** WORK	16.1
Simple past: I **WORKED** – regular	47
irregular	33
Perfect: I **HAVE** WORKED – regular	48
irregular	33
Pluperfect: I **HAD** WORKED	50

H   Special types of verb

Grammatical topic	Section(s)
Inseparable verbs: **begrijpen, ont**moeten etc.	32
Separable verbs: **opbellen, uit**gaan etc.	64
Reflexive verbs: **zich** wassen etc.	61

I   How to form longer and more complex sentences

Grammatical topic	Section(s)
Conjunctions affecting word order: IF, BECAUSE etc.	17.2
Word order	78
Relative pronouns: WHO, WHICH etc.	62
Use of (om) . . . te + infinitive	30
Translating English -ING constructions	31

J   The use of more complex tenses and verbal constructions

Grammatical topic	Section(s)
Future perfect: I **WILL HAVE** WORKED	23.3
Conditional perfect: I **WOULD HAVE** WORKED	16.2
Hypothetical sentences with 'if': IF I **HAD** WORKED	27
Passive: I **WAS SEEN** (BY . . .)	46
Modal verbs in complex tenses:	
double infinitives	40.2(b,c), 78.2(d)
conditional perfect: **SHOULD HAVE/COULD HAVE**	40.2(d)

K   Extending vocabulary: rules for deriving words from other words

Grammatical topic	Section(s)
Adjectives used as nouns	4
Adjectives derived from other words	3
Nouns derived from other words	43
Verbs derived from other words	74
Diminutives	20
Professions	56
Female endings	22

Entries

---

4 ☞ *Appendix* for alphabetical list of irregular verbs.

Tables

Reference grammar

1   Accents

Written Dutch has two types of accent: (i) the accute accent ('), (ii) the diaeresis (¨) which are used as follows:

1.1
The acute accent indicates emphasis. It is usually placed over the first vowel in the word (unless it is a capital letter) or over the first *two* vowels if they are identical[1]

een zéér moeilijke positie	a VERY difficult position
kom dus nú!	so come NOW!
nog vóór niet ná de oorlog	BEFORE, not AFTER the war

Note that the accute accent is often used to distinguish the numeral *een* meaning 'one' from *een* meaning 'a':

hij dronk alleen een glas wijn	he only drank a glass of wine
hij dronk alleen één glas wijn	he drank only one glass of wine
Ik heb een kind. Eén kind is genoeg	I have a child. One child is enough

1.2
The diaeresis is placed over a vowel (most commonly *i* or *e*) in order to show that it is pronounced separately from the immediately preceding vowel in cases where the letters in question usually represent one vowel sound

geïnteresseerd	interested
geëngageerd	engaged/socially concerned
tweeëntwintig	twenty-two
melodieën	melodies

Note that in compound words (i.e. words made up of two or more words which can also appear independently), a hyphen is used instead of a diaeresis, according to the new Dutch spelling rules (☞ *Spelling,*), e.g. *Drie-eenheid* 'Holy Trinity', *na-apen* 'to ape'.

Some words borrowed from French always occur with an accent, e.g. *café* 'café', *privé* 'private', *efficiënt* 'efficient', *à* 'at', as do a few Dutch words, e.g. *hé* 'hey', *hè?* 'eh?'

2   Adjectives

An adjective is a word used to describe a noun or pronoun. In English and Dutch, it is that part of speech which may occur between an article and a noun, e.g. 'the INTERESTING story', 'an EXPENSIVE wine', although it may also be placed after a verb, e.g. 'the story is INTERESTING', 'the wine is EXPENSIVE', 'she was BEAUTIFUL'. In Dutch, adjectives occurring before nouns often require a special ending. Consider the following rules:

---

1 Some Dutch writers prefer to use a grave accent (`) instead, particularly with the letter *e*.

2.1 Adjectives before nouns

(a) In Dutch, an adjective used before a noun takes the ending -e*

het interessante verhaal	the interesting story
de / een dure wijn	the/an expensive wine
deze / die grote zwarte hond	this/that big black dog
dit / dat kleine kind	this/that small child
mijn / jouw / Theo's laatste les	my/your/Theo's last lesson
nieuwe boeken	new books

*Note that, when adding -*e*, one must observe the regular Dutch spelling changes, e.g. *groot – een grote vogel* 'a big bird', *stom – een stomme kat* 'a stupid cat', *lief – een lieve hond* 'a nice dog', *vies – het vieze varken* 'the dirty pig' (☞ *Spelling*).

(b) However, adjectives have no ending if they precede a SINGULAR NEUTER NOUN in an indefinite context: i.e. after *een* 'a', *geen* 'no/not a', *elk* 'each', *welk* 'which', *ieder* 'every', *menig* 'many', *veel* 'a lot of', *weinig* 'little', *zulk* 'such', *zo'n* 'such a'

EEN **interessant** *verhaal*	an interesting story
GEEN **warm** *water*	no warm water
ZO'N **mooi** *gezicht*	such a pretty face
ELK/WELK **klein** *kind*	each/which small child
VEEL/WEINIG **vers** *brood*	a lot of/little fresh bread

This also applies when the adjective is preceded by nothing (i.e. by no article or pronoun):

gezond *eten*	healthy eating
het is **hard** *werk*	it's hard work

Table 1. Summary of adjective endings

	COMMON GENDER		NEUTER	
	definite	**indefinite**	**definite**	**indefinite**
singular	**-e** de oude man	**-e** een oude man	**-e** het oude huis	**-0** een **oud** huis
plural	**-e** oude mannen/huizen			

2.2 The rules given in 2.1 also apply to adjectives standing alone which refer to a noun mentioned before

ik heb een grote auto en jij een kleine	I have a big car and you have a small one
ik heb een **mooi** *gezicht en jij een* **lelijk**	I have a pretty face and you have an ugly one

2.3 Adjectives used after a verb have no ending

het verhaal is **interessant**	the story is interesting
de auto is **groot**	the car is big

2.4 EXCEPTIONS: The following types of adjectives never take an -*e* ending

(a) Adjectives ending in -*en*

het **gestolen** *geld*	the stolen money	*het* **stenen** *huis*	the stone house
de **open** *deur*	the open door	*een* **dronken** *man*	a drunk man

(b) Some adjectives of foreign origin

de **lila** *jurk*	the lilac dress	**nylon** *kousen*	nylon stockings
de **beige** *trui*	the beige sweater	**sexy** *mannen*	sexy men

(c) *links* 'left' and *rechts* 'right' often have special forms in -*er* prefixed to nouns

de **linker**kant	the left (hand) side	*het* **rechter**been	the right leg

 In more formal styles of written Dutch, whole phrases can be used as adjectives and are placed before a noun. In these cases, the last word of the phrase takes the ending (where necessary), e.g. *het* **door krakers bewoond-e** *huis* 'the house inhabited by squatters', *de* **gisteren door de politie gearresteerd-e** *inbrekers* 'the burglars arrested by the police yesterday' (*literally* 'the by squatters inhabited house', 'the yesterday by the police arrested burglars').

 In some cases, the -*e* ending may be absent in set phrases or in particular stylistic contexts which cannot be adequately captured by a rule: for instance, when referring to the innate characteristics of (especially male) human beings preceded by *een*, e.g. *een* **groot, indrukwekkend** *man* 'a great, impressive man', or when part of a proper name or fixed expression with *het*, e.g. *het* **centraal** *station* 'the central station', *het* **publiek** *bestel* [non-commercial Dutch TV].

3   Adjectives derived from other words

In English, adjectives may be derived from nouns, verbs, or other adjectives by the addition of specific endings, e.g. HAIR-Y, DRINK-ABLE, BLUE-ISH. In Dutch, the situation is similar, e.g. *mann***elijk** 'manly', *drink***baar** 'drinkable', *groen***ig** 'greenish'; yet, as there is usually no simple one-to-one correspondence between the Dutch and English endings, it is difficult to set out hard and fast rules for adjective derivation in Dutch. On the whole, each adjective must be learnt individually, although it may be helpful to foreign learners to identify the most common adjective-forming endings in Dutch. The following are given as a rough guide only:

3.1   Common adjective-forming endings

(a) -*elijk* (or sometimes -*lijk*[2]) is a very common ending added to nouns and verb stems. It sometimes corresponds to English '-ly'

*mann***elijk**	masculine/manly	*schrift***elijk**	written
*vrouw***elijk**	feminine	*geld***elijk**	monetary
*vriend***elijk**	friendly	*sterf***elijk***	mortal

---

2 The *e*-less variations -*lijk* and -*loos* tend to be used after words ending in an unstressed syllable, e.g. *jammer***lijk** 'miserable', *ouder***lijk** 'parental', *adem***loos** 'breathless', and words ending in a long vowel (written as two vowels) followed by *l*, *r* or *n*, e.g. *natuur***lijk** 'natural', *persoon***lijk** 'personally', *doel***loos** 'aimless'.

*Note that the verb STEM is the infinitive minus *-en* with the necessary spelling changes (☞ *Spelling*) and is identical to the first person singular present form, e.g. *sterven* 'to die' – (*ik*) **sterf** '(I) die'.

(b) *-ig* is mostly added to nouns (and occasionally to adjectives) and often corresponds to English '-y'

*ha**rig***	hairy		*sap**pig***	juicy
*ro**zig***	rosy		*gelu**kkig***	happy
*hand**ig***	handy		*blauw**ig***	bluey/blueish

(c) *-baar* is added to verb stems* and often corresponds to English '-able'/'-ible'

*eet**baar***	edible		*eer**baar***	honourable
*drink**baar***	drinkable		*bewijs**baar***	provable
*houd**baar***	maintainable		*benijd**baar***	enviable

*See * above.

(d) *-s* is the most common ending used to denote nationalities and to derive adjectives from place names

*Ier**s***	Irish		*Nederland**s***	Dutch
*Engel**s***	English		*Amsterdam**s***	from Amsterdam
*Schot**s***	Scottish		*Berlijn**s***	from Berlin

(e) *-vol*, *-eloos* (or sometimes *-loos*²), *-achtig*, and *-vormig* often correspond to English '-ful', '-less', '-like', and '-shaped' respectively

*hoop**vol***	hopeful		*boom**achtig***	tree-like
*nutte**loos***	useless		*leraar**achtig***	teacher-like
*gedachte**loos***	thoughtless		*peer**vormig***	pear-shaped

Note that, when deriving most adjectives, one must observe the regular Dutch spelling changes, e.g. *haar – ha**r**ig, sap – sap**p**ig, man – man**n**elijk* etc. (☞ *Spelling*). The addition of *-achtig*, however, does not require any spelling changes, e.g. *boomachtig* (not ✗ *b**o**machtig*).

3.2 When negating adjectives in Dutch, it is common to use the prefix *on-* which generally corresponds to English 'un-'

***on**aardig*	unpleasant		***on**bewijsbaar*	unprovable
***on**drinkbaar*	undrinkable		***on**gelukkig*	unhappy

3.3 Past and present participles may also be used as adjectives (☞ *Perfect tense*, 48.1(b) and *Present participles*, 54.2(a))

gereserveerd	reserved		*lopend*	running
opgewekt	cheerful		*slapend*	sleeping

📖 Other adjective-forming endings are *-matig*, which is added to nouns to give the meaning 'with respect to / in relation to' and is particularly common in more formal styles of Dutch, e.g. *regel-**matig*** 'regular', *plan**matig*** 'according to plan/planned', and *-zaam* which is usually added to verbs to give the meaning 'inclined to', e.g. *spaar**zaam*** 'thrifty', *werk**zaam*** 'industrious'.

4 Adjectives used as nouns

In Dutch, many adjectives can be used as nouns:

4.1 To define human beings by physical or emotional characteristics, in which case an -e ending is used

*blind – de blind**e***	the blind person / the blind one
*blond – de blond**e***	the blond(e) / the blond(e) one
*bang – een bang**e***	a frightened person

These nouns have common gender (i.e. take *de*) and form their plurals by adding *-n*

4.2 To refer to an unspecified thing in sentences such as 'the nice thing is . . ./the strange thing is . . .', also using an -e ending

*het leuk**e** is . . .*	the nice thing is . . .
*het interessant**e** is . . .*	the interesting thing is . . .
*het leukst**e** is . . .*	the nicest thing is . . .
*het ergst**e** is . . .*	the worst thing is . . .

These nouns are always neuter (i.e. take *het*)

4.3 After words like *iets/wat* 'something', *niets* 'nothing', *veel* 'many', *weinig* 'few' when referring to things, in which case an -s ending is used

*leuk – iets leuk**s***	something nice
*slecht – niets slecht**s***	nothing bad
*lekker – veel lekker**s***	many tasty things

5 Adverbs

An adverb is a word used to describe a verb or an adjective. In English, adverbs usually take the ending '-ly', e.g. 'he sings BEAUTIFULLY', 'he was EXTREMELY stupid'. In Dutch, adverbs are usually identical to adjectives, e.g. *het weer is **slecht*** 'the weather is bad', *hij zingt **slecht*** 'he sings badly'. However, unlike adjectives (☞ *Adjectives*), they never take an -e ending:

*Ruud speelt heel **goed***	Ruud plays very well
*een **ongelofelijk** vieze kamer*	an incredibly dirty room
*een **indrukwekkend** grote keuken*	an impressively large kitchen
Contrast: *een indrukwekkend**e** keuken*	an impressive kitchen

6 ALL: Dutch equivalents

In Dutch there are, roughly speaking, five ways of translating English 'all':

6.1 *alle* usually occurs before nouns

alle STUDENTEN *moeten hard werken*	all students must work hard
alle WINKELS *zijn dinsdags open*	all shops are open on Tuesdays

6.2 *allen* can be used to replace nouns referring to human beings. It is more common in written Dutch than in spoken Dutch

allen *moeten komen*	everyone must come
zij gingen ***allen*** *op reis*	they all went on holiday

6.3 *allemaal* is a less formal alternative to *alle* and *allen*. It is particularly common in spoken Dutch and is often used to translate English 'all of them/us/you'. It occurs after nouns and pronouns and follows the verb

de STUDENTEN *moeten* ***allemaal*** *werken*	the students must all work
de WINKELS *zijn* ***allemaal*** *open*	the shops are all open
ZIJ *gingen* ***allemaal*** *op reis*	all of them went on holiday

6.4 *al* occurs before nouns preceded by *de/het*, a possessive pronoun ('my, your' etc.) or a demonstrative pronoun ('this, that' etc.)

al MIJN *studenten moeten werken*	all my students must work
al DE *winkels zijn dinsdags open*	all the shops are open on Tuesdays
al DE *jongens spelen voetbal*	all the boys play football

Table 2. Four translations of ALL

alle		jongens	spelen		voetbal
allen			spelen		voetbal
	de	jongens	spelen	**allemaal**	voetbal
al	de	jongens	spelen		voetbal

6.5 *alles* is used to translate English 'all' meaning 'everything' (and 'anything' when stressed)

is dat ***alles***?	is that all/everything?
dat is ***alles*** *wat ik weet*	that is all/everything I know
alles *is mogelijk*	anything/everything is possible

7　Apostrophes

In English and Dutch, apostrophes are used to show that a letter has been omitted, e.g. IT**'S** (IT IS), *zo'n* (*zo een*) 'such a'. In English, they are also used to indicate possession, e.g. FRED'S NEW HOUSE.

7.1 In Dutch, apostrophes are used to indicate possession only after (i) nouns ending in *s* and *z*, in which case no *-s* follows, (ii) nouns ending in a vowel other than *-e* (i.e. in *-a*, *-i*, *-o*, *-u*, *-y*) or (iii) after abbreviations

(i)　***Kees'*** *hond*	Kees's dog
(ii)　*met* ***Theo's*** *hulp*	with Theo's help
(iii)　*Gery* **G.***'s* *flat*	Gery G.'s flat

Contrast: ***Annes*** *hond, met* ***Jans*** *hulp,* ***Geerts*** *flat.*

7.2 Apostrophes are also used before the noun plural ending *-s* after words ending in a vowel other than *-e* and after abbreviations

wij zijn **collega's**	we are colleagues
zij houdt niet van **baby's**	she doesn't like babies
er staan drie **pc's** *op kantoor*	there are three PCs in the office

Contrast: *zij zijn* **meisjes**, *ik houd van* **films**, *er staan drie* **computers** *op kantoor*.

 Apostrophes are also used with expressions such as *'s morgens* 'in the mornings', *'s middags* 'in the afternoons', *'s avonds* 'in the evenings', *'s nachts* 'at night' (☞ *Time*, 69.2).

8 Articles: usage

An article is a word used to limit a following noun, e.g. 'A man', 'A horse', or give definiteness to a following noun, e.g. 'THE man', 'THE horse'. Generally speaking, there are two types of article in English and Dutch: the indefinite article 'a' (Dutch **een**) and the definite article 'the' (Dutch **de** or **het** depending on the gender and number of the following noun, ☞ *Gender*). As a rule, articles in Dutch are used in the same way as in English. However, there are some cases in which article usage differs in the two languages. Below is a list of contexts in which the use of the article in Dutch differs from that of English:

8.1 *Een* 'a' is omitted in Dutch

(a) When the verb is *zijn* 'to be', *worden* 'to become' or *blijven* 'to remain' with nouns denoting a profession or nationality/place of origin

hij was TANDARTS	he was a dentist
John is ENGELSMAN	John is an Englishman
ik wil ZANGER *worden*	I want to become a singer

When these nouns are preceded by an adjective, however, *een* is used:

hij was **een** SUCCESVOLLE *tandarts*	he was a successful dentist
John is **een** TYPISCHE *Engelsman*	John is a typical Englishman
ik wil **een** BEROEMDE *zanger worden*	I want to become a famous singer

(b) Usually after *als* 'as' immediately followed by a noun[3]

ALS *kind was hij erg stout*	as a child he was very naughty
ik beschouw hem ALS *broer*	I regard him as a brother

(c) Commonly after *zonder* 'without'

hij is ZONDER *vriendin aangekomen*	he arrived without a girlfriend
ik woon in een huis ZONDER *tuin*	I live in a house without a garden

---

3 Yet not when *als* means 'like', e.g. *hij gedraagt zich als een kind* 'he behaves like a child'.

8.2 *De/het* are omitted in Dutch

(a) With musical instruments after *spelen* 'to play' and *leren* 'to learn'

hij speelt heel goed GITAAR	he plays the guitar very well
ik leer FLUIT *spelen*	I am learning to play the flute

(b) Before dates when a month is specified (☞ *Days and months*, 18.2(a))

hij komt (op) maandag 15 MEI	he's coming on Monday, 15 May
het is zeventien NOVEMBER	it's the seventeenth of November

8.3 *De/het* are used in Dutch

(a) Before certain abstract and collective nouns

de MENS *wordt bedreigd*	mankind is under threat
de WETENSCHAP *maakt vooruitgang*	science is making progress
de NATUUR *verandert steeds*	nature is constantly changing

(b) With meals

het ONTBIJT *is klaar*	breakfast is ready!
je bent net op tijd voor de LUNCH	you're just in time for lunch

(c) With seasons

ik houd niet van de WINTER	I don't like winter
in de ZOMER *gaan wij naar Spanje*	in summer we're going to Spain

(d) With the names of streets, squares, bridges and parks

hij woont in de REMBRANDTSTRAAT	he lives in Rembrandt Street
ik zag hem in het VONDELPARK	I saw him in (the) Vondelpark

(e) With the names of languages after *in* 'in' and *uit* 'out (of), from'

hij zong in het ENGELS	he sang in English
het boek werd uit het GRIEKS *vertaald*	the book was translated from Greek

(f) After the prepositions *boven/over* 'over' and *onder* 'under' followed by a numeral

zijn vrouw is BOVEN *de veertig*	his wife is over forty
het is ONDER *de tien gulden*	it is under ten guilders

8.4 In Dutch, it is usually necessary to repeat the article for each noun

de jongens en de meisjes speelden	the boys and girls were playing
de man en de vrouw stonden te praten	the man and woman were talking
geef mij een kopje, een schoteltje,	give me a cup, saucer, spoon and
een lepel en een suikerpot	sugar-bowl

Note that this also applies to demonstratives ('this, that' etc.) and possessive pronouns ('my, your' etc.), e.g. *die jongens en die meisjes* 'those boys and girls', *mijn hond en mijn kat* 'my dog and cat'.

There are numerous set expressions and idioms in which article usage differs in Dutch and English. Some common examples are *naar **de** stad / naar **de** kerk* 'to town / to church', *in **de** stad / in **de** gevangenis* 'in town / in prison', *op straat / op tafel* 'on the street / on the table', *op kantoor* 'in the office'.

9   Blijven

The Dutch verb *blijven* 'to remain' can be combined with another verb (in the infinitive) to express a continuous or repeated action:

*de kat **blijft** naar de muis* KIJKEN	the cat keeps looking at the mouse
***blijft** u maar* ZITTEN*!*	please remain seated!
*de Jehova's getuigen **bleven*** BELLEN	the Jehovah's witnesses kept ringing
*Piet is de hele nacht **blijven*** WERKEN	Piet carried on working all night

In this type of construction, *blijven* behaves like a modal verb (☞ *Modal verbs*, 40.2).

10   BOTH: Dutch equivalents

In Dutch there are three ways of translating English 'both' (compare *ALL*, 6.1–6.3):

10.1   *beide* occurs before nouns

beide JONGENS *spelen voetbal*	both boys play football
beide OUDERS *zijn vrij streng*	both parents are fairly strict
beide FILMS *waren erg grappig*	both films were very funny

It can also stand in for nouns that have been omitted (unless the nouns in question refer to human beings, ☞ 10.2 below):

was de FILM *beter dan het* BOEK*?*	was the film better than the book?
*nee, **beide** waren even goed*	no, both were equally good

10.2   *beiden* can be used to replace nouns referring to human beings. It is more common in written Dutch than in spoken Dutch

verdient M.H. meer dan J.F.? -	does M.H. earn more than J.F.? -
*nee, **beiden** verdienen f 9.000*	no, both earn 9,000 guilders

10.3   *allebei* is a less formal alternative to *beide* and *beiden*. It is particularly common in spoken Dutch and is often used to translate English *both of them/us/you*. It occurs after nouns and pronouns and follows the verb

de FILMS *waren **allebei** saai*	the films were both boring
ZIJ *waren **allebei** saai*	both of them were boring
komt Jan of Geert vandaag?	is Jan or Geert coming today?
ZIJ *komen **allebei***	both of them are coming

Table 3. *The three translations of BOTH*

beide		jongens	spelen		voetbal
beiden			spelen		voetbal
	de	jongens	spelen	**allebei**	voetbal

11 Capital letters

In written Dutch, capital letters are generally used in much the same way as in written English. Note, however, the following differences:

11.1 The words *meneer* 'Mr' and *mevrouw* 'Mrs/Miss' are not written with a capital letter, unless they begin a sentence

ik kom met meneer van Lenthe   I'm coming with Mr van Lenthe
een brief van mevrouw Zuidema   a letter from Mrs Zuidema

11.2 Capital letters are not used with the names of days and months, unless they begin a sentence (☞ *Days and months*)

11.3 As in English, capital letters are used at the beginning of sentences and with proper nouns. Note, however, the following points

(a) when expressions of time beginning with 's appear at the beginning of a sentence, it is the letter after 's which is capitalised

's Woensdags ga ik zwemmen   On Wednesdays I go swimming
's Avonds gaat hij meestal uit   In the evenings he usually goes out

(b) when the combination *ij* is capitalised, both letters are affected

de Noordelijke IJszee   the Arctic Ocean

12 Colloquial Dutch

Dutch has quite a few grammatical constructions and features which are characteristic of the informal spoken language. They tend not to be written, unless the style of writing is particularly informal or is meant to represent everyday spoken Dutch. Some common ones are:

12.1 Unstressed pronouns (☞ *Personal pronouns* and *Possessive pronouns*)

(a) The unstressed personal pronouns *'k* (*ik*), *ie* (*hij*), *'t* (*het*), *'m* (*hem*), *ze* or *d'r* (*haar*)

'k heb 'm niet gezien   I haven't seen him
'k heb d'r niets gezegd[4]   I haven't told her anything

---

4 Note that the *d* in *d'r* is mostly not pronounced.

*komt **ie** vanavond?*	is he coming this evening?
***'t** is veel te moeilijk*	it's much too difficult

(b) The unstressed possessive pronouns *m'n* (*mijn*), *z'n* (*zijn*), *d'r* (*haar* or *hun*)

***m'n** fiets is kapot*	my bike is broken
*hij komt met **z'n** vrouw*	he's coming with his wife

12.2 Possessives of the type 'John his bike' meaning 'John's bike' etc.
(☞ *Possession*, 📖)

*dat is **Jan z'n** fiets*	that's John's bike
*waar zijn **Linda d'r** schoenen?*	where are Linda's shoes?

And, similarly, 'who his'?, 'who her'? etc. meaning 'whose'? (☞ *Question words*, 📖):

***wie z'n** hoed is dat?*	whose hat is that?
***wie d'r** ring is dat?*	whose ring is that?

12.3 Extensive use of diminutives (☞ *Diminutives*)

*ik heb een **kadootje** voor je*	I've got a (little) present for you
*wat een leuk **kamertje**!*	what a nice (little) room!
*ik ga **eventjes** naar buiten*	I'm just popping out for a minute

12.4 Extensive use of the perfect tense to refer to the past (☞ *Perfect tense*)

*ik **heb** allen één biertje **gedronken** en **ben** toen naar huis **gegaan***	I only had one beer and then went home

12.5 Use of the present tense for dramatic effect when referring to the past (☞ *Present tense*)

*ik **kom** binnen, **zie** hem op de grond liggen en **bel** direct een ambulance*	I come in, see him lying on the ground and phone for an ambulance immediately

12.6 The insertion of short 'filler' words to modify the tone of the sentence. Some common ones are

(a) *eens*, *even* and *maar* are often used to make a sentence, particularly a command, sound less abrupt. They may be rendered by English 'just' (or also 'go ahead' in the case of *maar*). Often, however, they are simply left untranslated

*kom gauw **eens** langs*	(just) come along soon
*wilt u me **even** helpen?*	(please) could you (just) help me?
*wacht **even***	(just) wait (a minute)
*gaat u **maar** zitten*	(go ahead), (just) take a seat

(b) *soms* often renders English 'happen to'/'by any chance'

*heb je mijn sleutel **soms** gezien?*	have you seen my key by any chance?
*als je het **soms** ziet . . .*	if you happen to see it . . .

(c) *hoor* is often inserted at the end of an utterance. It sometimes lends emphasis to what has just been said but is usually left untranslated

hij is erg rijk, **hoor**	he's very rich (you know)
kom je vanavond? – Ja, **hoor**	are you coming tonight? – (Oh) yes

(d) *zeg* is often inserted at the beginning of an utterance to catch the listener's attention and is used much in the same way as English 'hey' or 'listen'

zeg, *wat doe je vanavond?*	hey, what are you doing tonight?

(e) *toch* and *wel* are also common filler words with a number of different functions (☞ *Toch* and *Wel*).

13 Commas

In written Dutch, commas are generally used in much the same way as in written English. Note, however, the following differences:

13.1 Sentences containing more than one clause, e.g. [When Jane arrived$_{Clause\ 1}$] [John was not ready$_{Clause\ 2}$]

(a) If one of the clauses contains a verb which has been sent to the end (☞ *Word order*, 78.1(b)), a comma is used to separate the clauses

toen zij hem ZAG, *werd zij rood*	when she saw him she blushed
de man die mij gisteren BEZOCHT, *is leraar*	the man who visited me yesterday is a teacher
ik moet in een café werken, omdat ik geld nodig HEB	I have to work in a cafe because I need money[5]

Note that, as in English, a comma is not usually used before *dat* meaning 'that'

het regende zo hevig DAT *ik de bel niet hoorde*	it was raining so heavily that I did not hear the doorbell

(b) However, if the clauses have normal word order (i.e. the verb has not been sent to the end of the clause), there is usually no comma

Geert DRONK *wijn en Jan* AT *koekjes*	Geert drank wine and Jan ate biscuits
ik WIL *koffie maar er* IS *geen melk*	I want coffee but there's no milk

13.2 In English, words such as 'however', 'incidentally', 'surprisingly' etc. are usually separated off by commas when they occur after a verb within the sentence. This is not the case in Dutch

het blijft ECHTER *een ernstige kwestie*	it still is, however, a serious matter
ik heb TROUWENS *gehoord dat Jan wil verhuizen*	I heard, incidentally, that Jan wants to move house

---

5 Some Dutch people prefer to omit the comma if the clauses are short, e.g. *ik werk omdat ik geld nodig heb* 'I work because I need money', *hij vroeg mij of ik ziek was* 'he asked me if I was ill'.

13.3 In Dutch, a comma is used instead of a decimal point and, conversely, a full stop is used with numbers over a thousand

ƒ 25, 50	25.50 guilders
8,5 procent	8.5 per cent
2.500	2,500

14 Comparatives

The comparative is the form of the adjective used when comparing one person/thing to another, e.g. 'the shirt is CHEAPER than the tie'. In English, comparatives are formed either by adding '-er' to the adjective, e.g. TALL-ER, GREEN-ER, or, if the adjective has more than two syllables, by placing the word 'more' in front of it, e.g. MORE INTERESTING, MORE INTELLIGENT. The formation and use of comparatives in Dutch are as follows (☞ also *Superlatives*):

14.1 Formation of comparatives: Dutch comparatives are formed with *-er* (or *-der* if the adjective ends in *r*) irrespective of the length of the adjective*

mooier	nicer, prettier	*interessanter*	more interesting
goedkoper	cheaper	*moeilijker*	more difficult
duurder	more expensive	*verder*	further

*Note that, when forming comparatives, one must observe the regular Dutch spelling changes, e.g. *goedkoop – goedkoper* 'cheap – cheaper', *dik – dikker* 'fat – fatter', *boos – bozer* 'angry – angrier' etc. (☞ *Spelling*).

14.2 Comparatives follow the same rules as ordinary adjectives with regard to adding *-e* before nouns (☞ *Adjectives*)

een kleiner huis	a smaller house
het kleinere huis	the smaller house
de duurdere jurk	the more expensive dress

They may also stand in for nouns that have been omitted:

welk kind? – het oudere	which child? – the older one
welke jurk? – ik heb de goedkopere	which dress? – I have the cheaper one

14.3 Comparative constructions:

(a) The Dutch equivalent of 'than', as in 'X is bigger than Y' is *dan*, while the Dutch equivalent of 'as . . . as', as in 'X is (just) as big as Y' is *even . . . als*

*ik ben **jonger dan** hij*	I am younger than him
(☞ 📖 📖)	
*de student is **ouder dan** de leraar*	the student is older than the teacher
*Piet is **even oud als** zijn leraar*[6]	Pete is just as old as his teacher

---

6 Or *Piet is **net zo** oud als zijn leraar.*

(b) The Dutch equivalent of constructions such as 'bigger and bigger' etc. is formed with *steeds* + comparative

*Ludo wordt **steeds dikker***   Ludo is getting fatter and fatter

(c) The Dutch equivalent of constructions such as 'the more he eats, the fatter he gets' etc. is formed with *hoe* + comparative . . . *hoe* + comparative

hoe meer *ik eet,* ***hoe dikker*** *ik word*   the more I eat, the fatter I get

Table 4. Comparative constructions

A ʙ	A is **groter dan** B
A B	A is **even groot als** B
ᴀᴀᴬA	A wordt **steeds groter**
ᴀᴀ**A**	**Hoe groter** A wordt, **hoe dikker** A wordt

 Irregular comparatives: *goed* – ***beter*** 'good – better' and *kwaad* – ***erger*** 'bad – worse', *graag* – ***liever*** 'gladly – preferably' (☞ *Graag*, 26.2), *veel* – ***meer*** 'much – more', *weinig* – ***minder*** 'few – fewer/less'. Note the use of *minder* 'less' + adjective, e.g. *de **minder** belangrijke vergadering* 'the less important meeting' (☞ also *Superlatives*,).

Note that Dutch uses subject pronouns after *dan* and *als* unless the verb requires an object, e.g. SUBJECT *Jan is groter dan **ik/hij/wij*** etc. literally 'Jan is bigger than I/he/we etc.' versus OBJECT *hij vindt Linda aardiger dan **mij/hem/ons*** etc. 'he finds Linda nicer than me/him/us etc.'. This may cause problems for English speakers who tend to use the object pronouns in all cases, e.g. 'John is bigger than ME/HIM/US.' If in doubt as to whether a subject or object is needed, it is advisable to imagine what the whole sentence would have been, e.g. 'Jan is bigger than **I** am/**he** is/**we** are' etc. versus 'he finds Linda nicer than he finds **me/him/us**'.

15   Compound words

A compound word is a word made up of two or more other words which can also occur independently, e.g. 'house' + 'wife' → HOUSEWIFE, 'bed' + 'room' → BEDROOM. In Dutch, compound words are very common and can often be equivalent to whole phrases in English, e.g. ***geldzucht*** 'love of money', ***huisvader*** 'father of the family'. Some illustrative examples of Dutch compound words are given below, with the component parts (i.e. noun (N), adjective (A) and verb (V)) made explicit:[7]

15.1   Compound nouns

N+N	*deurknop*	door-handle	*huisdier*	domestic animal/pet
A+N	*kleingeld*	small change	*groothandel*	wholesale business
V+N	*eetkamer*	dining room	*denkwijze*	way of thinking

Note that the gender of compound nouns is determined by the **last** word in the compound:[8]

---

7 Note that stress usually falls on the first word within the compound.

8 For gender, ☞ separate entry.

*de kamer**huur***	rent	*het huur**huis***	rented house
*de land**bouw***	agriculture	*het bouw**land***	arable land

15.2 Compound adjectives

N+A	*ijzersterk*	very strong	*sneeuwwit*	as white as snow
A+A	*hardhorig*	hard of hearing	*kleinzielig*	small-minded
(V+A less common)				

15.3 Compound verbs

N+V	*huishouden*	to keep house	*speerwerpen*	to throw the javelin
A+V	*hardlopen*	to run (fast)	*grootdoen*	to show off/swagger
(V+V less common)				

 Sometimes a compound word may contain a connecting element *-s-, -e-, -er-* or *-en-* between two or more of its parts. It is often possible to predict the occurrence of these elements: *-s-* mostly occurs after nouns ending in *-ing, -heid* and *-en* (e.g. *verzekering**s**agent* 'insurance agent', *schoonheid**s**instituut* 'beauty parlour', *eten**s**tijd* 'meal-time'); *-en-* often occurs after nouns with a plural interpretation (e.g. *boek**en**kast* 'bookshelf', i.e. shelf for more than one book, *per**en**boom*[9] 'pear tree') and *-er-* occurs after the nouns *kind* 'child' and *ei* 'egg' (e.g. *kind**er**spel* 'child's play', *ei**er**dop* 'eggshell'). It must be noted, however, that these generalisations cannot account for all compounds (e.g. *boek**winkel* 'bookshop', *broek**s**pijp* 'trouser leg').

16 Conditional and conditional perfect tenses

The conditional is the tense used to refer to hypothetical situations. In English, there are two types of conditional: the (simple) conditional which uses 'would' plus a verb, e.g. 'I WOULD GO on holiday if I had the money', and the conditional perfect which uses 'would' plus the perfect tense, e.g. 'I WOULD HAVE GONE on holiday'. These conditional forms are also used in Dutch:

16.1 In Dutch, the conditional is formed with *zou* (plural *zouden*) plus the infinitive

Table 5. The conditional

SUBJECT	ZOUDEN	INFINITIVE
ik		
jij		
u (sing. and pl.)	zou	
hij/zij/het		werken 'work'
wij/jullie/zij	zouden	

Note that English progressives with BE + '-ing' have no direct equivalent in Dutch:

*ik **zou** hard **werken***   I would work hard   OR
                         I would be working hard

---

9 According to the new Dutch spelling rules, the linking *-e-* must be replaced by *-en-* in those cases where the first noun has a plural form in *-en*, e.g. old spelling: *per**e**boom* becomes *per**en**boom* in the new spelling (☞ *Spelling*,).

> *dat* **zou** *ik zeker niet* **doen**[10]   I would certainly not do that
> **zouden** *zij vroeger* **komen**, *als . . . ?*   would they come earlier if . . . ?
> *zij* **zouden** *naar de stad* **willen gaan**   they would like to go to town*

*The verb *willen* 'to want' has a special conditional form *wou* (plural *wouden*) which is often used to mean 'would like' and is common in spoken Dutch (☞ also *Graag*):

> *ik* **wou** *(graag) een half kilo tomaten*   I would like half a kilo of tomatoes
> *wij* **wouden** *(graag) 3 kaartjes kopen*   we would like to buy 3 tickets

16.2 The conditional perfect is formed with *zou* (plural *zouden*) plus the perfect

Table 6. The conditional perfect (full form)

Subject	ZOUDEN	Perfect
ik/jij/u hij/zij/het	zou	
		gewerkt hebben
wij/jullie/zij	zouden	
ik/jij/u hij/zij/het	zou	
		gekomen zijn
wij/jullie/zij	zouden	

Note that English progressives with BE + '-ing' have no direct equivalent in Dutch:

> *ik* **zou** *hard* **gewerkt hebben**   I would have worked hard   OR
> I would have been working hard

> *dat* **zou** *ik zeker niet* **gedaan hebben**   I certainly would not have done that
> **zouden** *zij vroeger* **gekomen zijn**?   would they have come earlier?
> *hij* **zou** *zijn auto* **verkocht hebben**[11]   he would have sold his car

Note that there is also a contracted form of the conditional perfect which is commonly used with *als* 'if', e.g. dat **had** *ik zeker niet* **gedaan**, *als . . .* 'I certainly would not have done

Table 7. The conditional perfect (contracted form)

Subject	HEBBEN/ZIJN	Past participle
ik/jij/u hij/zij/het	had	
		gewerkt
wij/jullie/zij	hadden	
ik/jij/u hij/zij/het	was	
		gekomen
wij/jullie/zij	waren	

---

10 ☞ *Word order*, 78.2(a).
11 The alternative word order *. . . hebben gedaan, . . . zijn gekomen* and *. . . hebben verkocht* is also possible (☞ *Word order*, 78.2(c)).

that if . . . ' (☞ *Hypothetical Sentences with **als*** 'if', 27.2), and with modal verbs, e.g. *ik **had** het niet **kunnen doen*** 'I would not have been able to do it', *ik **had** het niet **willen doen*** 'I would not have wanted to do it' (☞ *Modal Verbs*, 40.2(d)).

 Note that English 'would' is also used in other (non-hypothetical) constructions: (i) when referring to habitual actions in the past, e.g. 'he would get up at seven every morning' (='he used to get up . . .'), (ii) when asking polite questions, e.g. 'would you show me the letter?' In the first case, Dutch simply uses a past or perfect tense, e.g. *hij **stond** iedere morgen om zeven uur op* (☞ *USED TO*, 72.2), while in the second, the verb *willen* 'to want' is used, e.g. ***wilt** u mij de brief laten zien?* (☞ *Modal Verbs*,).

17 Conjunctions: AND, BUT, BECAUSE etc.

A conjunction is a word which links clauses together (i.e. that part of the sentence which contains at least one verb, usually with a subject), e.g. [John came round$_{\text{Clause 1}}$] **AND** [I made some tea$_{\text{Clause 2}}$], 'John wanted tea **BUT** I wanted coffee.' Conjunctions in Dutch may cause problems for English learners as some of them affect the word order of the following clause. The most common conjunctions in Dutch are given below:

17.1 Conjunctions which do not affect word order (also known as 'co-ordinating' conjunctions)

*Jan kwam langs **en** ik maakte thee*	Jan came round **and** I made tea
*Jan wilde thee **maar** ik wilde koffie*	Jan wanted tea **but** I wanted coffee
*ik ging naar bed **want** ik was moe*	I went to bed **because** I was tired
*ga jij uit **of** blijf jij thuis?*	are you going out **or** are you staying at home?

17.2 Conjunctions which send the verb to the end of the following clause (☞ *Word Order*, 78.1(b))

*mijn zoon was ziek, **toen** hij klein* WAS	my son was ill **when** he was little
*ik weet **dat** jij mij leuk* VINDT	I know **that** you like me
*hij doet **alsof** hij iets bijzonders* WAS	he acts **as if** he were something special
***hoewel** hij jong* IS, *is hij erg rijk*	**although** he is young he is very rich
***zodra** ik klaar* BEN, *kom ik even langs*	**as soon as** I'm ready I'll come over
***terwijl** ik in bed* LAG, *brak de dief in*	**while** I was lying in bed the thief broke in

Note that, in the last three examples where the conjunction introduces the whole sentence, the second clause begins immediately with a verb (☞ *Word order*, 78.1(c, ii)).

Conjunctions which send the verb to the end are known as SUBORDINAT-ING conjunctions and Dutch has a considerable number of these. Some common ones are listed alphabetically in the table below.

Table 8. Conjunctions which send the verb to the end[12]

als	if/when	tenzij	unless
alsof	as if	terwijl	while
behalve dat	except that	toen	when (in past)
dat	that	tot(dat)	until
hoewel	although	wanneer	when
inzover(re) dat	to the extent that	voor(dat)	before
nu(dat)	now	zoals	just
of	whether[13]	zodat	so that
omdat	because[14]	zolang	as long as
na(dat)	after	zonder dat	without
sinds/sedert	since	zover	as far as

 There are other words which link clauses together but require a different word order to those set out above. For instance, words such as *anders* 'otherwise' and *daarom* 'that is why' must be immediately followed by the verb, e.g. *je moet opschieten,* **anders** KOM *je te laat* 'you have to hurry otherwise you'll be late', *hij wou me bezoeken,* **daarom** IS *hij vroeger weggegaan* 'he wanted to visit me, that's why he left earlier'. In the case of *dus* 'so/therefore' there are two alternatives, e.g. *ik was moe* **dus** GING *ik naar bed* or *ik was moe* **dus** *ik* GING *naar bed* (co-ordinating conjunction) 'I was tired so I went to bed.'

18   Days and months

18.1 The names of the days and months in Dutch are as follows. (Note that they are not written with a capital letter.)

Table 9. Days of the week

DE WEEK		HET WEEKEND	
maandag	Monday	zaterdag	Saturday
dinsdag	Tuesday	zondag	Sunday
woensdag	Wednesday		
donderdag	Thursday		
vrijdag	Friday		

---

12 ☞ also *Question words,* , for words such as **hoe** 'how', **wat** 'what', **waarom** 'why' etc. which can function like subordinating conjunctions, e.g. *ik weet niet* **hoe** *jij het doet* 'I don't know how you do it'.

13 Not to be confused with *of* meaning 'or' which does not affect word order.

14 Note that *want* also means 'because' but it does not send the verb to the end, e.g. *ik ben vroeger weggegaan want ik* **was** *moe* versus *ik ben vroeger weggegaan omdat ik moe* **was** 'I left earlier because I was tired'.

Table 10. Months

DE WINTER 'winter'		DE ZOMER 'summer'	
december	December	**juni**	June
januari	January	**juli**	July
februari	February	**augustus**	August
DE LENTE 'spring'		DE HERFST 'autumn'	
maart	March	**september**	September
april	April	**oktober**	October
mei	May	**november**	November

18.2 Dates

(a) When the month is specified, cardinal numbers are used and the definite article 'the' is not translated (☞ *Numbers*, 44.1)

*zaterdag **zestien** april 1966*	Saturday the sixteenth of April 1966
*het is **vijfentwintig** december*	it's the twenty-fifth of December
*het was **20** november 1936*	it was 20 November 1936

(b) When the month is omitted, ordinal numbers are used, along with the definite article *de* (☞ *Numbers*, 44.2)

de hoeveelste is het vandaag?	what is today's date?
*het is **de zevenentwintigste***	it's the twenty-seventh
*ik kom op **de 15e***	I'm coming on the 15th

18.3 Useful expressions

(op) maandag/dinsdag etc.	on Monday/Tuesday etc.
('s) zondags/('s) maandags/	on Sundays/Mondays/
*('s) woensdags**	Wednesdays
(op) zaterdagmorgen/-avond etc.	on Saturday morning/evening etc.
in oktober/november etc.	in October/November etc.
begin/eind januari etc.	at the beginning/end of January etc.
midden (formal *medio*) *augustus etc.*	in the middle of August
in de jaren tachtig/negentig	in the eighties/nineties

*Note *dinsdags/donderdags/vrijdags/zaterdags* without *'s*.

19 Demonstrative pronouns: THIS, THAT etc.

A demonstrative pronoun is a pronoun which points out a specific person or thing, differentiating it from other similar members of its class. In English, the demonstrative pronouns are THIS and THAT in the singular, THESE and THOSE in the plural, e.g. 'THIS man', 'THAT dog', 'THOSE sheep'. In Dutch, they are as follows:

19.1 Demonstrative pronouns occurring immediately before a noun

(a) THIS: *dit* is used before neuter nouns and *deze* before common-gender nouns
(☞ *Gender*)

dit HUIS *is te groot*	this house is too big
deze FLAT *is te klein*	this flat is too small

(b) THAT: *dat* is used before neuter nouns and *die* before common-gender nouns

zie jij **dat** MEISJE?	do you see that girl?
die MAN *is zo kaal als een biljartbal*	that man is as bald as a coot

(c) THESE: *deze* is used before all nouns

deze HUIZEN *zijn erg groot*	these houses are very big
deze TOMATEN *zijn nog groen*	these tomatoes are still green

(d) THOSE: *die* is used before all nouns

ik wil één van **die** HUIZEN *kopen*	I want to buy one of those houses
die OEFENINGEN *zijn veel te moeilijk*	those exercises are much too difficult

Note that the use of *dit/dat* corresponds to the use of *het* 'the' (e.g. *het huis, dit/dat huis*) while *deze/die* corresponds to *de* 'the' (e.g. *de man, deze/die man; de huizen, deze/die huizen*)

Table 11. Demonstrative pronouns

	COMMON GENDER	NEUTER
SINGULAR the this / that	de deze / die	**het** **dit / dat**
PLURAL the these / those	de deze / die	

19.2 Demonstrative pronouns can also stand in for nouns which have been omitted

dit huis is groot maar **dat** *is klein*	this house is big but that one is small
deze wijn is zoet maar **die** *zijn droog*	this wine is sweet but those are dry

19.3 When used independently (e.g. immediately before or after the verb 'to be', as in 'that is nice', 'these are my two children', 'is that true?') the Dutch equivalents are *dit* 'this' and *dat* 'that', EVEN WHEN REFERRING TO PLURALS

dit IS *mijn zus, Ans, en* **dat** ZIJN *haar kinderen*	this is my sister, Ans, and those are her children
dat IS *leuk*	that is nice
dit ZIJN *de beste aardbeien*	these are the best strawberries

📖 When the independent demonstrative pronouns *dit* and *dat* are used with a preposition (e.g. 'on', 'under', 'from', 'with' etc.), *hier* usually replaces *dit* and *daar* usually replaces *dat*. The preposition is then added at the end: e.g. 'after this' is not ✗ *na dit* but ***hier****na*, 'on that' is not ✗ *op dat* but ***daar****op*, 'between those' is not ✗ *tussen dat* but ***daar****tussen*.

 In English, it is common to omit demonstrative pronouns to avoid repetition, e.g. 'bring me that cup and [that] saucer', 'I like these apples and [these] oranges'. In Dutch, however, they are usually repeated, e.g. *breng mij **dat** kopje en **dat** schoteltje, ik houd van **deze** appels en **deze** peren* (☞ also *Articles*, 8.4).

20   Diminutives

A diminutive is a word form (usually a noun with a special ending) used chiefly to indicate smallness, although it may also be used to express endearment, contempt and other subtle nuances of meaning. In English, there are very few special diminutive forms (e.g. PIG**LET**, FLAT**LET**) and it is more usual simply to place the words 'small' or 'little' in front of the noun, e.g. 'the small table', 'his cute little face', 'an ugly little man'. With personal names, and a small number of ordinary nouns, '-y' may be added to express endearment, particularly when talking to children, e.g. 'Johnn**y**, look at the nice dogg**y**'. In Dutch, diminutives are extremely common, especially in the spoken language, and are usually formed by adding *-je* to a noun, e.g. *het huis**je*** 'the little house'. This ending has a number of alternative forms, however, depending on the phonetic shape of the noun to which it is added.

20.1   The formation of the diminutive[15]

(a) *-je* is the basic diminutive ending which is added to most nouns

*kind – kind**je***	little child	*schaap – schaap**je***	little sheep
*voet – voet**je***	little foot	*dak – dak**je***	little roof
*neus – neus**je***	little nose	*oog – oog**je***	little eye

(b) *-tje* is added to nouns which

(i) end in a vowel (*a, e, i, o, u*), *y, w* or *j*

*trui – trui**tje***	little jersey	*rij – rij**tje***	small queue
*ei – ei**tje***	little egg	*vrouw – vrouw**tje***	little woman

Note that nouns ending in one vowel (other than *e*) are written with two vowels in the diminutive: e.g. *oma – om**aa**tje* '(little) granny'; *foto – fot**oo**tje* '(small) photo'; contrast *dame – dametje* '(little) lady' (☞ *Spelling*, 65.2).

(ii) contain a long vowel or diphthong (written as two vowels) followed by *r, l* or *n*

*zoon – zoon**tje***	young son	*deur – deur**tje***	small door
*been – been**tje***	little leg	*uil – uil**tje***	small owl

(iii) end in unstressed *-er, -el* or *-en*

*vader – vader**tje***	daddy	*nagel – nagel**tje***	little nail
*deken – deken**tje***	little blanket	*borrel – borrel**tje***	little drink

---

15 In compound words it is always the last noun which determines the choice of diminutive ending, e.g. *kind**je** – kleinkind**je*** 'little grandchild', *mann**etje** – buurmann**etje*** 'little neighbour'.

(c) *-etje* is added to nouns containing a short vowel (written as one vowel) followed by *r, l n, m* or *ng*

*man – man**etje***	little man	*kar – karr**etje***	little cart
*bal – ball**etje***	little ball	*ding – ding**etje***	little thing
*lam – lamm**etje***	little lamb	*stem – stemm**etje***	little voice

Note that the final consonant of the noun is doubled to keep the preceding vowel pronounced short (☞ *Spelling*, 65.1(b)).

(d) *-kje* is added to nouns ending in unstressed *-ing* and the final *-g* is dropped

verrassing	surprise	→	*verrassin**kje***	little surprise
beweging	movement	→	*bewegin**kje***	little movement

(e) *-pje* is added to nouns ending in *-m*

*oom – oom**pje***	little uncle	*bezem – bezem**pje***	little broom
*duim – duim**pje***	little thumb	*worm – worm**pje***	little worm

Unless *-m* is immediately preceded by a short stressed vowel, e.g. *lam – lammetje* (☞ 20.1 (c)).

20.2 All diminutives are neuter (i.e. take *het*) and form their plurals by the addition of *-s*

*het hond**je***	the little dog	*de hond**jes***	the little dogs
*het man**etje***	the little man	*de man**etjes***	the little men

20.3 USAGE: The diminutive is used very frequently in spoken Dutch and also, to a lesser extent, in less formal styles of writing. In formal written Dutch, e.g. in the quality press, the diminutive is less common.

20.4 MEANING: The diminutive is used to express many subtle nuances of meaning which can only be grasped by listening to and reading as much Dutch as possible. Some of the more easily identifiable meanings expressed by the diminutive are given below as a rough guide.

(a) SMALLNESS

Roos heeft een (klein) **kindje**	Roos has a small child
hij nam een **stukje** *brood*	he took a small piece of bread

(b) ENDEARMENT

Toby is een lief **hondje**	Toby is a lovely little dog
kom op, **Jantje**	come on, Johnny

(c) CONTEMPT

dat was een raar **mannetje**	that was an odd little man
jij met je stomme **praatjes**	you with your stupid talk

20.4 Some ADVERBS may also have diminutive forms which are usually used to weaken the intensity of meaning. The diminutive ending for adverbs is *-jes* (or *-tjes*, *-etjes*, *-pjes* etc. according to the rules set out in 20.1 above).

*jullie gaan nu still**etjes** spelen*	now you go and play nice and quietly
*ruim je spullen net**jes** op*	clear your things away nice and neatly
*ik ga event**jes** naar buiten*	I'm just popping outside for a minute

The rules set out in 20.1 above cannot account for all diminutives and there are some irregular forms (e.g. *jongen* – *jong**etje*** 'little boy') and some which are influenced by their noun plural forms (e.g. *schip* – *sche**epje*** 'little ship', *glas* – *gla**asje*** 'little glass', *pad* – *p**aadje*** 'little path', cf. the plurals *schepen*, *glazen*, *paden*, *Nouns: Plurals*, 42.2(a)). In addition, some diminutives may have a different meaning from their associated nouns, e.g. *kaart* 'map' – *k**aartje*** 'ticket', *schotel* 'dish' – *sch**oteltje*** 'saucer', *vriendin* 'female friend' – *v**riendinnetje*** 'girlfriend' and some may exist only as diminutives, e.g. *m**eisje*** 'girl'.

21 Er

The Dutch word *er* causes difficulties for English learners of Dutch as it is used in a number of different grammatical constructions and does not always correspond to the same English word.

21.1 Generally speaking, *er* has four main functions

(a) SUBJECT: *Er* is used to introduce a subject. This corresponds to English 'there', as in 'there is', 'there are', 'there was' etc.

***er** is niemand thuis*	there is no one at home
***er** waren veel goede concerten*	there were many good concerts on
*is **er** een boekhandel in de buurt?*	is there a bookshop in the vicinity?

Note that verbs such as *zitten* 'to sit', *staan* 'to stand', *liggen* 'to lie', *lopen* 'to walk, run' are commonly used after *er*, where English would simply use the verb *to be*:

***er** STOND een theepot op tafel*	there was a teapot on the table
***er** ZIT een bedelaar op de straat*	there is a beggar in the street
***er** LOPEN veel mensen in het park*	there are many people in the park

(b) PLACE: *Er* occurs as the unstressed form of *daar*, expressing location. This corresponds to English 'there', as in e.g. 'I'll see you there tomorrow' and is usually placed after the subject and verb

*HIJ HEEFT **er** vannacht geslapen*	he slept there last night
*hoe lang WILLEN WIJ **er** blijven?*	how long do we want to stay there?

Where an object is present, *er* usually follows it:

*ik heb HET KADO **er** gisteren gekocht*	I bought the present there yesterday

(c) 'IT'/'THEM' REPLACEMENT: *Er* replaces *het/hem* 'it' and *ze* 'them' when used with a preposition (☞ *Prepositions*,). As in 21.1(b), *er* follows the subject and verb, while the preposition appears at the end of the sentence[16]

---

16 But before verbs and parts of verbs that have been sent to the end (☞ *Word order*, 78.1(b), 78.2).

PRAAT HIJ *er ooit* **over**? (✗ *over het*)　　does he ever talk about it?
IK WEET **er** *heel weinig* **van** (✗ *van het*)　　I know very little about it?
IK HEB **er** *niet* **om** *gelachen* (✗ *om het*)　　I did not laugh at it

Note that *er* only replaces pronouns referring to things and not to human beings:

mooie VROUWEN? *Ik droom* **van hen**　　beautiful women? I dream of them
grote snelle AUTO's? *Ik droom* **ervan**[17]　　big fast cars? I dream of them

(d) QUANTITY: When placed before numbers and expressions of quantity, *er* corresponds to English 'of it' or 'of them', as in 'I have three of them'. Note, however, that, unlike the English equivalents, *er* is obligatory here[18]

hoeveel kaartjes hebben zij?　　how many tickets do they have?
Jaap heeft **er** TWEE *maar*　　Jaap has two (of them) but
Geert heeft **er** GEEN　　Geert doesn't have any (of them)

Table 12. Functions of er

SUBJECT	er is niemand thuis
PLACE	hij is **er** niet
'IT/THEM' REPLACEMENT	hij praat **er**over / hij praat **er** niet over
QUANTITY	hij heeft **er** een / twee / veel

21.2　Rules governing the co-occurrence of different types of *er*

(a) Only type (a) [SUBJECT] and type (d) [QUANTITY] may occur together

er *zijn veel cafés in Leiden*　　there are many cafes in Leiden
er *zijn* **er** *veel in Leiden*　　there are many (of them) in Leiden
BUT NOT ✗ **er** *zijn* **er** **er** *veel*　　there are many (of them) there

Otherwise the sentence must be reformulated:

hoeveel flats heeft hij in Parijs?　　how many flats has he in Paris?
hij heeft **er** [PLACE] *één flat*　　he has one flat there
hij heeft **er** [QUANTITY] *één*　　he has one
NOT ✗ *hij heeft* **er** **er** *één*　　he has one there

(b) Type (c) ['IT'/'THEM' REPLACEMENT] is simply omitted if another *er* is present

er *is een boek over geschreven*　　a book has been written about it
　　NOT ✗ **er** *is een boek* **er**over *geschreven*
er *lachen veel mensen om*　　there are many people laughing at it
　　NOT ✗ **er** *lachen* **er** *veel mensen om*

 Er always occurs with the verb *uitzien* 'to look/appear', e.g. *deze druiven zien* **er** *heel goed uit* 'these grapes look very good', and usually with the verb *aankomen* 'to arrive' when the destination is not

---

17 When nothing comes between *er* and the preposition they are written as one word.
18 Compare French *en*, e.g. *j'*en *ai trois* 'I have three (of them)'.

specified, e.g. *Jaap is **er** om tien uur aangekomen* 'Jaap arrived at ten o'clock.'[19] In addition, SUBJECT
er often appears in constructions with the verb *gebeuren* 'to happen/occur', e.g. *wat is **er** (met jou)
gebeurd?* 'what has happened (to you)?', ***er** is niets gebeurd* 'nothing has happened'.

22   Female endings

In English, certain nouns denoting female humans and animals have a special feminine
ending, e.g. MANAGER**ESS**, LION**ESS**. This only occurs with a handful of examples,
however, as most English nouns can refer to either sex, e.g. 'the student', 'the teacher',
'the German'. By contrast, Dutch has a number of special endings which are commonly
used when referring to females, particularly with certain professions, nationalities and
animals, e.g. *student**e*** 'female student', *Duits**e*** 'German woman', *leeuw**in*** 'lioness'.
Generally speaking, there are three common female endings in Dutch (and four more
restricted ones), the choice of which cannot be easily predicted by rule and must simply
be learned in conjunction with each noun. There are, however, general tendencies governing the choice of these endings which may be helpful to foreign learners. The following are given as a rough guide only:

22.1   *-ster*: Nouns ending in *-er* referring to males usually form their female equivalents with *-ster* (☞ *Professions*)

werker	worker	→	*werk**ster***	female worker
speler	player	→	*speel**ster***	female player
schoonmaker	cleaner	→	*schoonmaak**ster***	female cleaner
uitgever	publisher	→	*uitgee**f**ster**	female publisher

22.2   *-e*: Nouns of French origin and nouns denoting nationality usually have a female form in *-e*

*cliënt**e***	female client	*Iers**e***	Irish woman
*psycholog**e***	female psychologist	*Engels**e***	English woman
*pianist**e***	female pianist	*Schots**e***[20]	Scottish woman

22.3   *-in*: This ending is used with a small number of nouns, usually not referring to professions, and with some animal names:

*vriend**in***	female friend	*tijger**in***	tigress
*vijand**in***	female enemy	*ber**in***	female bear
*koning**in***	queen	*pauw**in***	pea-hen

Note that, when adding any of these endings, one must observe the regular Dutch
spelling changes, e.g. *beer – b**e**rin, psycholoog – psycholo**g**e, speler – spee**l**ster, uitgever – uitgee**f**ster*
etc. (☞ *Spelling*).

 Less general female endings are (i) *-es*, e.g. *lerar**es**/onderwijzer**es*** 'female teacher', *zanger**es*** 'female
singer', (ii) *-esse* (cf. masc. *-aris*), e.g. *secretaris – secretar**esse*** 'secretary', (iii) *-euse* (cf. masc. *-eur* from

---

19 Unless some sort of indirect object is present, e.g. *zij kwamen met een kadootje aan* 'they arrived with a
    (small) present'.

20 Note that the feminine form of most nationalities is formed by adding *-e* to the corresponding
    adjective ending in *-s* and not to the masculine noun (☞ *Adjectives derived from other words*, 3.1(d)).

French), e.g. *masseur – masseuse* 'masseur – masseuse', (iv) *-trice* (cf. masc. *-teur* from French), e.g. *acteur – actrice* 'actor – actress', *directeur – directrice* 'director', *conducteur – conductrice* 'conductor / ticket collector'.

23 Future and future perfect tenses

The future tense is used either to refer to future time, e.g. 'the weather will be nice tomorrow', or to express an assumption, e.g. 'John will (probably) be in London by now'. In English, there are two types of future tense: the (simple) future tense which uses 'will' with a verb, e.g. 'John WILL GO on holiday', and the future perfect tense which uses 'will' with a verb in the perfect tense, e.g. 'John WILL HAVE GONE on holiday'. These future forms are also used in Dutch.

23.1 In Dutch, the future tense is formed with *zullen* (singular *zal*, plural *zullen*) plus the infinitive

Table 13. The future

SUBJECT	ZULLEN	INFINITIVE
ik	zal	
jij	zal/zult	
u (sing. and pl.)	zal/zult	
hij/zij/het	zal	werken 'work'
wij/jullie/zij	zullen	

Note that tenses in Dutch do not have special progressive alternatives (cf. English BE + . . . 'ing'):

ik zal hard werken	I will work hard OR
	I will be working hard
de lessen zullen makkelijk zijn	the lessons will be easy
zal jij het moeilijk vinden?	will you find it difficult?
Jan zal nu in Utrecht zijn[21]	Jan will now be in Utrecht

23.2 There are, however, alternative ways of referring to future time

(a) *Gaan* 'to go' plus the infinitive is used in much the same way as English 'going to'

| *ik ga een nieuw baantje zoeken* | I'm going to look for a new job |
| *mijn leraar gaat een boek schrijven* | my teacher is going to write a book |

Note that *gaan* is not used with *komen* 'to come' or with *gaan* itself (e.g. *ik ✗ ga naar de bioscoop gaan* 'I'm going to go to the cinema').

---
21 ☞ *Word order*, 78.2(a).

(b) It is very common in Dutch to use the present tense to refer to the future, especially when there is already some reference to the future in the sentence (e.g. 'tomorrow', 'next week', 'when?' etc.)

*Jos **komt** MORGEN naar het feestje*	Jos is coming to the party tomorrow
*ik **ben** VANAVOND niet thuis*	I will not be at home this evening
*WANNEER **is** het klaar?*	when will it be ready?

23.3 The future perfect is formed with *zullen* plus the perfect tense:

Table 14. The future perfect

Subject	ZULLEN	Perfect
ik	zal	
jij/u	zal/zult	
hij/zij/het	zal	gewerkt hebben
wij/jullie/zij	zullen	
ik	zal	
jij/u	zal/zult	
hij/zij/het	zal	gekomen zijn
wij/jullie/zij	zullen	

Note that tenses in Dutch do not have special progressive alternatives (cf. English BE + . . . 'ing'):

*ik **zal** hard **gewerkt hebben***	I will have worked hard OR
	I will have been working hard
*ik **zal** hem vóór zondag **gezien hebben***	I will have seen him by Sunday
*zij **zullen** vóór midden mei **gegaan zijn***	they will have gone by mid May
*hij **zal** al een fax **gestuurd hebben**[22]*	he will have already sent a fax

24 Geen

The Dutch word *geen* is used to translate English 'not a', 'not any' or 'no' when followed by a noun (or by an adjective plus noun). Thus, the Dutch equivalent of 'he is not a good writer' is not ✗ *hij is **niet een** goede schrijver* but *hij is **geen** goede schrijver*. Other examples are:

is dat een vrouw?	is that a woman?
*dat is **geen** VROUW – dat is een man!*	that's not a woman, it's a man!
*ik heb **geen** witte DRUIVEN nodig*	I don't need any green grapes
*Ans heeft **geen** GELD en **geen** VRIENDEN*	Ans has no money and no friends
*Jo wil **geen** ADVOCAAT worden*	Jo doesn't want to become a lawyer

---

22 The alternative word order . . . *hebben gezien*, . . . *zijn gegaan*, . . . and *hebben gestuurd* is also possible (☞ *Word order*, 78.2(c)).

Note that *niet één* is used to mean 'not one', e.g. **niet één** *mens is gekomen* 'not one person came'.

25 Gender

In English, nouns do not have grammatical gender and there is only one definite article, 'the'. By contrast, Dutch nouns may be either common gender nouns or neuter nouns, the former taking the definite article *de* and the latter *het*, e.g. **de man** 'the man', **de vrouw** 'the woman', **het kind** 'the child', **het huis** 'the house'.[23] (Note that *een* 'a' is the same for both genders, e.g. *een man, een vrouw, een kind* etc., as is the plural *de* 'the', e.g. *de mannen, de vrouwen, de kinderen* etc., ☞ **Table 15** below). It is difficult to establish hard and fast rules for assigning gender in Dutch, although certain general tendencies can be observed. As around two thirds of nouns are common gender nouns while only one third is neuter, it is perhaps easier for the student to identify which types of nouns are neuter and then assign common gender to the rest.

25.1 Neuter nouns

(a) All diminutives (☞ *Diminutives*)

het kindje	little child	*het neusje*	little nose
het voetje	little foot	*het meisje*	girl

(b) All infinitives used as nouns (☞ *Nouns derived from other words*, 43.2(a))

het eten	eating	*het zingen*	singing
het drinken	drinking	*het denken*	thinking

(c) All nouns of the type 'the good thing', 'the bad thing' etc. (☞ *Adjectives used as nouns*, 4.2)

het leuke	the nice thing	*het beste*	the best thing
het stomme	the stupid thing	*het ergste*	the worst thing

(d) All nouns of the form *ge . . . te* (☞ *Nouns derived from other words*,)

*het **ge**bergte*	mountain range	*het **ge**beente*	bones
*het **ge**dierte*	animals	*het **ge**steente*	stones

(e) All colours

het rood	red	*het groen*	green
het wit	white	*het geel*	yellow

(f) All well-known metals

het goud	gold	*het ijzer*	iron
het zilver	silver	*het lood*	lead

---

23 The term 'common gender' refers to original masculine and feminine nouns which have now merged into one gender class.

(g) Points of the compass

het noorden	north	*het oosten*	east
het zuiden	south	*het zuidwesten*	south-west

(h) All words ending in *-um, -aat, -sel* or *-isme*

*het decor**um***	decorum/appearances	*het vertel**sel***	story
*het result**aat***	result	*het fasc**isme***	fascism

(i) Most nouns beginning with the prefixes *ge-, be-* and *ver-*, but not those ending in *-ing* (☞ *Nouns derived from other words*, 43.2(b), 43.3)

het gefluister	whispering	*het bereik*	reach, range
het gepiep	chirping/squeaking	*het begin*	beginning
het beklag	complaint	*het verlies*	loss

(j) Some other commonly used nouns

het boek	book	*het kleinkind*	grandchild*
het brood	bread	*het land*	land/country
het geld	money	*het raam*	window
het haar	hair	*het uur*	hour
het huis	house	*het water*	water
het kind	child	*het werk*	work

*The gender of compound words is determined by the last noun in the compound (☞ *Compound words*, 15.1).

Table 15. Use of articles according to gender and number

	COMMON	NEUTER
SINGULAR 'the'	de de man	het het huis
PLURAL 'the'	de de mannen/huizen	
INDEFINITE 'a'	een een man/huis	

25.2 Gender and pronouns

(a) Non-humans: in English, 'it' is usually used to refer to non-human nouns while Dutch uses *hij* (object *hem*) for common gender nouns and *het* for neuter nouns[24]

DE *kat?* **Hij** *heeft de muis gegeten*	the cat? It has just eaten the mouse
DE *auto? Ik heb* **hem** *net gekocht*	the car? I've just bought it
HET *huis? Ik heb* **het** *net verkocht*	the house? I've just sold it

---

24 With prepositions, however, 'it' is translated by *er* (☞ *Er*, 21.1(c)).

English 'they' is translated by *zij/ze* and 'them' by *ze* (when referring to non-human nouns):

DE *huizen? Ik heb* **ze** *net verkocht*   the houses? I've just sold them

(b) When referring to humans, *hij* 'he' (object *hem*), *zij/ze* 'she' (object *haar/ze*) and *zij/ze* 'they' (object *hen/hun/ze*) are used in much the same way as English, irrespective of the grammatical gender of the noun (☞ also *Personal pronouns*)

DE *actrice? Ik vind* **haar** *heel mooi*   the actress? I find her very beautiful
HET *meisje?* **Zij** *werkt bij de bank*   the girl? She works at the bank
HET *broertje van Wim?* **Hij** *is ziek*   Wim's younger brother? He is ill
DE *meisjes? Ik vind* **hen / hun** *aardig*   the girls? I like them

Table 16. Translations of 'it' and 'they' (non-human)

	COMMON (e.g. de auto)	NEUTER (e.g. het huis)
IT subject	hij hij is nieuw	het het is nieuw
IT object	hem ik heb hem gekocht	het ik heb het gekocht
THEY	zij/ze zij/ze zijn nieuw	
THEM	ze ik heb ze gekocht	

 Note that while some grammatical endings, e.g. *-heid* and *-isme*, are linked to a particular gender (i.e. common and neuter respectively) others, e.g. *-schap*, are not (e.g. **de broederschap** 'brotherhood' but **het vaderschap** 'fatherhood'). Some nouns may have two genders, e.g. **de** or **het omslag** 'envelope', and sometimes a change in gender denotes a change in meaning e.g. **de blik** 'look, glance' versus **het blik** 'tin', **de portier** 'porter' versus **het portier** 'door of a vehicle'.

 In Belgium and the south of The Netherlands, *zij/ze* 'she' (object *haar* 'her') is often used not only to refer to female humans but also to non-human nouns which were originally feminine in gender, e.g. *de kat?* **Zij** *heeft de muis gegeten* 'the cat? It has eaten the mouse', *de deur? Ik heb* **haar** *dicht gedaan* 'the door? I have shut it'.

26 *Graag*

The Dutch word *graag* is an adverb which conveys the meaning 'willingly' or 'with pleasure' (compare German *gern(e)*). It appears after verbs and is best translated into English by using 'to like' with the verb in question, e.g. *ik speel* **graag** *voetbal* 'I like playing football'.[25]

---

25 Contrast *leuk vinden* and *houden van* which are used with nouns and pronouns, e.g. *hij vond* **de film** *leuk* 'he liked the film', *hij vond* **haar** *leuk* 'he liked her', *ik houd van* **opera** 'I like/love opera'.

26.1 Use of *graag*[26]

DOE *jij het* **graag***?*	do you like doing it?
ik BEZOEK *hem (niet)* **graag**	I (do not) like visiting him
hij GAAT *heel* **graag** *naar het theater*	he really likes going to the theatre
WILT *u koffie? Ja,* **graag**	do you want a coffee? Yes, please.

Note that *graag* is very often used in 'would like' constructions using the conditional of *willen* 'to want'(☞ *Conditional and conditional perfect tenses*, 16.1):

ik WOU **graag** *een biertje*	I would like a beer
ik ZOU **graag** *naar huis* WILLEN *gaan*	I would like to go home

26.2 The comparative form of *graag* is *liever* and the superlative is *het liefst*. These forms are best translated by 'to prefer' (or 'would rather') and 'to like best' respectively

Jaap WOONT **liever** *alleen*	Jaap prefers to live alone
ik ZOU **liever** *wijn dan bier* DRINKEN	I would rather drink wine than beer
Piet LEEST **het liefst** *griezelromans*	Piet likes reading horror stories best

27 Hypothetical sentences with *als*: IF

In English, hypothetical sentences referring to future time are often expressed using the simple past tense followed by the conditional, e.g. 'if I WORKED harder I WOULD EARN more money' (i.e. it is still possible in the future). Hypothetical sentences referring to the past are expressed using the pluperfect tense followed by the conditional perfect, e.g. 'if I HAD WORKED harder I WOULD HAVE EARNED more money' (i.e. it is no longer possible).[27]

27.1 In Dutch, the same tense patterns may be used (☞ also *Conditional and conditional perfect tenses*)

als ik harder **werkte**,	if I worked harder
zou *ik meer geld* **verdienen**	I would earn more money
als ik harder **gewerkt had**,	if I had worked harder
zou *ik meer geld* **verdiend hebben**	I would have earned more money

But there are also alternatives:

27.2 'If I worked . . .': Some Dutch speakers prefer to use the conditional in both parts of the sentence

als ik harder **zou werken**,	if I worked harder
zou ik meer geld verdienen	I would earn more money

---

26 Generally speaking, *graag* follows the same word order rules as *niet, nooit, ook* etc. (☞ *Niet*).
27 ☞ also the separate entries for the individual tenses.

27.3 'I would have earned . . .': It is very common to use a contracted form of the conditional perfect which is identical to the pluperfect

als ik harder gewerkt had,	if I had worked harder
had *ik meer geld* **verdiend**	I would have earned more money

Other examples are:

als ik die wijn **gedronken had**,	if I had drunk that wine
had *ik hoofdpijn* **gekregen**	I would have got a headache
als ik vroeger **opgestaan was**,	if I had got up earlier
had *ik tijd voor het ontbijt* **gehad**	I would have had time for breakfast
als de bus om zes uur **vertrokken was**,	if the bus had left at six o'clock
was *ik om acht uur* **aangekomen**	I would have arrived at eight

28 Imperative

The imperative is the form of the verb used to give an order or command, e.g. 'COME here'! In Dutch there are three basic imperative forms depending on who is being addressed:

28.1 Most commonly, the bare verb stem is used

ga *rechtdoor*	go straight on
kijk!	look!
laat *mij het doen*	let me do it

The verb STEM is the infinitive minus *-en* with the appropriate spelling changes (☞ *Spelling*) and is identical to the first person singular present form, e.g. *gaan – ik* **ga** 'I go', *kijken – ik* **kijk** 'I look', *leven – ik* **leef** 'I live' etc.

Note that, especially in spoken Dutch, *eens* and *even* 'just' are often added to make the command sound less harsh, and *maar* is often used to mean 'just' or 'go ahead':

kom morgen **eens** *langs*	(just) come along tomorrow
wacht **even**!	(just) wait!
schrijf me **maar** *een brief*	(go ahead), write me a letter

28.2 When being very polite, the *u* form is used

vult u *dit formulier in*	(please) fill in this form
betaalt u *aan de kassa*	(please) pay at the cash desk
blijft u *maar zitten*	(please) (just) remain seated

28.3 If a verb has a separable prefix this is sent to the end of the clause (☞ *Separable verbs*)

doe *een das* **om**, *want het is koud*	put a scarf on because it's cold
kijk uit!	look out!

28.4   English 'let us/let's' plus a verb is often rendered by *laten we* + infinitive

laten we *gaan*	let's go
laten we *maar thuisblijven*	let's just stay at home

28.5   When the command is general and no one particular person is being addressed, the infinitive is often used. This is particularly common on public signs

*NIET **ROKEN***	NO SMOKING
*NIET **AANRAKEN***	DO NOT TOUCH
TREKKEN/DUWEN	PULL/PUSH

 Note that the verb *zijn* has the irregular imperative *wees* (and the polite form *weest u*), e.g. ***wees*** *niet bang* 'don't be afraid'.

 In formal written Dutch, a special plural imperative ending in *-t* is sometimes used, e.g. ***verstuurt*** *f100 aan . . .* '(please) send 100 guilders to . . .'

<h1>29   Indefinite pronouns: SOME, ANY, EACH etc.</h1>

An indefinite pronoun is a word which refers to persons or things which are not specific. The most common ones in English are SOME, SOMEBODY, SOMETHING, ANY, ANYBODY, ANYTHING, EACH, EVERY, EVERYBODY, EVERYTHING, NOBODY, NOTHING, ALL and NO/NOT ANY. Sometimes these pronouns are difficult to translate into Dutch as they may have more than one meaning. Some of the more problematic cases are dealt with below.

29.1   SOME: The Dutch equivalents of 'some' are *sommige* and *enige/enkele/wat*

(a) *sommige* is used to denote a group of people or things, particularly where a contrast is implied

sommige *huizen zijn erg duur*	some houses are very expensive
sommige *mensen hebben geen smaak*	some people have no taste

(b) *enige, enkele* or, less formally, *wat* are used to express an indefinite quantity. *Wat* is commonly used with nouns which do not usually have a plural, e.g. *suiker* 'sugar', *melk* 'milk' etc.

*ik heb **enige / enkele / wat** foto's gezien*	I saw some photos
*hij heeft nog **wat** geld bij hem*	he still has some money on him

29.2   ANY: The Dutch equivalents of 'any' are *ieder(e)/elk(e)* and *enig(e)/wat*[28]

(a) *ieder(e)* and *elk(e)* are used interchangeably to mean 'no matter which'

*jij zou **iedere / elke** wijn drinken*	you would drink any (sort of) wine
***ieder / elk** huis is beter dan een flat*	any house is better than a flat

---

28   The forms with *-e* are used everywhere except before singular neuter nouns (compare *Adjectives,* 2.1).

(b) *enig*(e) or, less formally, *wat* are used in questions. *Wat* is commonly used with nouns which do not usually have a plural (compare 29.1(b))

*zie jij **enige / wat** champignons?*	can you see any mushrooms?
*heb jij **wat** melk?*	have you any milk?

In negative sentences with '(not) any', *geen* is usually used, e.g. *ik heb **geen** melk* 'I don't have any milk' (☞ *Geen*).

29.3 EACH, EVERY: The Dutch equivalents of 'each' and 'every' are *ieder*(e) and *elk*(e) which are used interchangeably[28]

ieder / elk *boek kost f 50*	each book costs 50 guilders
*Jaap gaat **iedere / elke** dag zwemmen*	Jaap goes swimming every day

29.4 SOMEBODY, ANYBODY, NOBODY, EVERYBODY

(a) *iemand* is used to mean 'somebody'. It also translates 'anybody' in questions

iemand *heeft mijn fiets gestolen*	somebody has stolen my bike
*heeft **iemand** een sigaret?*	does anybody have a cigarette?

(b) *niemand* is used to mean 'nobody'. It also translates 'anybody' in negative contexts

niemand *komt vanavond*	nobody is coming tonight
*hij houdt van **niemand***	he does not love anybody

(c) *Iedereen* and, less commonly, *allen* (☞ *ALL*, 6.2) are used to mean 'everybody'. They also translate 'anybody' when stressed

iedereen *heeft dit boek gelezen*	everybody has read this book
*hij praat met **iedereen***	he talks to everybody / anybody
iedereen *kan deze oefening doen*	anybody can do this exercise

29.5 SOMETHING, ANYTHING, NOTHING, EVERYTHING

(a) *iets* and, more colloquially, *wat* are used to mean 'something'. They also translate 'anything' in questions

*ik heb net **iets / wat** gehoord*	I have just heard something
*heeft hij **iets / wat** gezegd?*	did he say anything?

(b) *niets* is used to mean 'nothing'. It also translates 'anything' in negative contexts

*de arme man heeft **niets***	the poor man has nothing
*hij houdt van **niets***	he does not like anything

(c) *alles* is used to mean 'everything'. It also translates 'anything' when stressed (☞ *ALL*, 6.5)

*ik heb **alles** verloren*	I've lost everything
*heb jij **alles** gehoord?*	did you hear everything?
alles *is mogelijk*	anything is possible

29.6   For ALL and NO/NOT ANY, ☞ *ALL* and *Geen* respectively

 When the indefinite pronouns *sommige/enige* 'some', *alle* 'all', *veel* 'many', *andere* 'other' and *verscheidene* 'various' stand in for nouns referring to humans, they take *-n* in the plural, e.g. **sommigen/anderen/allen/velen** *hebben geen smaak* 'some/others/all/many have no taste'.

30   Infinitives and use of (*om*) . . . *te*

The infinitive is the part of the verb which is always given in dictionaries and does not change its form to show person, number and tense. In English, it consists of the verb stem usually preceded by 'to', e.g. 'to WORK', 'to GO', 'to DO'. In Dutch, the infinitive consists of the verb stem plus *-en* (or *-n*), e.g. *werken, gaan, doen* and, depending on the construction in which it occurs, it may be used either on its own, with *te* or with *om . . . te*, e.g. *ik kan* **komen** 'I can come', *hij begon* **te lachen** 'he began to laugh', *ik werk* **om** *geld* **te verdienen** 'I work to earn money'.[29] In many cases, *te* and *om . . . te* are used interchangeably, although there is now a general tendency to prefer *om . . . te* (☞ for examples). Therefore, it is advisable for students to use *om . . . te* in all but the following cases:

30.1   The infinitive is used without (*om*) . . . *te*

(a) After modal verbs, *laten* and *blijven* (☞ *Modal verbs, Laten, Blijven*)

ik WIL/KAN/MOET/MAG **komen**	I want to/can/must/am allowed to come
hij LAAT *mij het* **doen**	he lets me do it

(b) After *zullen/zou(den)* in the future and conditional (☞ *Future and future perfect tenses, Conditional and conditional perfect tenses*)

het ZAL *morgen* **regenen**	it will rain tomorrow
wij ZOUDEN *liever* **wachten**	we would rather wait

(c) When used as an imperative (☞ *Imperative*, 28.3)

niet **roken**!	no smoking!

(d) After verbs of sensation (e.g. *zien* 'to see', *horen* 'to hear', *voelen* 'to feel') and *komen* 'to come', *gaan* 'to go', *vinden* 'to find', *leren* 'to teach', *helpen* 'to help'

ik ZIE *jou graag* **werken**	I like to see you working[30]
zijn moeder HOORDE *hem* **vloeken**	his mother heard him swearing
zij GAAT *iedere dag* **zwemmen**	she goes swimming every day

Note that these verbs are similar to modal verbs, *laten* and *blijven* in that they use an infinitive in the perfect and pluperfect tenses when they co-occur with another verb (☞ also *Word order*, 78.2(d)):

zijn moeder had hem HOREN **vloeken**	his mother had heard him swearing
zij is iedere dag GAAN **zwemmen**	she went swimming every day

---

29   Note that the infinitive (with or without *te*) usually appears at the end of the clause (☞ *Word order*, 78.2(a)).

30   ☞ also *-ING constructions*.

30.2 The infinitive is used only with *te*

(a) With verbs of position, e.g. *zitten* 'to sit', *staan* 'to stand', *liggen* 'to lie' and *lopen* 'to walk'. In these cases, English uses an '-ing' construction

Roos STOND *op de bus* **te wachten**	Roos stood waiting for the bus
Geert ZAT *naar de radio* **te luisteren**	Geert sat listening to the radio
Ruud LAG *de hele dag* **te slapen**	Ruud lay sleeping all day
Kees LIEP **te zingen**	Kees was walking along singing

(b) With some other verbs, e.g. *beginnen* 'to begin', *proberen* 'to try', *durven* 'to dare', *hoeven* 'to need', *weten* 'to know how to/to manage to'

PROBEER *het* **te raden**	try and guess
het BEGINT **te regenen**	it's beginning to rain
jij HOEFT *niet* **te gaan**, *als jij niet wilt*	you needn't go if you don't want

(c) After certain prepositions, e.g. *zonder* 'without', *in plaats van* 'instead of', *door* 'by'

ik zei het ZONDER **te denken**	I said it without thinking
hij nam het ZONDER *iets* **te zeggen**	he took it without saying anything
ik keek tv IN PLAATS VAN *uit* **te gaan**	I watched TV instead of going out

30.3 English infinitives which follow an object, e.g. 'he asked *me* TO COME', 'I want *you* TO STAY', 'I told *the man* what TO DO', are translated not by infinitives in Dutch but more loosely by whole clauses

hij verwacht **dat ik kom**	he is expecting me to come
ik vroeg hem **of hij kon wachten**	I asked him to wait
hij zei haar **wat zij moest doen**	he told her what to do
ik weet niet **wat ik moet zeggen**	I don't know what to say

Meaning literally 'he expects that I come', 'I asked him whether he could wait', 'he told her what she had to do', 'I don't know what I have to say'.

 Here is a list of examples using infinitives with *om . . . te*. Note that all objects, expressions of time, manner and place, adjectives, adverbs and prepositions are placed between *om* and *te*: e.g. *hij neemt een uur vrij* **om** *naar de tandarts* **te gaan** 'he is taking an hour off to go to the dentist', *hoeveel kost het* **om** *hier* **te parkeren?** 'how much is it to park here?', *hij is te moe* **om** *stout* **te zijn** 'he's too tired to be naughty', *het is erg moeilijk* **om te doen** 'it is very difficult to do', *ik heb een telefoonkaart gekocht* **om** *jou op* **te bellen** 'I bought a phonecard to ring you up' (☞ *Separable verbs*, 64.4). *Om . . . te* always occurs when the infinitive is at the beginning of a sentence, e.g. **Om** *het duidelijk* **te maken**, *het interesseert me niet* 'To make it clear, I'm not interested', or when the infinitive refers to a preceding noun, e.g. *het is een interessant programma* **om** *naar* **te kijken** 'it's an interesting programme to watch'.

31 -ING constructions: Dutch equivalents

In English, verb[31] forms in '-ing', such as 'workING', 'playING', 'beING' etc., are particularly difficult to translate into Dutch, as different grammatical constructions are

---

31 For -'ing' forms used as adjectives and adverbs, ☞ *Present participles*.

needed depending on the context in which the '-ing' form occurs. This section outlines some common occurrences of '-ing' and their Dutch equivalents:

31.1 English progressive forms such as 'I AM READING a book', 'he WAS PLAYING football' etc. have no direct equivalent in Dutch, and are simply translated in the same way as the corresponding non-progressive form

*ik **drink** een kopje thee*	I drink/am drinking a cup of tea
*wij **praatten** over het werk*	we talked/were talking about work

Note that if a speaker wishes to stress the progressive aspect, s/he can do so in other ways (☞ *Progressive forms*, 57.2).

31.2 -ING forms are rendered by the INFINITIVE in Dutch

(a) When used after verbs of sensation (e.g. *zien* 'to see', *horen* 'to hear', *voelen* 'to feel') and after *komen* 'to come', *gaan* 'to go', *vinden* 'to find', *leren* 'to teach'

*ik ZIE jou graag **werken***	I like to see you working
*zijn moeder HOORDE hem **vloeken***	his mother heard him swearing
*zij GAAT iedere dag **zwemmen***	she goes swimming every day

(b) When used in short headings, titles and commands

*het boek heet 'Geld **Sparen'***	the book is called 'Saving Money'
*niet **roken***	no smoking

31.3 And by *te* + INFINITIVE

(a) With verbs of position, e.g. *zitten* 'to sit', *staan* 'to stand', *liggen* 'to lie' and *lopen* 'to walk'

*Roos STOND op de bus **te wachten***	Roos stood waiting for the bus
*Geert ZAT naar de radio **te luisteren***	Geert sat listening to the radio
*Theo LAG aan zijn vriendin **te denken***	Theo lay thinking of his girlfriend
*Kees LIEP **te zingen***	Kees was walking along singing

(b) After certain prepositions, e.g. *zonder* 'without', *in plaats van* 'instead of', *door* 'by'[32]

*zij gingen ZONDER **te betalen***	they left without paying
*hij nam het ZONDER iets **te zeggen***	he took it without saying anything
*ik keek tv IN PLAATS VAN uit **te gaan***	I watched TV instead of going out
*DOOR harder **te werken**, krijgt hij hogere cijfers*	by working harder he gets higher grades

31.4 -ING forms are often used instead of passives with the verb 'to need' in English, e.g. 'my car needs repairing'. This is rendered by *moeten* plus a passive in Dutch (☞ *Passive*)

*al dit werk MOET **gedaan worden***	all this work needs doing
*mijn jurk MOET **gewassen worden***	my dress needs washing

---

32 Yet if there are two **different** subjects, a whole clause beginning with *dat* is needed, e.g. 'I left without **him** seeing me': *ik ging weg zonder **dat hij mij zag**.*

31.5 In English, the relative pronouns 'who', 'which' and 'that' may be omitted and an '-ing' construction used. This is not possible in Dutch (☞ *Relative pronouns*)

*de man **die** de krant **leest**, is mijn vader*	the man reading the newspaper is my father
*ken je de vrouw **die zingt**?*	do you know the woman singing?

31.6 When in doubt, -ING constructions are best translated loosely using whole clauses in Dutch

*ik kan me niet vorstellen **dat zij komt***	I can't imagine her coming
***toen wij** in de stad **reden**, zagen wij een ongeluk*	driving into town, we saw an accident
*ik las het boek **en lachte** in mezelf*	I read the book, laughing to myself
*nadat **hij** zijn moeder **bezocht had***	after visiting his mother
*ik streek terwijl **ik** naar de tv **keek***	I ironed while watching TV

 In written Dutch, and especially in the literary language, present participles may be used to translate English verb forms in '-ing' when beginning a sentence or following a comma (☞ *Present participles,*).

32 Inseparable verbs

Dutch has a number of verbs which are derived from nouns, adjectives and, in particular, other verbs by adding the prefixes **be-**, **her-**, **ont-**, **ver-**, **ge-** and **er-** . These are called 'inseparable prefixes' because they are never separated from the verb (contrast *Separable verbs*).

32.1 When using inseparable verbs in Dutch one must bear two general points in mind

(a) Their inseparable prefixes are always unstressed. (The stressed syllables are underlined)

*hij **her**haalde de zin drie keer*	he repeated the sentence three times
*wie **ont**dekte deze brief?*	who discovered this letter?
*de trein **ver**trekt om twee uur*	the train is leaving at two o'clock
*ik moet iets met jou **be**spreken*	I must discuss something with you

(b) They form their past participles without ge- (☞ *Perfect tense*, 48.2(a))

*het werd drie keer **her**haald*	it was repeated three times
*wie heeft deze brief **ont**dekt?*	who discovered this letter?
*de trein is al **ver**trokken*	the train has already left
*wij hebben het al **be**sproken*	we have already discussed it

32.2 MEANING: Although, generally speaking, inseparable prefixes do not have clearly definable meanings and must be interpreted within the context of the verb with which they occur, it is sometimes possible to observe general *tendencies* whereby a particular prefix is connected with a specific meaning or function. The following are given as a rough guide only.

(a) *be-* is commonly used to derive transitive verbs (i.e. those taking a direct object)

ik wil eindigen/DE BRIEF *be*ëindigen	I want to finish / to finish the letter
ik wil reizen/DE WERELD *be*reizen	I want to travel / to travel the world
de zon schijnt/*be*schijnt DE VELDEN	the sun is shining / shining on the fields

Sometimes the derived verb has a slightly different (or even completely different) meaning from the original verb:

noemen	to name	→	*be*noemen	to appoint/nominate
spreken	to speak	→	*be*spreken	to discuss
keren	to turn	→	*be*keren	to convert (religious)

(b) *her-* often corresponds to English 're-' meaning 'again'

*her*enigen	to reunite	*her*lezen	to re-read
*her*vormen	to reform	*her*schrijven	to rewrite
*her*drukken	to reprint	*her*zien	to revise

(c) *ont-* is often added to reverse the action described by a verb. In this way it is similar to English 'un-', 'dis-' and 'de-'

*ont*sluiten	to unlock	*ont*kleden	to undress
*ont*erven	to disinherit	*ont*dekken	to discover
*ont*cijferen	to decipher	*ont*koppelen	to declutch

It may also render English 'away':

*ont*nemen	to take away	*ont*lopen	to run away
*ont*glippen	to slip away	*ont*komen	to get away/escape

(d) *ver-* is the most widely used of the inseparable prefixes and conveys a variety of meanings. Some common ones are

(i) To change appearance or state (derived from adjectives)

*ver*beteren	to improve	*ver*slechteren	to deteriorate/worsen

(ii) To die or come to an end (from nouns, adjectives and verbs)

*ver*hongeren	to starve to death	*ver*drogen	to dry up

(iii) To cover something with a material (derived from nouns):

*ver*gulden	to gild	*ver*pakken	to pack/package

(iv) To do something incorrectly (when reflexive)

*zich ver*spreken	to make a slip of the tongue
*zich ver*tellen	to miscount
*zich ver*slikken	to swallow something the wrong way

(e) *ge-* and *er-* are not as common as the prefixes listed in 32.2(a–d) and cannot be associated with clearly definable meanings

*ge*denken	to commemorate	*er*kennen	to acknowledge
*ge*bieden	to command	*er*varen	to experience

41

33   Irregular verbs[33]

Roughly speaking, there are three types of irregular verb in English and Dutch: (i) verbs which have irregular forms in the present and past tenses, e.g. English BE – AM – IS - ARE – WAS – BEEN etc., (ii) verbs which only have irregular forms in the past, e.g. GO – WENT, SEND – SENT, (iii) verbs which have a regular vowel change in the past. In (iii), the vowel changes are 'regular' in that they follow certain patterns shared by a number of similar verbs, e.g. SING – SANG, RING – RANG, SWIM – SWAM on the one hand, FIND – FOUND, BIND – BOUND, GRIND – GROUND on the other. These are commonly known as 'strong' verbs and can be divided into seven subgroups in Dutch according to the basic patterns of vowel change (☞ 33.3 below). Note that the past participles of strong verbs in Dutch always end in *-en*.

33.1   Verbs which are irregular in the present and past

(a) Modal verbs (☞ *Modal verbs*, 40.1)

(b) *hebben* 'to have'

ik **heb**	I have	*wij* **hebben**	we have
jij **hebt**	you have (informal)	*jullie* **hebben** (rarer **hebt**)	you (pl.) have
u **heeft** (or **hebt**)	you have (formal)		
hij/zij/het **heeft**	he/she/it has	*zij* **hebben**	they have
ik/jij/u/hij/zij/het	**had**	I, you, you, he, she, it had	
wij/jullie/zij	**hadden**	we, you(pl.), they had	
ik heb etc.	**gehad**	I have etc. had (past participle)	

(c) *zijn* 'to be'

ik **ben**	I am	*wij* **zijn**	we are
jij **bent**	you are	*jullie* **zijn**	you (pl.) are
u **bent** (or **is**)	you are		
hij/zij/het **is**	he/she/it is	*zij* **zijn**	they are
ik/jij/u/hij/zij/het	**was**	I was, you were, he/she/it was	
wij/jullie/zij	**waren**	we/you(pl.)/they were	
ik ben etc.	**geweest**	I have etc. been (past participle)	

(d) *zullen* 'will'

ik **zal**	I will	*wij* **zullen**	we will
jij **zal** (or **zult**)	you will	*jullie* **zullen**	you (pl.) will
u **zal** (or **zult**)	you will		
hij/zij/het **zal**	he/she/it will	*zij* **zullen**	they will
ik/jij/u/hij/zij/het	**zou**	I was, you were, he/she/it would	
wij/jullie/zij	**zouden**	we/you(pl.)/they would	

no past participle

---

33 ☞ *Appendix* for alphabetical list of irregular verbs.

(e) *komen* 'to come'

ik **kom** (not *koom*)	I come	wij **komen**	we come
jij **komt**	you come	jullie **komen**	you(pl.) come
u **komt**	you come		
hij/zij/het **komt**	he/she/it comes	zij **komen**	they come

ik/jij/u/hij/zij/het	**kwam**	I was, you were, he/she/it came
wij/jullie/zij	**kwamen**	we/you(pl.)/they came
ik ben etc.	**gekomen**	I have etc. come (past participle)

33.2 Verbs which are irregular in the past

(a) Verbs with irregular simple past forms (and past participles)

Inf.	Past Sing.	Past Pl.	Past Part.	
brengen	*bracht*	*brachten*	*gebracht*	bring
denken	*dacht*	*dachten*	*gedacht*	think
doen	*deed*	*deden*	*gedaan*	do
gaan	*ging*	*gingen*	*gegaan*[z]	go[34]
jagen	*joeg/*	*joegen/*	*gejaagd*	chase
		jaagde	*jaagden*	hunt
kopen	*kocht*	*kochten*	*gekocht*	buy
plegen	*placht*	*plachten*	———	be used to[35]
slaan	*sloeg*	*sloegen*	*geslagen*	hit
staan	*stond*	*stonden*	*gestaan*	stand
vragen	*vroeg*	*vroegen*	*gevraagd*	ask
weten	*wist*	*wisten*	*geweten*	know
worden	*werd*	*werden*	*geworden*[z]	become
zeggen	*zei*	*zeiden*	*gezegd*	say
zien	*zag*	*zagen*	*gezien*	see
zoeken	*zocht*	*zochten*	*gezocht*	look for

(b) In addition, the following verbs have irregular past participles in -*en* but their simple past forms are regular

bakken – *gebakken*	bake	**raden** – *geraden*	guess
barsten – *gebarsten*	burst	**scheiden** – *gescheiden*	separate
braden – *gebraden*	roast	**spannen** – *gespannen*	stretch
brouwen – *gebrouwen*	brew	**stoten** – *gestoten*	push
heten – *geheten*	be called	**vouwen** – *gevouwen*	fold
lachen – *gelachen*	laugh	**wassen** – *gewassen*	wash
laden – *geladen*	load	**weven** – *geweven*	weave
malen – *gemalen*	grind	**zouten** – *gezouten*	salt

---

34 [z]= verbs taking *zijn* as an auxiliary in the (plu)perfect; [h/z]= verbs taking *hebben* or *zijn* (☞ *Perfect tense*, 48.3 and 48.4).

35 Used in formal Dutch (☞ *USED TO*, 72.1).

33.3 'Strong' verbs with a vowel change in the simple past (and past participle). Below is a list of the most commonly used verbs, i.e. the infinitive, past singular, past plural and past participle:

(a) Group 1

ij	*ee*	*e*	*e*[36]	
bijten	*beet*	*beten*	*gebeten*	bite
blijken	*bleek*	*bleken*	*gebleken*[z]	appear
blijven	*bleef*	*bleven*	*gebleven*[z]	stay
drijven	*dreef*	*dreven*	*gedreven*[h/z]	float/propel
glijden	*gleed*	*gleden*	*gegleden*[h/z]	slide/glide
grijpen	*greep*	*grepen*	*gegrepen*	grasp/seize
kijken	*keek*	*keken*	*gekeken*	look/watch
krijgen	*kreeg*	*kregen*	*gekregen*	receive/get
lijden	*leed*	*leden*	*geleden*	suffer
lijken	*leek*	*leken*	*geleken*	seem/resemble
prijzen	*prees*	*prezen*	*geprezen*	praise
rijden	*reed*	*reden*	*gereden*[h/z]	ride/drive
rijzen	*rees*	*rezen*	*gerezen*[z]	rise
schijnen	*scheen*	*schenen*	*geschenen*	shine/seem
schrijven	*schreef*	*schreven*	*geschreven*	write
snijden	*sneed*	*sneden*	*gesneden*	cut
spijten	*speet*	*speten*	*gespeten*	be sorry[37]
splijten	*spleet*	*spleten*	*gespleten*	split
stijgen	*steeg*	*stegen*	*gestegen*[z]	rise/climb
verdwijnen	*verdween*	*verdwenen*	*verdwenen*[z]	disappear
vermijden	*vermeed*	*vermeden*	*vermeden*	avoid
wijzen	*wees*	*wezen*	*gewezen*	point out
zwijgen	*zweeg*	*zwegen*	*gezwegen*	be silent

(b) Group 2

ui/ie	*oo*	*o*	*o*	
(i) **buigen**	*boog*	*bogen*	*gebogen*	bend
druipen	*droop*	*dropen*	*gedropen*	drip
duiken	*dook*	*doken*	*gedoken*[h/z]	dive
fluiten	*floot*	*floten*	*gefloten*	whistle
kruipen	*kroop*	*kropen*	*gekropen*[h/z]	creep/crawl
ruiken	*rook*	*roken*	*geroken*	smell
schuiven	*schoof*	*schoven*	*geschoven*[h/z]	shove/push
sluipen	*sloop*	*slopen*	*geslopen*	sneak/skulk
sluiten	*sloot*	*sloten*	*gesloten*	shut
snuiven	*snoof*	*snoven*	*gesnoven*	sniff

---

36 Note that consonant changes and the use of double and single vowels (e.g. *bleef – bleven*) are determined by the regular Dutch spelling rules (☞ *Spelling*).

37 *Spijten* is usually used witih *het* and the object pronoun: e.g. *het spijt me* 'I'm sorry'; *het speet hem* 'he was sorry'.

spruiten	*sproot*	*sproten*	*gesproten*[z]	sprout
spuiten	*spoot*	*spoten*	*gespoten*	spout/squirt
zuigen	*zoog*	*zogen*	*gezogen*	suck

Also:

spugen	*spoog*	*spogen*	*gespogen*	spit
	(spuugde)	*(spuugden)*	*(gespuugd)*	

(ii)

bedriegen	*bedroog*	*bedrogen*	*bedrogen*	deceive
bieden	*bood*	*boden*	*geboden*	offer
genieten	*genoot*	*genoten*	*genoten*	enjoy
gieten	*goot*	*goten*	*gegoten*	pour
kiezen	*koos*	*kozen*	*gekozen*	choose
liegen	*loog*	*logen*	*gelogen*	tell lies
schieten	*schoot*	*schoten*	*geschoten*	shoot
verbieden	*verbood*	*verboden*	*verboden*	forbid
verliezen	*verloor*	*verloren*	*verloren*	lose
vliegen	*vloog*	*vlogen*	*gevlogen*[h/z]	fly
vriezen	*vroor*	*vroren*	*gevroren*	freeze

Also:

scheren	*schoor*	*schoren*	*geschoren*	shave/shear
wegen	*woog*	*wogen*	*gewogen*	weigh

(c) Group 3

i/e + n/m/r/l   o   o   o

(i)

beginnen	*begon*	*begonnen*	*begonnen*[z]	begin
binden	*bond*	*bonden*	*gebonden*	bind
dringen	*drong*	*drongen*	*gedrongen*[h/z]	push forward
drinken	*dronk*	*dronken*	*gedronken*	drink
dwingen	*dwong*	*dwongen*	*gedwongen*	force
klinken	*klonk*	*klonken*	*geklonken*	sound
krimpen	*kromp*	*krompen*	*gekrompen*	shrink
spinnen	*spon*	*sponnen*	*gesponnen*	spin
springen	*sprong*	*sprongen*	*gesprongen*[h/z]	jump
stinken	*stonk*	*stonken*	*gestonken*	stink
vinden	*vond*	*vonden*	*gevonden*	find
winden	*wond*	*wonden*	*gewonden*	wind
winnen	*won*	*wonnen*	*gewonnen*	win
wringen	*wrong*	*wrongen*	*gewrongen*	wring
zingen	*zong*	*zongen*	*gezongen*	sing
zinken	*zonk*	*zonken*	*gezonken*[z]	sink

Also:

schrikken	*schrok*	*schrokken*	*geschrokken*[z]	be frightened

(ii)

gelden	*gold*	*golden*	*gegolden*	be valid
schelden	*schold*	*scholden*	*gescholden*	abuse/revile
schenken	*schonk*	*schonken*	*geschonken*	pour (a drink)
smelten	*smolt*	*smolten*	*gesmolten*[h/z]	melt
zenden	*zond*	*zonden*	*gezonden*	send/broadcast

zwellen	*zwol*	*zwollen*	*gezwollen*[z]	swell
zwemmen	*zwom*	*zwommen*	*gezwommen*[h/z]	swim

Also:

treffen	*trof*	*troffen*	*getroffen*	hit
trekken	*trok*	*trokken*	*getrokken*	pull
vechten	*vocht*	*vochten*	*gevochten*	fight

Note that a small group of verbs has *ie* in the past singular and plural instead of *o(o)*: e.g. **helpen – hielp – hielpen – geholpen** 'to help', **sterven – stierf – stierven – gestorven**[z] 'to die', **werpen – wierp – wierpen – geworpen** 'to throw'.

(d) Group 4

e	*a*[38]	*a*	*o*	
bevelen	*beval*	*bevalen*	*bevolen*	command
breken	*brak*	*braken*	*gebroken*	break
nemen	*nam*	*namen*	*genomen*	take
spreken	*sprak*	*spraken*	*gesproken*	speak
steken	*stak*	*staken*	*gestoken*	stab
stelen	*stal*	*stolen*	*gestolen*	steal

(e) Group 5

i/e	*a*	*a*	*e*	
(i) **bidden**	*bad*	*baden*	*gebeden*	pray
liggen	*lag*	*lagen*	*gelegen*	lie
zitten	*zat*	*zaten*	*gezeten*	sit
(ii) **eten**	*at*	*aten*	*gegeten*	eat
geven	*gaf*	*gaven*	*gegeven*	give
lezen	*las*	*lazen*	*gelezen*	read
meten	*mat*	*maten*	*gemeten*	measure
treden	*trad*	*traden*	*getreden*[z]	step/tread
vergeten	*vergat*	*vergaten*	*vergeten*[h/z]	forget
vreten	*vrat*	*vraten*	*gevreten*	eat (of animals)

(f) Group 6

a	*oe*	*oe*	*a(o)*	
dragen	*droeg*	*droegen*	*gedragen*	carry/wear
graven	*groef*	*groeven*	*gegraven*	dig
slaan	*sloeg*	*sloegen*	*geslagen*	hit
varen	*voer*	*voeren*	*gevaren*[h/z]	sail

Also:

zweren	*zwoer*	*zwoeren*	*gezworen*	swear (an oath)

---

38 Note the use of short *a* in the singular versus long *a* in the plural in Groups 4 and 5, e.g. *breken – brak – braken, nemen – nam – namen,* NOT ✗ *breken – brak – brak**k**en, nemen – nam – nam**m**en.*

(g) Group 7

a / ang	ie / ing	ie / ing	vowel as infinitive	
(i) **blazen**	*blies*	*bliezen*	*geblazen*	blow
laten	*liet*	*lieten*	*gelaten*	let
slapen	*sliep*	*sliepen*	*geslapen*	sleep
vallen	*viel*	*vielen*	*gevallen*[z]	fall
Also:				
houden	*hield*	*hielden*	*gehouden*	hold
lopen	*liep*	*liepen*	*gelopen*[h/z]	walk
roepen	*riep*	*riepen*	*geroepen*	shout/call
heffen	*hief*	*hieven*	*geheven*	lift
(ii) **hangen**	*hing*	*hingen*	*gehangen*	hang
vangen	*ving*	*vingen*	*gevangen*	catch

 Although it can be said that most verbs with *ij* and *ui* in the infinitive are strong, this is not always the case. Some common exceptions are *benijden* 'to envy', *bevrijden* 'to free', *huilen* 'to cry', *gebruiken* 'to use', *verhuizen* 'to move house' which are all regular.

 Most (but not all) verbs derived from irregular verbs are also irregular, e.g. *begrijpen* 'to understand' follows the same vowel change pattern as *grijpen* (☞ Group 1): **begrijpen – begreep – begrepen – begrepen**, *bezoeken* 'to visit' follows the same pattern as *zoeken* (☞ 33.2(a)): **bezoeken – bezocht – bezochten – bezochten**. Other examples are **verwijzen** 'to refer to' from *wijzen*, **overlijden** 'to pass away' from *lijden*, **vergelijken** 'to compare' from *lijken*, **verbinden** 'to connect' from *binden*, **bewegen** 'to move' from *wegen* etc.

34   KNOW: *weten* or *kennen*?

Generally speaking, there are two ways of translating English 'to know' into Dutch:

34.1   *Weten* is used to mean 'to know' a fact

ik **weet** *dat hij getrouwd is*	I know that he is married
weet *je zijn telefoonnummer?*	do you know his telephone number?
wanneer komt hij? ik **weet** *het niet*	when is he coming? I don't know

34.2   *Kennen* means 'to know' in the sense of 'to be acquainted with' (e.g. a person, place, story)

ik **ken** *haar man niet*	I don't know her husband
hij **kent** *Londen heel goed*	he knows London very well
ja, die film **ken** *ik*	yes, I know that film

35   *Laten*

When used together with an infinitive, the verb *laten* 'to let, to leave' has two basic functions in Dutch:[39]

---

39 When used only with a direct object and no other verb, *laten* corresponds to English *leave*, e.g. *ik laat mijn jas hier* 'I'll leave my coat here'.

35.1 It corresponds to English 'let'

laat *mij het* ZIEN	let me see it/show me it
hij heeft haar niet ***laten*** KOMEN	he has not let her come
laten *we naar huis* GAAN	let's go home

35.2 It conveys the meaning 'to have something done' (by someone else)

Linda ***laat*** *haar kamer* VERVEN	Linda is having her room painted
waar kan ik dit ***laten*** REPAREREN?	where can I get/have this repaired?
Piet heeft zijn auto ***laten*** WASSEN	Piet has had his car washed

The last example shows that, like the modal verbs, *laten* forms its perfect tense using an infinitive instead of the participle *gelaten* when occurring with another verb (☞ *Modal Verbs*, 40.2(b-c)).

36 Letter writing

As in English, formal letters in Dutch usually follow a set pattern with regard to layout and introductory and final wording while informal letters to family, friends and acquaintances can be set out in any form. 36.1 below provides a sample of a formal letter in Dutch. Common expressions and abbreviations used in formal and informal letters are given in 36.2.

36.1 Formal letter

Amsterdam, 16 april 1998	Place and date
Dhr. F. van Houten **Karel Doormanlaan 45** **7772 XW Hardenberg**	Name and address of addressee
Geachte heer van Houten,	Dear Mr etc
....	Paragraphs usually begin at the marginal line.
....	One line is usually left between paragraphs
Hoogachtend,	Yours faithfully/sincerely
G. Dijkstra	*Signature*
Mevr. G. Dijkstra **De Boelelaan 14** **1081 HV Amsterdam**	Sender's name and address

36.2 Useful expressions and abbreviations

(a) Formal letters: beginnings and endings

Dhr.	Mr
Mevr. (or *Mw*).	Mrs/Miss/Ms
t.a.v.[40]	For the attention of
Ons / Uw kenmerk:	Your/our reference:
Betreft: / Onderwerp:	Re:
Geachte heren (or *Mijne heren*)	Dear Sirs
Geachte heer / mevrouw	Dear Sir/Madam
Geachte heer / mevrouw B	Dear Mr/Mrs B
Hoogachtend	Yours faithfully/sincerely
Met vriendelijke groeten	With best wishes

(b) Informal letters: beginnings and endings

Beste Jan / meneer B / mevrouw B	Dear Jan/Mr B/Mrs. B
Hallo Jan	Hello Jan (less formal)
Lieve Jan	Dear Jan (to family/close friends)
Vriendelijke (or *hartelijke*) *groeten*	With best wishes / All the best
Dag / Tot ziens / Groetjes	Bye / See you / All the best (less formal)
Liefs	Love (to someone you love)

(c) Useful phrases for formal letters

• *Hartelijk dank voor uw brief*	Many thanks for your letter
• *Met verwijzing naar uw brief / ons telefoongesprek van 12.11.97*	With reference to your letter / our telephone conversation of 12.11.97
• *Ik zou u dankbaar zijn, als u . . .*	I would be grateful if you . . .
• *Het spijt mij zeer, maar ik ben niet in staat om . . .*	I am very sorry, but I am unable to . . .
• *Zou u zo vriendelijk willen zijn mij nadere inlichtingen te verstrekken*	Would you please send me further details/information
• *Bijgesloten treft u aan . . .*	Please find enclosed . . .
• *Bij voorbaat* (*hartelijk*) *dank voor uw medewerking*	In advance, thank you (very much) for your co-operation
• *Ik hoop spoedig iets van u te mogen vernemen*	I look forward to hearing from you soon
• *Hopelijk ben ik u hiermee van dienst geweest*	I hope that I have been of assistance to you (in this matter)

37 LIVE: *leven* or *wonen*?

Generally speaking, there are two ways of translating English 'to live' into Dutch:

37.1 *Leven* is used to mean 'to be alive'

*zijn broer **leeft** niet meer*	his brother is no longer alive
***leven** je grootouders nog?*	are your grandparents still alive?

---

40 Short for *ter attentie van*. When writing to firms, the name of the firm precedes the name of the addressee, e.g. *Smit Auto's, t.a.v. Dhr. P. Smit, Leidsestraat 12, 1234 Rotterdam.*

`37.2` *Wonen* means 'to live' in a place (i.e. 'to reside', 'to dwell')

zijn broer **woont** *in Brugge*	his brother lives in Bruges
waar **woon** *je?*	where do you live?

38 MAY/MIGHT: Dutch equivalents

In English, the words 'may' and 'might' are often used to express possibility, e.g. 'I may/might come'. When used in this way, they are translated into Dutch as follows:

`38.1` The most common way of rendering 'may/might' expressing possibility is to use *misschien* 'perhaps' with the verb in question

hij komt **misschien** *niet*	he may/might not come
misschien *is het niet mogelijk*	it may/might not be possible
misschien *willen zij het niet doen*	they may/might not want to do it

`38.2` Otherwise the modal verb *kunnen* 'to be able to/can' may be used, either in the present or conditional (☞ *Modal verbs*)

hij **kan** *het gedaan hebben*	he may have done it
zij **kunnen** *hem gezien hebben*	they may have seen him
dat **zou** *best wel* **kunnen**	that may well be

39 MEAN: *betekenen, bedoelen* or *menen*?

Generally speaking, there are three ways of translating English 'to mean' into Dutch:

`39.1` *Betekenen* is used in the sense of 'to signify' (e.g. to refer to the meaning of a word or action/situation)

wat **betekent** *'hyperbolisch'?*	what does 'hyperbolical' mean?
kijk! – grijze wolken. Dat **betekent**	look! – grey clouds. That means
dat het zal regenen	that it is going to rain

`39.2` *Bedoelen* refers to what a person intends or wants to say

wat **bedoel** *je daarmee?*	what do you mean by that?
zij zegt nooit wat zij **bedoelt**	she never says what she means
hij is zo saai. Wie **bedoel** *je?*	he is so boring. Whom do you mean?
ik **bedoel** *haar man*	I mean her husband

`39.3` *Menen* is used in the sense of 'to mean what you say'

meen *je dat echt?*	do you really mean that?
ik **meen** *het niet (echt)*	I don't (really) mean it

40 Modal verbs

Modal verbs are used, usually together with another verb, to express ability, e.g. 'I CAN cook', possibility, e.g. 'I MAY come', permission, e.g. 'MAY I call you John?', obligation, e.g. 'I MUST go' or volition, e.g. 'I WANT to dance.' In Dutch there are four modal verbs: *kunnen* 'to be able to', *mogen* 'to be allowed to', *moeten* 'to have to' and *willen* 'to want to':

40.1 Formation of modal verbs. (Irregular forms are given in bold print.)

	kunnen 'be able to/can'	**moeten** 'have to/must'	**mogen** 'be allowed to/may'[41]	**willen** 'want to'
Pres. *ik*	**kan**	*moet*	**mag**	*wil*
jij	*kunt/* **kan**	*moet*	**mag**	*wilt/* **wil**
u	*kunt*	*moet*	**mag**	*wilt*
hij etc.	**kan**	*moet*	**mag**	**wil**
wij	*kunnen*	*moeten*	*mogen*	*willen*
jullie	*kunnen*	*moeten*	*mogen*	*willen*
zij	*kunnen*	*moeten*	*mogen*	*willen*
Past *ik/jij/u/hij*	**kon**	**moest**	**mocht**	*wilde/* **wou**[42]
wij/jullie/zij	**konden**	**moesten**	**mochten**	*wilden/* **wouden**
Past participle	*gekund*	**gemoeten**	**gemogen**	*gewild*

40.2 Use of modals together with other verbs

(a) Modals are used with the infinitive forms of other verbs (without *om* or *te*)

kunt *u mij* HELPEN?	can you help me?
ik **moest** *in Nijmegen* OVERSTAPPEN	I had to change trains in Nijmegen
mag *ik het geluid wat zachter* ZETTEN?	may I turn down the volume?
ik **wilde/wou** *met de baas* SPREKEN	I wanted to speak to the boss

(b) In the perfect and pluperfect tenses, the INFINITIVE form of the modal is used instead of the past participle and it always comes before the other verb (☞ *Word order*, 78.2(d))[43]

heb *je hem* **mogen** ZIEN?	were you allowed to see him?
ik **had** *mijn auto niet* **kunnen** STARTEN	I had not been able to start my car
zij **hadden** *thuis* **moeten** BLIJVEN*	they had had to stay at home

*Note that modals always form their (plu)perfect with *hebben*. The verb with which the modal co-occurs does not affect the choice of auxiliary.

(c) The same word order is used in the future and conditional tenses

jij **zal** *het niet meer* **moeten** DOEN	you'll not have to do it any more
we **zullen** *nog niet* **mogen** GAAN	we'll not be allowed to go yet
ik **zou** *later* **kunnen** KOMEN	I would be able to / could come later

---

41 *May* and *might* expressing possibility are rendered by *kunnen* or *misschien* (☞ *MAY/MIGHT*).

42 *Wou* (plural *wouden*) is an informal alternative to *wilde(n)* and is common in spoken Dutch. It is also used to mean 'would like', e.g. *ik* **wou** *graag meer hebben* 'I would like to have more'.

43 If the modal is used on its own, however, the past participle is used as normal, e.g. *ik heb het niet* **gewild** 'I did not want it'.

(d) Conditional perfect sentences with modal verbs are best rendered by the contracted forms *had(den) moeten* 'would have had to/should have', *had(den) kunnen* 'would have been able to/could have', *had(den) willen* 'would have wanted to' and *had(den) mogen* 'would have been allowed to' (☞ *Conditional and conditional perfect tenses*, 16.2)

je **had** *harder* **moeten** *werken*[44]	you should have worked harder
ik **had** *niet* **kunnen** *komen*	I could not have come
zij **hadden** *niet* **willen** *gaan*	they would not have wanted to go
wij **hadden** *niet langer* **mogen** *blijven*	we would not have been allowed to stay longer

The non-contracted versions, which are also correct but less commonly used, would be *je* **zou** *harder* **hebben moeten** *werken*, *ik* **zou** *niet* **hebben kunnen** *komen*, *zij* **zouden** *niet* **hebben willen** *gaan* and *wij* **zouden** *niet langer* **hebben mogen** *blijven*.

 WORD ORDER: 1. When modals are sent to the end of the clause (e.g. after certain conjunctions like *dat* 'that', *omdat* 'because' etc.) they usually precede the other infinitive, e.g. *ik weet dat hij niet naar school* **wil** *gaan* 'I know that he does not want to go to school', although the alternative order *ik weet dat hij niet naar school gaan* **wil** is also permissible. 2. If the auxiliary verbs *hebben* and *zullen/zou(den)* need to be sent to the end, they always come before the modal and infinitive, e.g. *omdat ik mijn auto niet* **had** *kunnen starten* 'because I had not been able to start my car', *omdat jij het niet meer* **zal** *moeten doen* 'because you'll not have to do it any more', *omdat jij harder* **had** *moeten werken* 'because you would have had to work harder' (☞ *Word order*, 78.2 (b) and (d)).

 Notes on translation: (i) *moeten* translates English 'have to', 'must' and also 'should/ought to', e.g. *jij* **moet** *komen* 'you must/have to/should come'. If it is negated it always means 'must not/should not', e.g. *jij* **moet** *niet komen* 'you must not/should not come'. To render the meaning 'do not have to/need not', *hoeven niet te* is used, e.g. *jij* **hoeft** *niet* **te** *komen* 'you don't have to/needn't come'; (ii) in polite questions, *willen* and *kunnen* are often used in the present tense to translate English 'would' and 'could' respectively, e.g. **wilt** *u mij naar de luchthaven brengen?* 'would you take me to the airport (please)?', **kunt** *u dit voor mij faxen?* 'could you fax this for me (please)'?

 Constructions using a modal followed by a verb in the perfect, e.g. 'he MUST have done it', 'he CAN'T have seen it' etc. are common in both English and Dutch, e.g. *hij* **moet** *het gedaan hebben*, *hij* **kan** *het niet gezien hebben* etc.

41 Niet

The Dutch word *niet* 'not' is used to negate sentences, e.g. *Jan werkt* **niet** 'Jan does not work.' The position of *niet* in the sentence depends on the type of words and phrases with which it occurs. This is a fairly complicated matter and often causes problems for foreign learners. The following rules are given as a rough guide:[45]

---

44 Not to be confused with the supposition *je moet harder gewerkt hebben* 'you must have worked harder'.

45 Note that *ook* 'also/as well', *ook niet* 'not . . . either', *nog* 'still', *nog niet* 'not . . . yet', *nooit* 'never', *graag* 'gladly' and *toch* 'however', follow the same word order as *niet*, e.g. *Jan werkt* **ook niet** 'Jan does not work either', *Jan werkt* **nooit** 'Jan never works', *Jan werkt* **graag** 'Jan likes to work' (☞ *Graag*). This also applies to *wel*, the opposite of *niet*, e.g. *Jan werkt* **wel** 'Jan DOES work' (☞ *Wel*, 76.1).

41.1 Generally speaking, it is advisable to place *niet* at the end of the clause

*Jan leest **niet***	Jan does not read
*Jan wil deze krant **niet***	Jan does not want this newspaper
*Jan werkt volgende week **niet***	Jan is not working next week
*Jan woont er **niet***	Jan does not live there

Examples with more than one clause (indicated by square brackets) are: [*Jan leest **niet***], [*omdat hij geen tijd heeft*] 'Jan does not read because he doesn't have any time', [*Jan woont er **niet***] [*maar ik wel*] 'Jan doesn't live there but I do', [*ik ken de vrouw **niet***] [*die om de hoek woont*] 'I don't know the woman who lives around the corner.'[46]

41.2 There are, however, certain classes of words that are usually PRECEDED by *niet*

(a) Parts of verbs and prefixes which have been sent to the end (☞ *Word order*, 78.2(a) and *Separable verbs*, 64.2)

*sorry, ik kan u **niet** HELPEN*	sorry, I cannot help you
*Jan heeft het boek **niet** GESCHREVEN*	Jan has not written the book
*ik bel jou **niet** OP*	I am not phoning you

(b) Phrases with adjectives and adverbs

*de oefening is **niet** (te) MOEILIJK*	the exercise is not (too) difficult
*ik voel me **niet** GOED*	I do not feel well
*hij zingt **niet** SLECHT*	he does not sing badly

(c) Phrases with prepositions

*Jan houdt **niet** VAN opera*	Jan does not like opera
*hij denkt **niet** AAN zijn vrouw*	he is not thinking of his wife
*ik ga volgende week **niet** OP vakantie*	I am not going on holiday next week

(d) Indefinite pronouns

*hij komt **niet** ELKE dag*	he does not come every day
*er waren **niet** VEEL mensen in de bar*	there were not many people in the bar
*hij weet **niet** ALLES*	he does not know everything

Table 17. Position of niet

Subject+verb	Object	Expression of time	NIET	adjective/adverb/ preposition/ indef. pronoun	Element sent to end
ik lees			niet		
ik lees		vandaag	niet		
ik lees	de krant	vandaag	niet		
ik lees	de krant	vandaag	niet	snel/helemaal	
ik lees	de krant	vandaag	niet	in de trein	
ik lees	de krant		niet	elke dag	
ik heb	de krant	vandaag	niet		gelezen

---

46 Yet some speakers prefer to keep relative clauses (i.e. those beginning with WHO or WHICH / THAT) together with their preceding nouns, e.g. *ik ken de vrouw **die om de hoek woont** niet.*

41.3 In longer clauses containing combinations of the word classes listed in 41.2 above, the usual position of *niet* is as follows

(a) *niet* usually precedes adjectives, adverbs and indefinite pronouns rather than prepositions

*Jo voelde zich **niet** GOED in Turkije*	Jo did not feel well in Turkey
*ik rijd **niet** SNEL op de autoweg*	I do not drive fast on the motorway
*ik denk **niet** ELKE dag aan mijn vrouw*	I do not think of my wife every day

(b) *niet* usually precedes prepositions rather than verbs and prefixes sent to the end

*ik heb **niet** IN Amsterdam gewoond*	I did not live in Amsterdam
*ik heb **niet** AAN mijn vrouw gedacht*	I did not think of my wife
*ik bel jou **niet** VÓÓR zaterdag op*	I will not ring you before Saturday

If there is more than one phrase introduced by a preposition, *niet* usually precedes the first preposition, e.g. *ik ga **niet** MET mijn baas NAAR Amsterdam* 'I'm not going to Amsterdam with my boss.'

41.4 If a noun occurs after the verb *zijn* 'to be', *niet* may EITHER precede the noun (and any articles or pronouns with which it occurs) OR follow it

*dat is **niet** HET PROBLEEM /*	that is not the problem
*dat is HET PROBLEEM **niet***	
*ik ben **niet** JE VRIEND /*	I am not your friend
*ik ben JE VRIEND **niet***	

Note that this is only the case with nouns and not, for example, with pronouns:

*dat was HEM **niet***	that was not him
(NOT ✗ *dat was **niet** HEM*)	

41.5 *Een* 'a' is usually not preceded by *niet* or any phrase ending in *niet* (e.g. *ook niet* 'not either', *nog niet* 'not yet'). Instead, *geen*, *ook geen* and *nog geen* are used (☞ *Geen*)

*ik wil **geen** kopje koffie*	I do not want a cup of coffee
*hij wil **ook geen** kind hebben*	he does not want a child either
*zij hebben **nog geen** huis gevonden*	they have not found a house yet

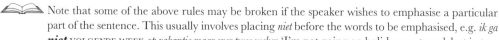 Note that some of the above rules may be broken if the speaker wishes to emphasise a particular part of the sentence. This usually involves placing *niet* before the words to be emphasised, e.g. *ik ga **niet** VOLGENDE WEEK op vakantie maar over twee weken* 'I'm not going on holiday next week but in two weeks' time', *ik wil **niet** DEZE ENGELSE KRANT kopen maar die Nederlandse* 'I do not want to buy this English newspaper but that Dutch one.'

42 Noun plurals

In English, noun plurals are formed by adding -*s* to the noun in question, e.g. 'table**s**', 'chair**s**', with a few irregular exceptions, e.g. 'men', 'feet', 'sheep'. In Dutch, the situation is slightly more complex as there are **two** regular plural endings, **-en** and **-s** as well as a number of irregular forms, e.g. *de hond – de honden* 'the dog(s)', *de tafel – de tafels* 'the table(s)', *het kind – de kinderen* 'the child(ren)'. Note that the article is always *de* before plural nouns.

42.1 Distribution of -en and -s

(a) *-en* (pronounced without the *-n*) is the most frequent plural ending added to most nouns

*boek – boek**en***	book(-s)		*haar – har**en***	hair(-s)
*man – mann**en***	man (- men)		*been – ben**en***	leg(-s)
*jas – jass**en***	coat(-s)		*druif – druiv**en***	grape(-s)
*kat – katt**en***	cat(-s)		*huis – huiz**en***	house(-es)

Note that, when adding *-en*, one must observe the regular Dutch spelling changes, e.g. *man – man**n**en, been – be**n**en, huis – huiz**en, druif – druiv**en* etc. (☞ *Spelling*).

(b) *-s* is added to nouns ending in the unstressed syllables *-el, -em, -en, -er* (also *-aar(d), -erd, -ier* when referring to people) and to most nouns ending in a vowel

*tafel – tafel**s***	table(-s)		*tante – tante**s***	aunt(-s)
*bodem – bodem**s***	floor(-s)		*dame – dame**s***	lady(-ies)
*jongen – jongen**s***	boy(-s)		*huisje – huisje**s***	little house(-s)
*bakker – bakker**s***	baker(-s)		*tuintje – tuintje**s***	little garden(-s)

Note that nouns ending in a vowel other than *-e* add an apostrophe before *-s*, e.g. *collega's* 'colleagues', *baby's* 'babies', *paraplu's* 'umbrellas'. Abbreviations also have a plural form in *-'s*, e.g. *tv's* 'TVs' (☞ *Apostrophes*).

42.2 Irregular forms

(a) A small group of nouns containing a short vowel (written as one vowel) do not double the following consonant in the plural before *-en*. This means that the plural vowel is pronounced long. Some common ones are

bad – baden	bath(-s)		*gat – gaten*	hole(-s)
blad – bladen	leaf(-ves) of book		*glas – glazen*	glass(-es)
dag – dagen	day(-s)		*graf – graven*	grave(-s)
slot – sloten	lock(-s)		*pad – paden*	path(-s)
spel – spelen	game(-s)		*weg – wegen*	road(-s)/way(-s)
slag – slagen	blow(-s)/slap(-s)		*god – goden*	god(-s)

Not, as one would expect, *bad – ✗ badden, dag – ✗ daggen, weg – ✗ weggen* etc. (contrast the regular forms *kat – kat**t**en* 'cat(s)', *bed – be**d**den* 'bed(s)', + *Spelling*, 65.1(b)).

(b) A few neuter nouns take the plural ending *-eren* (or *-deren* if the noun ends in *-n*). Some common ones are

*kind – kind**eren***	child(-ren)		*lied – lied**eren***	song(-s)
*ei – ei**eren***	egg(-s)		*blad – blad**eren***	leaf(-ves)
*been – been**deren***	bone(-s)		*lam – lamm**eren***	lamb(-s)
*rad – rad**eren***	wheel(-s)		*kalf – kalv**eren***	calf(-ves)

(c) Nouns ending in *-heid* have a plural in *-heden*

*mogelijkheid – mogelijk**heden***	possibility(-ies)
*bijzonderheid – bijzonder**heden***	speciality(-ies)
*fijnheid – fijn**heden***	nicety(-ies)

(d) Some other common irregular plurals are

*stad – st**e**den*	town(-s)	*koe – koe**i**en*	cow(-s)
*schip – sch**e**pen*	ship(-s)	*vlo – vloo**i**en*	flea(-s)
*gelid – gel**e**deren*	joint(-s)	*kleren*	clothes (no sing.)
*lid – l**e**den*	member(-s)	*goederen*	goods (no sing.)

 The rules in 42.1 have a number of exceptions. Some common ones are *broers* 'brothers', *zoons* (but also *zonen*) 'sons', *reden**en*** 'reason(s)', *artikel**en*** 'article(s)', *lerar**en*** 'teachers', *second**en*** 'seconds', *zee**ën*** 'seas'. Most foreign words, which the Dutch still regard as foreign, take *-s* (e.g. *films* 'films', *album**s*** 'albums', *club**s*** 'clubs', *acteur**s*** 'actors', *actrice**s*** 'actresses') except those ending in stressed *-ie* which usually take *-ën* (e.g. *theorie**ën*** 'theories'). Some nouns may take **either** *-(e)n* **or** *-s* (e.g. *ziekt**en*** or *ziekte**s*** 'diseases', *typ**en*** or *type**s*** 'types', *koloni**ën*** or *kolonie**s*** 'colonies', *zon**en*** or *zoon**s*** 'sons') where the plural in *-en* is often associated with a more formal style. Some nouns of Latin origin maintain their original Latin plural forms, e.g. *musicus – music**i*** 'musician(s)', *historicus – historic**i*** 'historian(s)'.

 Note that weights and measurements, such as *kilo, meter, liter* etc., usually remain singular in Dutch, e.g. *drie **meter*** 'three metres', *twee **kilo** tomaten* 'two kilos of tomatoes', *vier **liter** water* 'four litres of water' etc.

43   Nouns derived from other words

A noun is a word used to name a person, thing or concept, e.g. 'man', 'table', 'joy'. In English and Dutch, it is that part of speech which may occur after an article and may be either singular or plural, e.g. 'a man' – 'the men' (☞ *Noun plurals*). Nouns may be either simple, e.g. 'dog', or derived from verbs, e.g. 'to walk' – 'the WALK', adjectives, e.g. 'happy' – 'HAPPINESS', or other nouns, e.g. 'garden – GARDENER', either by the addition of an ending, e.g. 'garden**er**', or by simply using other parts of speech as nouns without changing their form, e.g. 'the walk'. In Dutch the situation is similar, e.g. *drinken – **het drinken*** 'to drink – the drinking', *gek – gek**heid*** 'mad – madness', *fiets – fiets**er*** 'bike – cyclist'; yet, as there is usually no simple one-to-one correspondence between the Dutch and English endings, it is difficult to set out hard and fast rules for noun derivation in Dutch. On the whole, each noun must be learnt individually, although it may be helpful to foreign learners to identify the most common ways of deriving nouns in Dutch. The following are given as a rough guide only:

43.1   Common noun-forming endings

(a) *-ing* is a very common ending added to verb stems (i.e. the infinitive minus *-en*) and usually indicates the result of an action. It often corresponds to English '-ing' or '-tion'

*de vertal**ing***	translation	*de reserver**ing***	reservation
*de vull**ing***	filling (in tooth)	*de teken**ing***	drawing
*de ontvoer**ing***	kidnapping	*de verleng**ing***	lengthening

(b) -*heid* is mostly added to adjectives to form abstract nouns. It often corresponds to English '-ness' or '-(i)ty'

*de gek***heid**	madness	*de lelijk***heid**	ugliness
*de bijzonder***heid**	speciality	*de moeilijk***heid**	difficulty

Note, however, that a small group of adjectives form their abstract nouns with -*te* which often corresponds to English '-th':

*de leng***te**	length	*de breed***te**	breadth
*de hoog***te**	height	*de sterk***te**	strength

(c) -*je*, -*tje*, -*etje* etc. are added to nouns to form diminutives, e.g. *het huisje* 'little house', *het broertje* 'little brother' (☞ *Diminutives*).

(d) -*er* is often added to verbs to indicate a profession, e.g. *de werker* 'the worker', *de schrijver* 'the writer' (☞ *Professions*).

(e) -*ster*, -*e*, -*in* etc. are added to nouns referring to masculine humans and animals to form the female counterpart, e.g. *de schrijfster* 'authoress', *de leeuwin* 'lioness' (☞ *Female endings*).

(f) -*e* is added to adjectives to form nouns of the type *de blinde* 'the blind person', *de blonde* 'the blond(e)', *het leuke* 'the nice thing', *het ergste* 'the worst thing' etc. (☞ *Adjectives used as nouns*).

43.2 Verbs used as nouns

(a) It is very common in Dutch to use infinitives as nouns. These often correspond to English nouns ending in '-ing'

het eten	eating/food	*het zingen*	singing
het drinken	drinking	*het denken*	thinking
het leven	life/living	*het luisteren*	listening

(b) If, however, the verb begins with an inseparable prefix (e.g. *be-*, *ver-*, etc., ☞ *Inseparable verbs*) it is usually the STEM which is used as a noun[47]

*het ***begin**	beginning	*het ***ver**blijf	stay/residence
*het ***be**klag	complaint	*het ***ver**trek	departure
*het ***be**sluit	conclusion	*het ***ver**lies	loss

Note that the verb STEM is the infinitive minus -*en* with the necessary spelling changes (☞ *Spelling*) and is identical to the first person singular present form, e.g. *beginnen* – *ik* **begin** 'I begin', *blijven* – *ik* **blijf** 'I stay'.

43.3 Nouns can also be derived by adding *ge-* to verb stems. This often indicates a repetitive or protracted action and may have pejorative overtones

*het ***ge**fluister	whispering	*het ***ge**jammer	moaning
*het ***ge**piep	whistling/chirping	*het ***ge**hamer	hammering
*het ***ge**babbel	prattle/chatter	*het ***ge**doe	doings/goings-on

---

47 Yet note that some verbs with inseparable prefixes have corresponding nouns ending in -*ing*, e.g. *de bediening* 'service', *de vergadering* 'meeting'.

Among the less common endings (and prefixes) are **-schap**, **-dom**, **-nis** and **ge-. . .-te**. When added to nouns *-schap* and *-dom* may indicate a collective, e.g. *de broeder***schap** 'brotherhood', *het mens***dom** 'humanity'. *-schap* is also used to signify a function, e.g. *het moeder***schap** 'motherhood', *het vader***schap** 'fatherhood' or, when added to adjectives, a condition, e.g. *de zwanger***schap** 'pregnancy'. *-nis* is added to some adjectives and verbs, e.g. *de duister***nis** 'darkness', *de begrafe***nis** 'burial/funeral', and *ge-. . .-te* is added to some nouns to give a collective interpretation, e.g. *het ge*berg**te** 'mountain range', *het ge*steen**te** 'stones', *het ge*vogel**te** 'birds/poultry'. In addition, prepositional prefixes are occasionally used to derive nouns from other nouns, e.g. **voor***stad* 'suburb', **over***jas* 'overcoat', **achter***kamer* 'back room'.

 Note that most nouns derived from verbs (☞ 43.1(a) and 43.2(b)) can be replaced by infinitives when the speaker wishes to emphasise the **action** described by the verb, e.g. *het beklag* 'complaint' vs. **het beklagen** '(the act of) complaining', **het vertrek** 'departure' vs. **het vertrekken** '(the act of) departing', **de vertaling** 'translation' vs. **het vertalen** '(the act of) translating' etc., e.g. *ik begrijp het boek wel maar* **het vertalen** *ervan is moeilijk* 'I (do) understand the book but translating it is difficult'.

44 Numbers

Generally speaking, numbers in English and Dutch can be divided into three categories: (i) cardinal numbers, e.g. *one, two, three* etc., (ii) ordinal numbers, e.g. *first, second, third* etc., and (iii) fractions, e.g. *a half, a quarter* etc.:

44.1 Cardinal numbers in Dutch (irregular forms are given in bold)

0 *nul*	20 ***twintig***	100 *honderd*
1 *een(één)**	21 *eenentwintig*	101 *honderdéén*
2 *twee*	22 *tweeëntwintig***	102 *honderdtwee*
3 *drie*	23 *drieëntwintig*	115 *honderdvijftien*
4 *vier*	24 *vierentwintig*	200 *tweehonderd*
5 *vijf*	25 *vijfentwintig*	201 *tweehonderdéén*
6 *zes*	26 *zesentwintig*	230 *tweehonderddertig*
7 *zeven*	27 *zevenentwintig*	300 *driehonderd*
8 *acht*	28 *achtentwintig*	400 *vierhonderd*
9 *negen*	29 *negenentwintig*	500 *vijfhonderd*
10 *tien*	30 ***dertig***	600 *zeshonderd*
11 *elf*	31 *eenendertig*	700 *zevenhonderd*
12 *twaalf*	32 *tweeëndertig*	800 *achthonderd*
13 ***dertien***	33 *drieëndertig*	900 *negenhonderd*
14 ***veertien***	40 ***veertig***	1000 *duizend*
15 *vijftien*	50 *vijftig*	1001 *duizendéén*
16 *zestien*	60 *zestig*	2000 *tweeduizend*
17 *zeventien*	70 *zeventig*	3080 *drieduizendtachtig*
18 *achttien*	80 ***tachtig***	4012 *vierduizendtwaalf*
19 *negentien*	90 *negentig*	5020 *vijfduizendtwintig*

2576	*tweeduizendvijfhonderdzesenzeventig*
100.000***	*honderdduizend*
1.000.000	*een miljoen*
1.000.000.000	*een miljard*

* In contexts where confusion between the number *een* and the indefinite article *een* 'a' may arise, acute accents are placed over the number (☞ *Accents*, 1.1)

** *en* meaning 'and' (e.g. 'two and twenty') always has a diaeresis above the *e* when preceded by another *e* to indicate that the vowels are pronounced separately (☞ *Accents*, 1.2).

*** Note the use of full stops in Dutch where English would use commas.

44.2 Ordinal numbers are usually formed from cardinal numbers by adding the ending *-de* (or *-ste* after *-t*, *-d*, and *-ig*). The Dutch abbreviation corresponding to English 'th' is e

1e **eerste**	11e *elfde*	21e *eenentwintig**ste***
2e *tweede*	12e *twaalfde*	30e *dertig**ste***
3e **derde**	13e *dertiende*	40e *veertig**ste***
4e *vierde*	14e *veertiende*	50e *vijftig**ste***
5e *vijfde*	15e *vijftiende*	60e *zestig**ste***
6e *zesde*	16e *zestiende*	75e *vijfenzeventig**ste***
7e *zevende*	17e *zeventiende*	100e *honderd**ste***
8e *acht**ste***	18e *achttiende*	101e *honderd**eerste***
9e *negende*	19e *negentiende*	1000e *duizend**ste***
10e *tiende*	20e *twintig**ste***	1.000.000e *miljoen**ste****

*Note the use of *-ste* here.

44.3 Fractions: As in English, ordinal numbers are used with most fractions, e.g. *een derde* 'one third', *een zestiende* 'one sixteenth'

1/2 *een half* (☞)	3/4 *driekwart*	0,5 *nul komma vijf**
1/4 *een kwart*	1 1/2 *anderhalf*	1,25 *één komma*
2/5 *twee vijfde*	2 1/2 *twee-en-een-half*	*vijfentwintig*
1/8 *een achtste*	3 1/4 *drie-en-een-kwart*	

*Note the use of commas in Dutch where English would use decimal points.

44.4 Useful expressions with numbers

*twee **plus/min/keer/gedeeld door** zes*	two plus/minus/times/divided by six
vierkante *meter*	square metres
*twee **gulden** twintig* (or ƒ 2,20)	two guilders twenty
Geert is negenentwintig (**jaar oud**)	Geert is twenty-nine (years old)
*Jaap is **begin** twintig*	Jaap is in his early twenties
hij is (**achter/midden**) *in de dertig*	he is in his (late/mid) thirties
*zij is **boven/onder de** veertig*	she is over/under forty
*ik begon **op mijn** vierde **jaar***	I began at the age of four
*een appel **of** vijf/tien/twintig* etc.	about five/ten/twenty etc. apples
*een man **of** vijftig/honderd*	about fifty/a hundred people
*de **op één na** grootste stad*	the second largest town
*het **op vier na** armste land*	the fifth poorest country

Note that expressions such as 'two of us', 'four of them' etc. are rendered by the use of *met ons* and *met z'n* respectively followed by the cardinal number plus *-en* (with the appropriate accents and spelling changes, ☞ *Accents* and *Spelling*):

wij waren **met ons** tweeën **/** drieën   there were two/three of us
zij zijn **met z'n** vieren **/** vijven **/** zessen   there are four/five/six of them

 Note that *half, anderhalf, twee-en-half* etc. act as adjectives and may therefore take endings, e.g. *het* **halve** *brood* 'half of the bread', *twee-en-een-**halve** dag*[48] 'two and a half days' (☞ *Adjectives*, 2.1). In addition to the adjective *half* there is also a noun *de helft* e.g. *ik heb **de helft** van het boek geschreven* or *ik heb het **halve** boek geschreven* both mean 'I have written half of the book.'

45   Objects: direct and indirect

Some verbs occur with both a direct and an indirect object. In these cases, the **direct** object is the direct recipient of the action described by the verb, e.g. 'John gave THE MONEY', 'Jane wrote THE LETTER', while the **indirect** object is the recipient of the direct object, as well as of the action described by the verb, e.g. 'John gave the money TO HIS EX-WIFE', 'Jane wrote the letter TO THE HEADMASTER.' The relative order of direct and indirect objects after the verb is very similar in English and Dutch, as is the use of 'to' in English and its equivalent *aan* in Dutch:

45.1   When the direct object is a NOUN

(a) The direct object is followed by *aan* + indirect object

Jan gaf DE BLOEMEN **aan** *zijn vrouw*   Jan gave the flowers to his wife
ik schreef EEN BRIEF **aan** *hem*   I wrote a letter to him

This is often used when the speaker wishes to stress the indirect object.

(b) As in English, it is also possible to have the reverse order: i.e. indirect object + direct object without *aan*, particularly with verbs such as *geven* 'to give', *sturen* 'to send', *schrijven* 'to write' etc.

Jan gaf **zijn vrouw** DE BLOEMEN   Jan gave his wife the flowers
ik schreef **hem** EEN BRIEF   I wrote him a letter

45.2   When the direct object is a PRONOUN, e.g. 'it', 'them', 'her' etc., it must come first and the indirect object is preceded by *aan*

Jan gaf ZE **aan** *zijn vrouw*   Jan gave them to his wife
Piet vertelde HET **aan** *zijn vriend*   Piet told it to his friend

If BOTH objects are pronouns, *aan* may be dropped, unless the indirect object is to be emphasised:

Jan heeft ZE **haar** *gegeven*   Jan has given her them*
Piet heeft HET **hem** *gestuurd*   Piet has sent him it*
Jan heeft ZE **aan haar** *gegeven*   Jan has given them to her

*Note the different order in English.

---

48 The noun is always singular after *anderhalf, twee-en-een-half* etc.

45.3 Common verbs taking indirect objects

behoren aan	to belong to	*schrijven aan*	write to
bijdragen aan	to contribute to	*sturen aan*	send to
geven aan	give to	*uitleggen aan*	explain to
laten zien aan	show to	*vertellen aan*	tell (to)
lenen aan	lend to	*voorstellen aan*	to introduce to
leveren aan	deliver to	*wennen aan*	to get used to

46   Passive

The passive voice is used to shift the emphasis from the **agent** of the verb (i.e. the doer) to the **recipient** of the action described by the verb. For example, the passive equivalent of a sentence such as 'John kissed me' is I WAS KISSED BY JOHN. Often, the passive is used when the speaker does not wish to specify an agent, e.g. 'I was kissed'. Passive sentences in English are formed by using the verb 'to be' plus the past participle, e.g. 'I am kissed', 'I was kissed', 'I have been kissed' etc. In Dutch, the passive is formed by the use of **worden** 'to become', or in the perfect tenses **zijn** 'to be', plus the past participle (☞ *Perfect tense*, 48.1(b) for past participles):

46.1   Formation of the passive

(a) In the present, the simple past, the future and the conditional, the appropriate tense of the verb *worden* is used with the past participle

Table 18. The passive with worden

Present	ik	word		
	jij/u/hij	wordt	slecht	behandeld
	wij/jullie/zij	worden		
Past	ik/jij/u/hij	werd	slecht	behandeld
	wij/jullie/zij	werden		
Future	ik/jij/u/hij	zal	slecht	behandeld **worden**
	wij/jullie/zij	zullen		
Conditional	ik/jij/u/hij	zou	slecht	behandeld **worden**
	wij/jullie/zij	zouden		

1. *Jan **wordt** slecht behandeld*   Jan is treated badly
2. *Jan **werd** slecht behandeld*   Jan was treated badly
3. *Jan **zal** slecht behandeld **worden***   Jan will be treated badly
4. *Jan **zou** slecht behandeld **worden***   Jan would be treated badly

Note that the passive can also be used with modal verbs such as *moeten* 'to have to / must' and *kunnen* 'to be able to':

het boek **moet** GELEZEN WORDEN			the book must be read	
het werk **kon** *niet* GEDAAN WORDEN[49]			the work could not be done	

(b) In the perfect tenses, i.e. the perfect, pluperfect, future perfect and conditional perfect, the appropriate tense of the verb *zijn* is used with the past participle

Table 19. The passive with zijn

Perfect	ik	ben		
	jij/u	bent	slecht	behandeld
	hij	is		
	wij/jullie/zij	zijn		
Pluperfect	ik/jij/u/hij	was	slecht	behandeld
	wij/jullie/zij	waren		
Future Perfect	ik/jij/u/hij	zal	slecht	behandeld **zijn**
	wij/jullie/zij	zullen		
Conditional Perfect	ik/jij/u/hij	zou	slecht	behandeld **zijn**
	wij/jullie/zij	zouden		

1. *Jan* **is** *slecht behandeld*　　Jan has been treated badly
2. *Jan* **was** *slecht behandeld*　　Jan had been treated badly
3. *Jan* **zal** *slecht behandeld* **zijn**　　Jan will have been treated badly
4. *Jan* **zou** *slecht behandeld* **zijn**[50]　　Jan would have been treated badly

The use of *zijn* in the above cases may be confusing to English speakers, as it resembles the English non-perfect passives. Thus, one must bear in mind that sentences such as *Jan* **is** *slecht behandeld* correspond to English 'Jan HAS BEEN treated badly' and not ✗ 'Jan IS treated badly'.

46.2　The agent (i.e. the 'doer' of the action) is introduced by *door* (English 'by')

zij WERDEN **door** *de politie* BEZOCHT	they were visited by the police
de jongen IS **door** *zijn hond* GEBETEN	the boy has been bitten by his dog
mijn huiswerk WAS **door** *de leraar* GECORRIGEERD	my homework had been marked by the teacher

46.3　When the passive sentence is of a general nature (i.e. when there is no agent specified and the recipient of the verbal action is either absent or indefinite) it is common to insert *er* (☞ *Er*, 21.1)

er WERD *veel schade* AANGERICHT	there was a lot of damage done
er *kon niets* GEREPAREERD WORDEN	nothing could be repaired

---

49 The alternative word order *worden* + Past Part. is also possible, e.g. *Jan zal slecht* **worden** *behandeld*, *het werk kon niet* **worden** *gedaan* etc. (☞ *Word order*, 78.2(c)).
50 The alternative word order *zijn* + Past Part. is also possible, e.g. *Jan zou slecht* **zijn** *behandeld* etc.

    er WERD *niet meer* GEPRAAT   there was no more talking
    er WORDT *een liedje* GEZONGEN   a song will be sung

Note that definite nouns (i.e. those preceded by 'the', 'this/that' or 'my/your/his' etc.) do not co-occur with *er*, e.g. HET *liedje wordt gezongen* 'the song will be sung', NOT ✗ *er wordt het liedje gezongen*.

46.4   USE OF THE PASSIVE: The passive is very common in both written and spoken English. In Dutch, however, it is less common, particularly in the spoken language

(a) Often, a passive sentence in English is simply rendered by an active (i.e. non-passive) construction in Dutch

e.g. 'he has been bitten by his dog'

    hij is door zijn hond gebeten   he has been bitten by his dog
    zijn hond heeft hem gebeten   his dog has bitten him

(b) Where no agent is specified, Dutch may use *men* 'one' (less formally *je*[51] 'you'), *ze* 'they', *iets* 'something', *iemand* 'someone', *niemand* 'no one' etc

e.g. 'the problem cannot be solved'

    het probleem kan niet opgelost worden   the problem cannot be solved
    men *kan het probleem niet oplossen*   one cannot solve the problem
    je *kunt het probleem niet oplossen*   you cannot solve the problem
    niemand *kan het probleem oplossen*   no one can solve the problem

e.g. 'he had been seen'

    hij was gezien   he had been seen
    iemand *had hem gezien*   someone had seen him
    ze *hadden hem gezien*   they had seen him

 Verbs taking indirect objects (☞ *Objects: direct and indirect*, 45.3) and objects with prepositions (☞ *Prepositions*, **Table 31**) may cause difficulties for English students as, in Dutch, these objects remain as such while, in English, they become subjects, e.g. '**I** was told nothing' is not ✗ *ik werd niets verteld* but *er werd niets* **aan mij** *verteld* (or *er werd* **mij** *niets verteld* or **mij** *werd niets verteld*), '**she** had been given flowers' is not ✗ *zij was bloemen gegeven* but *er waren bloemen* **aan haar** *gegeven* (or *er waren* **haar** *bloemen gegeven*), '**he** cannot be relied upon any more' is not ✗ *hij kan niet meer op gerekend worden* but *op hem kan niet meer gerekend worden*. Note the use of *er* with the indirect objects (literally '**there** was nothing told to me', '**there** were flowers given to her').

47   Past tense (simple past)

Both English and Dutch have a simple past tense, otherwise known as the *imperfect* or *preterite*. In English, the simple past tense of regular verbs is formed by adding '-ed', e.g. I WORK**ED**. In Dutch, it is formed by adding either *-te* or *-de* (plural *-ten* or *-den*) to the verb stem, e.g. *ik werk**te** 'I worked', *wij maak**ten** 'we made', *jij huil**de** 'you cried'. The rules for the formation and use of the simple past in Dutch are set out below. Verbs with irregular past tense forms are dealt with under *Irregular verbs*.

---

51 But never *jij* 'you'.

47.1 Regular verbs add EITHER *-te(n)* OR *-de(n)* to the verb stem in the simple past[52]

hij hoopte	he hoped
zij speelden	they played

The verb STEM is the infinitive minus *-en* with the appropriate spelling changes (☞ *Spelling*) and is identical to the first person singular present form, e.g. *hopen* – *ik* **hoop** 'I hope', *spelen* – *ik* **speel** 'I play', *leven* – *ik* **leef** 'I live'.

Note that English progressives with BE + '-ing' have no direct equivalent in Dutch:

hij hoopte	he hoped OR
	he was hoping

(a) *-te(n)* is added to stems ending in voiceless consonants (i.e. *t, k, f, s, ch, p*).*
Note that *-te(n)* is also added to stems already ending in *-t* which leads to a doubling of the consonant:

werken – werkte	work(ed)	*hopen – hoopte*	hope(d)
lachen – lachte	laugh(ed)	*straffen – strafte*	punish(ed)
missen – miste	miss(ed)	*praten – praatte*	talk(ed)

*These consonants are contained in the words **'t kofschip** and **'t fokschaap** which are often taught to Dutch school children as mnemonics.

(b) *-de(n)* is added to all other stems, even to those already ending in *-d* which leads to a doubling of the consonant

huilen – huilde	cry(ied)	*gooien – gooide*	throw (threw)
leren – leerde	learn(ed)	*plagen – plaagde*	tease(d)
plannen – plande[53]	plan(ned)	*landen – landde*	land(ed)

Note that stems ending in *-f* and *-s* which correspond to an infinitive with *-v* and *-z* respectively add *-de(n)* in accordance with the infinitive consonants:

leven – leefde	live(d)	*reizen – reisde*	travel(led)

Table 20. The simple past

VERB		STEM	PAST SINGULAR (ik, jij, u, hij, zij, het)	PAST PLURAL (wij, jullie, zij)
hopen	'hope'	hoop	**hoop-te**	**hoop-ten**
maken	'make'	maak	**maak-te**	**maak-ten**
blaffen	'bark'	blaf	**blaf-te**	**blaf-ten**
wassen	'wash'	was	**was-te**	**was-ten**
dromen	'dream'	droom	**droom-de**	**droom-den**
bellen	'ring'	bel	**bel-de**	**bel-den**
geloven	'believe'	geloof	**geloof-de**	**geloof-den**
vrezen	'be afraid'	vrees	**vrees-de**	**vrees-den**

---

52 Compare the rules for the addition of *g-* . . . *-t* and *ge-* . . . *-d* in the past participle (☞ *Perfect tense*, 48.1(b)).

53 Note that verbs borrowed from English such as *plannen* 'to plan', *scoren* 'to score a goal', *speechen* 'to speechify' etc. also follow these rules, e.g. *plande, scoorde, speechte*.

47.2 If the verb has a separable prefix such as *op-, in-, uit-, mee-* etc., it is sent to the end of the clause or sentence (☞ *Separable verbs*, 64.2)

*Jo bel**de** haar moeder iedere dag* OP   Jo rang her mother up every day
*hij leg**de** alles aan de politie* UIT   he explained everything to the police

47.3 USE: The simple past in English may correspond EITHER to the simple past OR to the perfect in Dutch. In practice, it is the perfect which is more commonly used, especially in spoken Dutch (☞ *Perfect tense*, 48.5(b)). There are, however, cases in which the simple past is preferred.

(a) When telling a story or narrating a series of events in the past (especially in written Dutch)

*Kees **zette** de radio af en **rolde** een*   Kees turned off the radio and rolled a
    *sigaret. Zijn zus **opende** de deur,*   cigarette. His sister opened the door,
    lachte** verlegen en **verontschuldigde   gave an embarrassed laugh and
    zich   apologised

(b) After *toen* meaning 'when'

TOEN *ik met hem **praatte***   when I talked to him
TOEN *jij vanavond **kookte***   when you cooked this evening
TOEN *mijn broer in Leiden **woonde***   when my brother lived in Leiden

(c) The simple past is often used with the following very common verbs: *hebben* 'to have', *zijn* 'to be', *weten* 'to know', *denken* 'to think', *zeggen* 'to say', *zien* 'to see' and modal verbs (☞ *Modal verbs*)

ik DACHT *dat ik het bij me **had***   I thought I had it with me
hij WIST *niet dat zij ongelukkig **was***   he didn't know that she was unhappy
ik KON *niet met hem praten*   I could not talk to him

 Note that the simple past in Dutch is also used to translate English pluperfects in expressions with 'for', 'since' and 'how long'?, e.g. 'I had lived / been living there for five years' *ik **woonde** er al vijf jaar*, 'he had worked / been working with his brother since April' *hij **werkte** sinds april met zijn broer*, 'how long had you known Jan?' *hoe lang **kende** u Jan al?*, meaning literally 'I lived there already five years', 'he worked since April with his brother', 'how long did you know Jan already?' It may also translate English pluperfects before 'when' if an '-ing' form is used, e.g. 'I had been reading the newspaper when he arrived' *ik **las** de krant toen hij aankwam* (☞ *Pluperfect tense,*).

48   Perfect tense

In English, the perfect tense is used to refer to actions in the past which are still relevant to the present, e.g. 'I HAVE MADE a cake' (*and it has not yet been eaten*). It is formed using the verb 'have' in the present tense plus a past participle, e.g. I HAVE MADE, YOU HAVE MADE, HE HAS MADE etc. The formation and use of the perfect tense in Dutch are as follows:

48.1 Formation of the perfect

(a) Most verbs form their perfect tense using *hebben* plus a past participle

Table 21. The perfect tense with hebben

SUBJECT	HEBBEN	PAST PARTICIPLE	
ik	heb		
jij	hebt		
u (sing. and pl.)	hebt/heeft		
hij/zij/het	heeft	gewerkt	'worked'
wij/jullie/zij	hebben		

ik **heb** *heel hard* **gewerkt**	I have worked very hard
wij **hebben** *al twee keer* **gespeeld**[54]	we have played twice (already)

Note that English progressives with BE + -'ing' have no direct equivalent in Dutch:

ik **heb gewerkt**	I have worked OR
	I have been working

(b) Regular past participles are formed by adding *ge-* plus the endings *-t* or *-d*[55] to the verb stem. (For irregular past participles ☞ *Irregular verbs*.)

ge*hoop***t**	hoped
ge*zeg***d**	said

The verb STEM is the infinitive minus *-en* with the appropriate spelling changes (☞ *Spelling*) and is identical to the first person singular present form, e.g. *hopen – ik* **hoop** 'I hope', *zeggen – ik* **zeg** 'I say', *leven – ik* **leef** 'I live'.

(i) *-t* is added to stems ending in voiceless consonants (i.e. *t, k, f, s, ch, p*).* Note, however, that stems already ending in *-t* do not double the consonant

werken – **ge***werk***t**	work(ed)	*straffen –* **ge***straf***t**	punish(ed)
hopen – **ge***hoop***t**	hope(d)	*kosten –* **ge***kost**	cost(cost)
missen – **ge***mis***t**	miss(ed)	*praten –* **ge***praat**	talk(ed)

*These consonants are contained in the words *'t* **k***o***fsch***i***p** and *'t* **f***o***ksch***aa***p** which are often taught to Dutch school children as mnemonics.

(ii) *-d* is added to all other stems, except those already ending in *-d*

huilen – **ge***huil***d**	cry(ied)	*studeren –* **ge***studeer***d**	study(ied)
leren – **ge***leer***d**	learn(ed)	*plagen –* **ge***plaag***d**	tease(d)
plannen – **ge***plan***d**	plan(ned)[56]	*landen –* **ge***land**	land(ed)

---

54 ☞ *Word order*, 78.2(a).

55 Compare the rules for the addition of *-te* and *-de* in the simple past (☞ *Past tense*, 47.1).

56 Note that verbs borrowed from English such as *plannen* 'to plan', *scoren* 'to score a goal', *speechen* 'to speechify' etc. also follow these rules, e.g. *gepland, gescoord, gespeecht.*

Note that stems ending in *-f* and *-s* which correspond to an infinitive with *-v* and *-z* respectively add *-d* in accordance with the infinitive consonants:

leven – geleefd   live(d)   *reizen – gereisd*   travel(led)

Table 22. Past participles[57]

VERB		STEM	PAST PARTICIPLE
hopen	'hope'	hoop	**ge-hoop-t**
maken	'make'	maak	**ge-maak-t**
blaffen	'bark'	blaf	**ge-blaf-t**
missen	'miss'	mis	**ge-mis-t**
dromen	'dream'	droom	**ge-droom-d**
bellen	'ring'	bel	**ge-bel-d**
loven	'praise'	loof	**ge-loof-d**
vrezen	'be afraid'	vrees	**ge-vrees-d**

48.2   Verbs with prefixes (☞ *Inseparable verbs* and *Separable verbs*)

(a) Verbs with the inseparable prefixes *be-, her-, ont-, ver-, ge-* and *er-* do not add *ge-* in the past participle

beseffen – beseft   realise(d)   *herkennen – herkend*   recognise(d)
geloven – geloofd   believe(d)   *ontdekken – ontdekt*   discover(ed)
vertalen – vertaald   translate(d)   *ontmoeten – ontmoet*   meet (met)

(b) Verbs with separable prefixes, such as *aan-, bij-, op- mee-, in-, uit-* etc., add *ge-* AFTER the prefix:

OP*bellen – opgebeld*   phone(d)
UIT*leggen – uitgelegd*   explain(ed)
AF*studeren – afgestudeerd*   graduate(d)

48.3   DOUBLE INFINITIVES: When modal verbs and some other verbs, such as *laten* 'to let', *blijven* 'to stay/remain', *zien* 'to see', *horen* 'to hear' etc. occur with a second verb, the perfect tense is formed not with the past participle but with an infinitive (☞ *Modal verbs*, 40.2(b) and *Infinitives* 30.1(d))

PRESENT *ik **kan** het niet vinden*   I cannot find it
PERFECT *ik **heb** het niet **kunnen** vinden* I have not been able to find it
PRESENT *hij **hoort** mij praten*   he hears me talking
PERFECT *hij **heeft** mij **horen** praten*   he has heard me talking

48.4   Verbs taking *zijn*

A relatively small number of verbs form their perfect tense not with *hebben* but with *zijn* 'to be'

---

57 Note that some past participles may also be used as adjectives, e.g. *de **gereserveerd-e** kamer* 'the reserved room' (☞ *Adjectives derived from other words*, 3.3).

Table 23. The perfect tense with zijn

SUBJECT	ZIJN	PAST PARTICIPLE	
ik	**ben**		
jij	**bent**		
u (sing. and pl.)	**bent/is**		
hij/zij/het	**is**	gegaan	'gone'
wij/jullie/zij	**zijn**		

zij **zijn** *naar de stad* **gegaan**	they have gone to town
wat **is** *er* **gebeurd**?	what has happened?

Some common verbs taking *zijn* in the perfect are

blijven	to stay	*stoppen/ophouden*	to stop
blijken	to appear/seem	*verdwijnen*	to disappear
gaan	to go	*verschijnen*	to appear
gebeuren	to happen	*worden*	to become
komen	to come	*zijn*	to be

To a certain extent, it is possible to predict which types of verb will take *zijn*. For details see below.

48.5 Verbs taking *hebben* OR *zijn*

Some verbs of motion can take either *hebben* or *zijn* depending on whether it is the ACTION that is stressed (*hebben*) or the DESTINATION/DIRECTION (*zijn*)

ik **heb** *de hele dag* **gefietst**	I have cycled all day (ACTION)
ik **ben** NAAR DE STAD **gefietst**	I have cycled to town (DESTINATION)

This rule applies to verbs which specify the manner in which one moves from A to B, e.g. **fietsen** 'to cycle', **lopen** 'to walk', **rennen** 'to run', **reizen** 'to travel', **rijden** 'to drive', **varen** 'to sail', **vliegen** 'to fly', **zwemmen** 'to swim' etc:

bent *u ooit* NAAR SPANJE **gevlogen**?	have you ever flown to Spain?
hebt *u ooit in een Boeing 747* **gevlogen**?	have you ever flown in a Boeing 747?
ben *jij* NAAR AMSTERDAM **gereden**? *nee,*	did you drive to Amsterdam? no, I didn't
ik **heb** *niet* **gereden**, *maar* **gelopen**!	drive, I walked!

48.6 USE: The perfect is more common in Dutch than in English

(a) It is used almost always to translate a perfect in English
(yet ☞ below)

ik **heb** *nooit een creditcard* **gebruikt**	I have never used a credit card
hij **heeft** *het boek al* **gelezen**	he has already read the book
de brief **is aangekomen**	the letter has arrived

(b) It is also used as an alternative to the simple past, especially in spoken Dutch. Thus, learners are advised always to use the perfect when referring to the past except in cases where the simple past is preferred (☞ *Past tense, 47.3*)

wij **hebben** *gisteren hard* **gewerkt**	we worked hard yesterday
ik **heb** *met Kerstmis te veel* **gegeten**	I ate too much at Christmas
de trein **is** *om twee uur* **vertrokken**	the train left at two o'clock

 Verbs taking *zijn* are usually intransitive (i.e. do not take a direct object) and many of them fall into two main categories: (i) VERBS DENOTING MOTION OR A CHANGE IN POSITION, e.g. *hij* **is** *naar huis* **gegaan** 'he has gone home', *ik* **ben** *te laat* **gekomen** 'I came too late'. Other examples are *vallen* 'to fall', *vertrekken* 'to depart', *opstaan* 'to get up', *instappen/uitstappen* 'to get in/out', *zinken* 'to sink', *ontsnappen* 'to escape' etc; (ii) VERBS DENOTING A CHANGE OF STATE OR CONDITION, e.g. *hij* **is** *agressiever* **geworden** 'he has become more aggressive'. Other examples are *sterven* 'to die', *geboren zijn* 'to be born', *groeien* 'to grow', *krimpen* 'to shrink', *verouderen* 'to grow old', *verwelken* 'to wither', *verkleuren* 'to change colour' etc. Note that *beginnen* 'to begin', *vergeten* 'to forget' and *volgen* 'to follow/pursue' are unusual in that they take *zijn* even when used transitively (i.e. with a direct object), e.g. *ik* **ben** *mijn nieuwe boek* **begonnen** 'I have begun my new book', *hij* **is** *haar adres* **vergeten** 'he has forgotten her address', *zij* **is** *haar leraar* **gevolgd** 'she has followed her teacher'.[58] All other verbs used transitively take *hebben*.

 Most verbs derived from verbs taking *zijn* also take *zijn* themselves, e.g. **aankomen** 'to arrive' from *komen*, **ondergaan** 'to undergo' from *gaan*, **opgroeien** 'to grow up' from *groeien*, **afvallen** 'to fall off / to lose weight', **invallen** 'to invade / (of a thought, idea etc.) to occur to someone' and **opvallen** 'to attract attention' from *vallen*.[59]

 The perfect tense in expressions with 'for', 'since' and 'how long'?, e.g. 'I have lived here for five years / since April' etc. are rendered not by the perfect but by the present tense in Dutch (☞ *Present tense,*).

49 Personal pronouns: I, YOU, HE etc.

A personal pronoun is a pronoun referring to one or more persons, e.g. 'I', 'you', 'he', 'she', 'we', 'they'. In addition, pronouns referring to inanimate objects (e.g. 'it', 'they') are usually dealt with under this heading. There are two types of personal pronoun in English: (i) subject pronouns which function as the subject of the sentence, e.g. 'I like coffee', 'WE play football', 'are THEY coming?'; (ii) object pronouns which function as the direct or indirect object, e.g. 'John likes ME', 'come with US', 'give THEM a drink' etc. In Dutch, the situation is very similar, although a number of differences should be noted (☞ 49.2). One particularly interesting difference is that some personal pronouns in Dutch have a special unstressed variant which is also used in writing. Rules for the use of stressed and unstressed pronouns are given in 49.3:

---

58 When transitive, *vergeten* may also be used with *hebben*, e.g. *ik heb mijn portemonnee vergeten* 'I have forgotten my purse'. *Volgen* is used with *hebben* in the sense of 'to follow a story or event', e.g. *ik heb het college gevolgd* 'I followed the lecture'.

59 Unless the derived verbs are transitive, e.g. *bekomen* 'to receive', *begaan* 'to commit', in which case they take *hebben*.

49.1 Personal pronouns in Dutch (unstressed forms are given in brackets)

Table 24. Subject pronouns used in spoken and written Dutch

SINGULAR		PLURAL	
ik	I	**wij (we)**	we
jij (je)	you (informal)	**jullie**	you (informal)
u	you (polite)	**u**	you (polite)
hij	he/(it, ☞ 49.2(b))		
zij (ze)	she	**zij (ze)**	they
het	it		

jij *en* ***ik*** *zijn goede vrienden*	you and I are good friends
hij *ging uit en* ***zij*** *bleef thuis*[60]	he went out and she stayed at home

Note that there are also unstressed forms of *ik* (***'k***), *hij* (***ie***) and *het* (***'t***) which are not usually written.

Table 25. Object pronouns used in spoken and written Dutch

SINGULAR		PLURAL	
mij (me)	me	**ons**	us
jou (je)	you (informal)	**jullie**	you (informal)
u	you (polite)	**u**	you (polite)
hem	him/(it, ☞ 49.2(b))		
haar	her	**hen/hun (ze)**	them (people)
het	it	**die**	them (things)

hij nodigde ***jou*** *en* ***mij*** *uit*	he invited you and me
ik praatte met ***hem*** *en toen met* ***haar***	I spoke to him and then to her

Note that there are also unstressed forms of *hem* (***'m***), *haar* (***ze*** or ***d'r***) and *het* (***'t***) which are not usually written.

49.2 Differences between English and Dutch personal pronouns

(a) YOU: The English pronoun 'you' has three equivalents in Dutch

(i) *JIJ* (unstressed *je*, object *jou/je*) is the informal word for 'you' in the singular. Generally speaking, it is used with family, friends and children (under 18). In addition, young adults usually use *jij/je/jou* with people of their own age

wil ***jij*** *nog een biertje?*	do you want another beer?
ik vind ***jou*** *heel aardig*	I really like you

---

60 Although the Dutch equivalents of 'she' and 'they' are identical, this rarely leads to confusion as they usually occur with a verb which differentiates singular and plural, e.g. *zij bleef thuis* 'she stayed at home' vs. *zij bleven thuis* 'they stayed at home'.

(ii) *JULLIE* (object *jullie*) is the plural equivalent of *jij/je/jou*

komen **jullie** ook mee?	are you (plural) coming too?
ik wil met **jullie** praten	I want to talk to you (plural)

(iii) *U* (object *u*) is the polite word for *you* in the singular and plural. Generally speaking, it is used with grandparents, strangers and more distant acquaintances[61]

waar werkt **u**?	where do you work? (sing. or pl.)
kan ik **u** helpen?	can I help you? (sing. or pl.)

Note that *u* usually occurs with a singular verb form even when referring to more than one person. If, however, the situation is not too formal, *jullie* with a plural verb form may be used instead of *u* in the plural.

(b) IT: As Dutch has grammatical gender, the translation of English 'it' depends on the gender of the noun being referred to, i.e. *het* refers to neuter nouns and *hij* (object *hem*) to common gender nouns (☞ *Gender*, 25.2)

het nieuwe boek? Nee, ik ken **het** niet	the new book? No, I don't know it
de rode auto? Nee, **hij** is niet van mij	the red car? No it's not mine
de computer? Ik heb **hem** net gekocht	the computer? I've just bought it

Note that the personal pronouns are only used when the noun they are referring to is not present. If, however, the noun is specified later in the sentence, 'it' is always translated by the more general *het*:

het is een rode auto/**hij** is rood	it is a red car / it is red
het is mijn computer/**hij** is van mij	it is my computer / it is mine
het is de mijne/**hij** is van mij	it is mine / it is mine[62]

(c) THEY: *Zij* (unstressed *ze*) is used unless the noun is specified later, in which case *het* is used

het zijn rode auto's/**zij** zijn rood	they are red cars / they are red
het zijn mijn bloemen/**zij** zijn van mij	they are my flowers / they are mine
het zijn de mijne/**zij** zijn van mij	they are mine / they are mine

(d) THEM (people)

(i) In spoken Dutch, *hun* (or unstressed *ze*) is the usual way of translating English 'them' referring to people:

ik heb **hun** bloemen gegeven	I gave them flowers
zie je **hun**?	can you see them?
hij praat graag met **hun**	he likes talking to them

---

61 Dutch has two ways of translating English *please* depending on the formality of the situation: (i) *alsjeblieft* is used with *je*, (ii) *alstublieft* is used with *u*.

62 Note that forms such as *de mijne/het mijne* 'mine' (☞ *Possession*, 51.4(b)) and *dezelfde/hetzelfde* 'the same' (☞ *SAME*) are also nouns.

(ii) In written Dutch, *hen* is used to translate 'them' when it is a direct object and when it follows a preposition. *Hun* is used for indirect objects (☞ *Objects: direct and indirect*)*

*onze directeur kan **hen** niet bereiken*	our manager cannot reach them
*hij heeft een afspraak met **hen***	he has an appointment with them
*hij heeft **hun** 1.000 pond gegeven*	he gave them (indirect obj.) £1,000

*It should be noted, however, that Dutch people often use *hun* in place of *hen*.

(e) THEM (things): *Ze* is the usual way of translating English 'them' referring to things. If special emphasis is required, however, *die* meaning 'those' is often used[63]

*ik koop **ze** niet*	I am not buying them
*nee, **die** koop ik niet*	no, I'm not buying **them** (**those**)
*ik neem **die** en **die** alstublieft*	I'll take **those** and **those**, please

49.3 Use of stressed and unstressed personal pronouns

(a) WRITTEN DUTCH: stressed and unstressed pronouns can be used interchangeably if no particular emphasis is required. As a rule, the more formal the piece of writing, the more likely it is that the stressed forms will be used

***zij/ze** vinden de lessen moeilijk*	they find the lessons difficult
*hij weet veel van **hen/ze***	he knows a lot about them
*kunt u **mij/me** helpen?*	can you help me?

If, however, emphasis **is** required (i.e. if the writer wishes to stress a pronoun and/or make some contrast), the stressed forms are used:

***zij** vinden het moeilijk maar **wij** niet*	**they** find it difficult but **we** don't
*hij weet veel van **hen** maar niets van **mij***	he knows a lot about **them** but nothing about **me**

(b) SPOKEN DUTCH: unstressed pronouns are usually used if no particular emphasis is required

*waar kom **je** vandaan?*	where do you come from?
*ik houd van **je***	I love you
***ze** wil het niet doen*	she doesn't want to do it
***we** hebben genoeg geld*	we've got enough money

If, however, emphasis **is** required (i.e. if the speaker wishes to stress a pronoun and/or make some contrast), the stressed forms are used:

*ik kom uit Leiden. En **jij**?*	I come from Leiden. And **you**?
*ik houd van **jou**, niet van hem*	I love **you**, not him
*hij wil het doen maar **zij** niet*	he wants to do it but **she** doesn't

---

63 In spoken Dutch, *die* may also replace other third person pronouns (translating English 'he/him', 'she/her', 'it', 'they/them' referring to people or things), e.g. *die studeren Engels* 'they study English', ***die** heb ik niet uitgenodigd* 'I haven't invited him/her/them'. In these cases, *die* does not necessarily indicate stress but is simply a matter of usage.

> **wij** *verdienen meer dan* **zij**　　　　**we** earn more than **them**
> 　　　　　　　　　　　　　　　　　　(☞)

 When *it* and *them* (referring to things) follow a preposition in English, they are translated not by the personal pronouns in Dutch but by *er* (stressed *daar*) with the preposition following, e.g. 'the new car? – do you know about it?' is not *de nieuwe auto?* – ✗ *weet jij van* **hem** but *de nieuwe auto? – weet jij* **er**van? (☞ *Er*, 21.1(c)).

English speakers must take care not to overuse the object pronoun in Dutch after *dan* 'than', e.g. SUBJECT *Jan is groter dan* **ik/hij/wij** etc. literally 'Jan is bigger than I/he/we' etc. versus OBJECT *hij vindt Linda aardiger dan* **mij/hem/ons** etc. 'he finds Linda nicer than me/him/us etc.'. If in doubt as to whether a subject or object is needed, it is advisable to imagine what the whole sentence would have been, e.g. 'Jan is bigger than **I** ᴀᴍ/**he** ɪѕ/**we** ᴀʀᴇ' etc. versus 'he finds Linda nicer than ʜᴇ ꜰɪɴᴅѕ **me/him/us**'.

50　Pluperfect tense

In English, the pluperfect tense is generally used to refer to events in the past which are no longer relevant to the present, e.g. 'I HAD MADE a cake' (*but it has now been eaten*). It is formed using the auxiliary verb 'have' in the simple past tense plus a past participle, e.g. I/YOU/HE HAD MADE etc. The formation and use of the pluperfect tense in Dutch is as follows:

50.1　Formation of the pluperfect in Dutch

(a) Most verbs form their pluperfect tense using the PAST tense of *hebben* (i.e. singular *had*, plural *hadden*) plus a past participle (☞ *Perfect tense* for past participles)

Table 26. The pluperfect tense with hebben

SUBJECT	HEBBEN	PAST PARTICIPLE	
ik jij u (sing. and pl.) hij/zij/het	had		
		gewerkt	'worked'
wij/jullie/zij	hadden		

> *ik* **had** *heel hard* **gewerkt**　　　　I had worked very hard
> *wij* **hadden** *al twee keer* **gespeeld**[64]　　we had played twice (already)

Note that English progressives with BE + -'ing' have no direct equivalent in Dutch:

> *ik* **had gewerkt**　　　　I had worked   OR
> 　　　　　　　　　　　　I had been working
> 　　　　　　　　　　　　(☞ also)

---

64 ☞ *Word order*, 78.2(a).

(b) Verbs forming their perfect tense with *zijn* also form their pluperfect with *zijn*: i.e. singular *was*, plural *waren* (☞ *Perfect tense* 48.3)

Table 27. The pluperfect tense with zijn

SUBJECT	ZIJN	PAST PARTICIPLE	
ik jij u (sing. and pl.) hij/zij/het	**was**	gegaan	'gone'
wij/jullie/zij	**waren**		

*zij **waren** naar de stad **gegaan***	they had gone to town
*het **was** al **gebeurd***	it had already happenend

The same applies to verbs which can take *hebben* OR *zijn* (☞ *Perfect tense* 48.4):

*ik **had** de hele dag **gefietst***	I had cycled all day
*ik **was** naar de stad **gefietst***	I had cycled to town

50.2 USE: The pluperfect in Dutch is generally used in the same way as the pluperfect in English (yet ☞ and below)

*zij **hadden** mij niet **gewaarschuwd***	they had not warned me
*de leraar **had** het slecht **uitgelegd***	the teacher had explained it badly
*het **was** een heel mooie dag **geweest***	it had been a very nice day

 The pluperfect tense in expressions with 'for', 'since' and 'how long', e.g. 'I had lived there for five years / since April' etc., are rendered not by the pluperfect but by the simple past tense in Dutch (☞ *Past tense*,).

 PLUPERFECT CONSTRUCTIONS WITH 'WHEN': When the action described by the verb is still continuing English uses a progressive form of the pluperfect (i.e. with 'been' + '-ing') and Dutch uses a SIMPLE PAST tense, e.g. 'Anna **had been drying** her hair WHEN the doorbell rang' *Anna föhnde haar haar* TOEN *er gebeld werd*, which makes it clear that Anna was still drying her hair at that precise moment. By contrast, if the action had already been completed, i.e. she had finished drying her hair beforehand, both English and Dutch use a straightforward pluperfect, e.g. 'Anna **had dried** her hair WHEN the doorbell rang' = *Anna **had** haar haar **geföhnd*** TOEN *er gebeld werd*.

51 Possession

In English, possession can be expressed in a number of different ways: e.g. 'the neighbour'S car', 'the first page OF the book', 'MY house', 'it is YOURS' etc. Such possessive constructions are also present in Dutch, although their usage differs somewhat from that of the English ones, especially with regard to the distribution of -*s*.

51.1 In Dutch, the possessive -*s* can only be used with people's names

*het was Marieke**s** idee*	it was Marieke's idea
*dat is niet Jan**s** vrouw*	that is not Jan's wife
*meneer Kok**s** lessen zijn interessant*	Mr Kok's classes are interesting

Note that abbreviations and names ending in a vowel other than -*e* (i.e. in -*a*, -*i*, -*o*, -*u*, -*y*) require an apostrophe before -*s*. Names ending in -*s* and -*z* take an apostrophe without the -*s* (☞ *Apostrophes*, 7.1):

Kees' hond en Anita's kat	Kees's dog and Anita's cat
JC's boekhandel	JC's bookshop

51.2 Otherwise, the most common way of expressing possession in Dutch is by using *van* 'of'[65]

*de schoenen **van** mijn dochter*	my daughter's shoes
*een vriend **van** mij*	a friend of mine
*de ouders **van** de studenten*	the students' parents
***van** wie is deze hoed?*	whose is this hat? (literally *of whom* . . .)

Note that *van* can also be used with people's names as an alternative to -(')*s*:

*dat is niet de vrouw **van** Jan*	that is not Jan's wife
*het was het idee **van** meneer Kramer*	it was Mr Kramer's idea

51.3 Possessive pronouns can also be used (☞ *Possessive pronouns*)

*dit is **ons** nieuwe huis*	this is our new house
***mijn** fiets is kapot*	my bike is not working
*zijn dat **uw** kinderen?*	are those your children?

51.4 When the noun is omitted, e.g. 'it is MINE/YOURS' etc., there are two ways of rendering the possessive

(a) The more formal way is to use *van* plus a stressed object pronoun (☞ *Personal pronouns, Table 25*)

Table 28. Possessives with van

SINGULAR		PLURAL	
van **mij**	mine	van **ons**	ours
van **jou**	yours (informal)	van **jullie**	yours (informal)
van **u**	yours (polite)	van **u**	yours (polite)
van **hem**	his	van **hun**	theirs
van **haar**	hers		

*de rok? – hij is **van mij**, niet **van haar***	the skirt? – it is mine, not hers
*het huis? – ja, het is **van ons***	the house? – yes, it is ours
*de koekjes? – zij zijn niet **van jou***	the biscuits? – they are not yours

When this type of possessive is used independently (i.e. when it does NOT follow the verb *zijn* 'to be') it is preceded either by *dat* 'that', for singular neuter nouns, or by *die* 'that/those', for all other nouns (☞ *Demonstrative pronouns*, 19.1):

---

65 Note that 'of' is often left unexpressed after nouns denoting a certain quantity of something, e.g. *een kilo rijst* 'a kilo of rice', *een kopje thee* 'a cup of tea', *een bos bloemen* 'a bunch of flowers'.

*de rok? – **die van mij** is mooier*	the skirt? – mine is nicer
*het huis? – **dat van jullie** is groter*	the house? – yours (pl.) is bigger
*de koekjes? – **die van hen** zijn lekker*	the biscuits? – theirs are lovely

And with names:

*de auto? – **die van Piet** is sneller*	the car? – Piet's is faster

(b) The less formal way is to add the ending -e to the possessive pronouns, thus making them into nouns. They are then preceded by either *de* or *het* depending on the gender of the omitted noun

Table 29. Possessive pronouns used independently as nouns

PRONOUN	NOUN	
mijn	de/het **mijne**	mine
jouw	de/het **jouwe**	yours (informal)
uw	de/het **uwe**	yours (polite)
zijn	de/het **zijne**	his
haar	de/het **hare**	hers
ons	de/het **onze**	ours
jullie	—	— (no corresponding noun)
uw	de/het **uwe**	yours (polite)
hun	—	— ('de/het hunne' is not used)

Note that, when adding *-e*, one must observe the regular Dutch spelling changes, e.g. *haar – ha**r**e, ons – on**z**e* (☞ *Spelling*).

DE *rok? – het is **de mijne**, niet **de hare***	the skirt? – it is mine, not hers
HET *huis? – Ja, het is **het onze***	the house? – yes, it is ours
DE *koekjes? – het zijn niet **de jouwe***	the biscuits? – they are not yours

'It' and 'them' are always translated by *het* in such constructions while in 51.4(a) above *het, hij* and *ze* are used depending on the gender and number of the omitted noun (☞ *Gender,* 25.2).

 As an alternative to the constructions with *van* and *-s* in 51.1 and 51.2, there is also a more colloquial way of expressing possession which is common in spoken Dutch but is usually not written, e.g. ***Jan z'n*** *vrouw* 'Jan's wife', ***de oude vrouw d'r*** *katten* 'the old woman's cats', ***de kinderen hun*** *schoenen* 'the children's shoes' (literally 'Jan his wife', 'the old lady her cats', 'the children their shoes') which always uses the unstressed form of the possessive pronoun (☞ *Possessive pronouns,* 52.1).

52   Possessive pronouns: MY, YOUR, HIS etc.

Possessive pronouns in English are derived from personal pronouns and are used to denote possession, e.g. 'MY house', 'YOUR car', 'ITS doors', 'THEIR friends'. This is also the case in Dutch although, as with personal pronouns, there are some differences regarding the use of variant forms that should be noted:

52.1 Dutch possessive pronouns (unstressed forms are given in brackets)

Table 30. Possessive pronouns used in spoken and written Dutch

SINGULAR		PLURAL	
mijn **jouw** (je) **uw**	my your (informal) your (polite)	**ons/onze** **jullie** (je) **uw**	us your (informal) your (polite)
zijn **haar** **zijn**	his her its	**hun**	their

jouw vrienden en *mijn* gezin   your friends and my family
zijn huis en *haar* auto   his house and her car

Note that there are also unstressed forms of *mijn* (**m'n**), *zijn* (**z'n**) and *haar* (**d'r**) which are not usually written.

52.2 Differences between English and Dutch possessive pronouns

(a) YOUR: The Dutch equivalent of 'your' has three variants corresponding to the three alternatives for 'you' (☞ *Personal pronouns*, 49.2(a))

(i) *JOUW* (unstressed *je*, ☞ 52.3(a)) is the informal singular corresponding to *jij/je*

is dat ***jouw*** *vriend?*   is that your friend?
heb jij ***je*** *jas meegenomen?*   do you have your jacket with you?

(ii) *JULLIE* (unstressed *je*, ☞ 52.3(b)) is the informal plural corresponding to *jullie*

ik vind ***jullie*** *huis erg mooi*   I think your (pl.) house is very nice
is dat ***jullie*** *auto?*   is that your (pl.) car?

(iii) *UW* is the polite singular and plural form corresponding to *u*

wat is ***uw*** *adres?*   what is your (sing./pl.) address?
u mag ***uw*** *sleutel hier laten*   you may leave your (sing./pl.) key here

(b) OUR: The Dutch equivalent of *our* has two variants: (i) *ons* is used before singular neuter nouns, (ii) *onze* is used elsewhere (i.e. before singular common gender nouns and all plural nouns)

dit is ***ons*** *nieuwe huis*   this is our new house
en dat is ***onze*** *nieuwe auto*   and that is our new car
heeft u ***onze*** *kinderen gezien?*   have you seen our children?

52.3 Use of stressed versus unstressed forms

(a) *Je*, the unstressed variant of *jouw*, is the norm in spoken and written Dutch unless the speaker/writer wishes to stress the pronoun and/or make some sort of contrast

*mag ik **je** fiets even lenen?*	may I borrow your bike?
*ja, maar wat is met **jouw** fiets?*	yes, but what about **your** bike?
*is dat **mijn** bier of **jouw** bier?*	is that **my** beer or **your** beer?

(b) In the plural, the stressed variant *jullie* is the norm. If, however, any other *jullie* has already been used in the same sentence, the unstressed variant *je* is preferred, as it is generally felt that more than one *jullie* in a sentence sounds clumsy

***jullie** huis is erg mooi*	your house is very nice
*willen jullie **je** huis verkopen?*	do you want to sell your house?
*jullie mogen **je** bagage hier laten*	you can leave your luggage here

52.4 Possessive pronouns may also be used independently as nouns to translate English 'mine', 'yours' etc. (☞ *Possession, Table 29*)

 In English, possessive pronouns are often omitted to avoid repetition, e.g. 'he is very proud of his house and [his] garden', 'where are your shoes and [your] socks?', 'she likes playing with her dog and [her] cat'. This is not usual in Dutch, e.g. *hij is erg trots op **zijn** huis en **zijn** tuin, waar zijn **je** schoenen en **je** sokken?, zij speelt graag met **haar** hond en **haar** kat* (☞ also *Articles*, 8.4).

53 Prepositions

A preposition is a word (or group of words) used before a noun or pronoun to relate it to other words in the sentence, e.g. 'it is UNDER the table', 'I looked AT you'. Prepositions in Dutch often cause problems for English learners as there is rarely a one-to-one correspondence between Dutch and English prepositions, e.g. English 'on' may correspond to Dutch *aan*, *op* or *in* depending on the context (☞ 53.1: ON). Furthermore, many prepositions have different meanings depending on whether they occur on their own or in a set phrase together with a verb, noun or adjective, e.g. ***aan** de rechterkant* 'ON the right-hand side' but *ik denk **aan** jou* 'I am thinking OF you', *ik ben trouw **aan** mijn land* 'I am loyal TO my country'. Therefore, it is impossible to cover all the meanings and nuances of Dutch prepositions in a way that is helpful to students and, for the most part, one must simply learn them on an ad hoc basis along with the phrases in which they occur.

The list given in 53.1 of the most common prepositions in English and their Dutch equivalents may be useful as a (very) rough guide to the general usage of prepositions and their basic meanings in Dutch. In addition, 53.2 and 53.3 list some useful Dutch phrases and commonly used verbs and adjectives which occur with unpredictable prepositions:

53.1 Common prepositions and their basic meanings

ABOUT = *over*

*ik lees een boek **over** de Romeinen*	I'm reading a book about the Romans
*hij praat graag **over** zijn werk*	he likes talking about his job

ABOVE/OVER

(i) *boven* is used with expressions of place

*de krans hangt **boven** de deur*	the wreath is hanging above the door
*hij woont **boven** een slagerij*	he lives over/above a butcher's shop

(ii) *boven* and *over* are used elsewhere

zijn vrouw is **boven / over** *de veertig*	his wife is over forty
er waren **boven / over** *de vijftig mensen*	there were over fifty people

ACCORDING TO = *volgens*

volgens *deze brief bent u 21 jaar oud*	according to this letter you are 21
volgens *mijn leraar ben ik lui*	according to my teacher I am lazy

AFTER = *na*

kom **na** *twee uur even langs*	come along after two o'clock
na *u!*	after you!

AGAINST = *tegen*

hij zette zijn fiets **tegen** *de muur*	he put his bike against the wall
ik ben **tegen** *de doodstraf*	I am against the death sentence

ALONG/PAST = *langs*

wij wandelen graag **langs** *de rivier*	we like walking along the river
hij is hier **langs** *gereden*[66]	he drove past here

APART FROM (☞ EXCEPT (FOR))

AROUND = *(rond)om*

zij verdwenen **om** *de hoek*	they disappeared around the corner
de padvinders zaten (rond)**om** *het vuur*	the scouts sat around the fire

AT

(i) *bij* is used with people's houses/businesses and with meals

ik was **bij** *de bakker en toen* **bij** *Jan*	I was at the baker's and then at Jan's
ik heb hem **bij** *het avondeten gezien*	I saw him at dinner

(ii) *om* is used with expressions of time

hij komt **om** *vier uur*	he is coming at four o'clock
de trein vertrekt **om** *half twee*	the train leaves at half past one

(iii) *aan* tends to be used elsewhere

Jeroen studeert **aan** *de universiteit*	Jeroen is (i.e. studies) at university
er is iemand **aan** *de deur*	there's someone at the door

BECAUSE OF = *vanwege/wegens*

ik kan **vanwege** *de hitte niet slapen*	I can't sleep because of the heat
hij valt op **vanwege** *zijn blauwe ogen*	he is striking because of his blue eyes

BEFORE = *vóór*

kom **vóór** *half zes even langs*	come along before half past five
laten we **vóór** *de lunch gaan fietsen*	let's go cycling before lunch

---

66 Note that *hier* 'here', *daar/er* 'there', and *waar* 'where' precede the preposition (☞ 📖 📖).

BEHIND = *achter*

*hij verscheen van **achter** een boom*	he appeared from behind a tree
*u mag **achter** de school parkeren*	you may park behind the school

BETWEEN = *tussen*

*hij stond **tussen** twee politieagenten*	he stood between two policemen
*je mag niet **tussen** de maaltijden eten*	you must not eat between meals

BY

(i) *bij* is used to mean 'near'

*Harald wachtte **bij** de deur*	Harald waited by the door
*Enschede ligt **bij** de Duitse grens*	Enschede is near the German border

(ii) *met* 'with' (or, more formally, *per*) is used with means of transport and post

*hij gaat liever **met** de trein*	he prefers travelling by train
*ik stuur u de boeken **met** de post*	I will send you the books by post

(iii) *vóór* is used with expressions of time

*ik doe het **vóór** dinsdag*	I'll do it by Tuesday
*jij moet **vóór** 1 mei klaar zijn*	you must be finished by 1 May

(iv) *door* is used in the passive to introduce the agent (i.e. the doer) of the verb (☞ *Passive*, 46.2)

*hij werd **door** zijn vrouw verlaten*	he was left by his wife
*zij waren **door** de politie bezocht*	they had been visited by the police

DURING = *gedurende/tijdens*

***tijdens** de oorlog was hij in Berlijn*	he was in Berlin during the war
***gedurende** de laatste vier jaar*	during the last four years

EXCEPT (FOR)/APART FROM = *behalve*/(more formally) *afgezien van*

*hij doet alles **afgezien van** werken*	he does everything except work
*niemand wil hem zien **behalve** ik*	no one wants to see him except me

FOR

(i) *voor* (without accents) is the basic Dutch equivalent:

*heeft u een tafel **voor** twee personen?*	do you have a table for two?
*ik heb iets leuks **voor** jou*	I have something nice for you

(ii) With expressions of time, *for* is often left unexpressed in Dutch (yet ☞ * and (iii) below)

ik was zes dagen in Leiden	I was in Leiden for six days
ik zat twee uur in het café te wachten	I sat waiting in the cafe for two hours

*Note, however, that *voor* is usually used with *gaan* 'to go' and *komen* 'to come' when referring to future time:

*hij komt **voor** een week naar Londen*	he is coming to London for a week
*ik ga **voor** zes dagen naar Leiden*	I am going to Leiden for six days

(iii) *al* 'already' is used with verbs in the present/simple past which translate an English perfect/pluperfect (☞ *Present tense,* 📖 *, and Past tense,* 📖 *)*

*hij werkt **al** een jaar bij ons*	he has worked at our place for a year
*zij woonden er **al** twee maanden*	they had lived there for two months

FROM/OFF

(i) *van* is the basic Dutch equivalent

*het is een cadeau **van** mijn collega*	it's a present from my colleague
*de appel is **van** de boom gevallen*	the apple fell from/off the tree

(ii) *uit* is used with names of towns, countries and languages

*kom jij **uit** Groningen?*	do you come from Groningen?
*het is **uit** het Engels vertaald*	it has been translated from English

(iii) *vandaan* renders *from* when no noun or pronoun follows

*waar kom jij **vandaan**?*	where do you come from?
*waar heeft hij die **vandaan**?*	where did he get those from?

IN(TO) (☞ also *INSIDE/WITHIN*)

(i) *in* is the basic Dutch equivalent

*kunt u dit **in** het Nederlands vertalen?*	can you translate this into Dutch?
*haar vriend is **in** de vijftig*	her boyfriend is in his fifties

(ii) *over* is used with expressions of time referring to the future

*de trein vertrekt **over** tien minuten*	the train is leaving in ten minutes[67]
*ik ga **over** een week naar Spanje*	I'm going to Spain in a week's time

IN FRONT OF = *vóór*

*ik stond **vóór** de bioscoop te wachten*	I stood waiting in front of the cinema
*ik had de fiets **vóór** het café gelaten*[68]	I had left the bike in front of the cafe

INSIDE/WITHIN = *binnen*

*kom **binnen***	come in/inside
*ik ben er **binnen** een half uur*	I'll be there within half an hour

IN SPITE OF = *ondanks*

***ondanks** de hitte had hij een jas aan*	in spite of the heat he had a jacket on
***ondanks** het feit dat hij rijk is, . . .*	in spite of the fact that he is rich, . . .

---

67 Contrast *hij heeft de brief **in** tien minuten geschreven* 'he wrote the letter in ten minutes'.
68 Note that *vóór* is often used where English would use 'outside', e.g. *de auto stopte vóór het huis* 'the car stopped outside the house'.

NEAR = *bij* (☞ also *BY*)

*ik woon **bij** het station*	I live near the station
*Enschede ligt **bij** de Duitse grens*	Enschede is near the German border

NEXT TO = *naast*

*het huis **naast** het onze is te koop*	the house next to ours is for sale
*kom **naast** mij zitten*	come and sit next to me

OF = *van*

*hij is een vriend **van** mij*	he is a friend of mine
*het was dom **van** haar*	it was stupid of her

Note that 'of' is often left unexpressed after nouns denoting a certain quantity of something, e.g. *een kilo tomaten* 'a kilo of tomatoes', *een stuk kaas* 'a piece of cheese', *een kopje thee* 'a cup of tea', *een bos bloemen* 'a bunch of flowers'.

ON(TO)

(i) *op* is the basic Dutch equivalent. It is used with horizontal objects, meaning 'on top of', and in many other contexts

*hij zette het boek **op** de plank*	I put the book on (top of) the shelf
***op** vrijdag kwam hij niet **op** tijd*	on Friday he was not on time

(ii) *aan* is used before vertical objects, meaning 'on the side of'

*het schilderij hangt **aan** de muur*	the painting is hanging on the wall
*de melkboer klopte **aan** de deur*	the milkman knocked on the door

(iii) *in* is used with vehicles

*ik zag hem **in** de trein zitten*	I saw him sitting on the train
*hoeveel mensen waren er **in** de bus?*	how many people were on the bus?

OPPOSITE = *tegenover*

*ik woon **tegenover** het ziekenhuis*	I live opposite the hospital
*zij zaten **tegenover** elkaar*	they sat opposite each other

OUT (OF) = *uit*

*hij gooide het boek **uit** het raam*	he threw the book out of the window
*zij heeft het **uit** wrok gedaan*	she did it out of spite

OVER (☞ *ABOVE*)

PAST = *voorbij* (after noun)/*langs*

*hij reed het huis **voorbij***	he drove past the house
*wij gingen **langs** een café*	we went past a cafe

ROUND (☞ *AROUND*)

SINCE = *sinds*/(more formally)*sedert*

*ik werk hier **sinds** vorige maand*	I've worked here since last month
*meneer Smits is **sedert** enige tijd ziek*	Mr Smits has been ill for some time

THROUGH = *door*

ik probeerde **door** *het raam te kijken*	I tried to look through the window
wij wandelden **door** *de stad*	we took a walk through the town

TO

(i) *aan* is used before indirect objects (☞ *Objects: direct and indirect*) and with certain adjectives

ik gaf de bloemen **aan** *mijn moeder*	I gave the flowers to my mother
hij is verslaafd **aan** *cocaïne*	he is addicted to cocaine

(ii) *to* and *towards* expressing direction are translated by *naar*. When no noun or pronoun follows, *naar* becomes *naartoe*[69]

hoe kom ik **naar** *het postkantoor?*	how do I get to the post office?
waar ga jij **naartoe***?*	where are you going (to)?

(iii) *to* and *towards* meaning 'with regard to/with respect to' are translated by *tegenover*

tegenover *mij is hij erg vriendelijk*	he's very friendly to(wards) me
hoe is hij **tegenover** *zijn vrouw?*	how is he towards his wife?

UNDER = *onder*

de hond zit **onder** *de tafel*	the dog is sitting under the table
het is **onder** *de tien gulden*	it costs under ten guilders

UNTIL = *tot*

jij moet **tot** *vanavond wachten*	you must wait until this evening
tot *morgen!*	until tomorrow! / see you tomorrow!

WITH

(i) *met* is the basic Dutch equivalent

hij ging **met** *zijn vriend zwemmen*	he went swimming with his friend
*wat ga jij er***mee** *doen?*[70]	what are you going to do with it?

(ii) *bij* is used with *wonen* 'to live' meaning 'at someone's house' and also with food and drink

hij woont **bij** *zijn ouders*	he lives with his parents
wil jij een koekje **bij** *de koffie?*	do you want a biscuit with the coffee?

WITHOUT = *zonder* (with omission of the article)

ga nooit **zonder** *paraplu uit!*	never go out without an umbrella!
ik kan het **zonder** *woordenboek doen*	I can do it without a dictionary

---

69 *Toe* on its own is used as a separable verb prefix, e.g. **toe***roepen* 'to call out to' (☞ *Separable verbs,* **Table 41**).

70 Following *er, daar* and *waar* (☞ 📖 📖) *met* becomes **mee**. *Mee* is also used as a separable verb prefix, e.g. **mee***spelen* 'to play with someone' (☞ *Separable verbs*).

53.2 Useful phrases with unpredictable prepositions

aan *tafel/de kust/de hemel* etc.	at the table / the coast / in the sky etc.
aan *de rechter-/linkerkant*	at/on the right/left hand side
heb je geld etc. **bij** *je?*	do you have any money etc. on you?
ik dacht **bij** *mezelf*	I thought to myself
bij *mooi weer*	in nice weather
in *het weekend*	at the weekend
met *Kerstmis/Pasen*	at Christmas/Easter
onder *vrienden/mensen* etc.	among friends/people etc.
op *school/kantoor/een feest* etc.	at school/the office/a party etc.
op *zoek naar*	in search of
volgens *mij/jou/hem/ons* etc.	in my/your/his/our etc. opinion

53.3 Common verbs and adjectives taking unpredictable prepositions

Table 31. Verbs with prepositions

afhangen **van**	depend on	luisteren **naar**	listen to
bang zijn **voor**	be afraid of	praten/spreken **met**	talk to
deelnemen **aan**	take part in	reageren **op**	react to
denken **aan**	think of/about	rekenen **op**	rely on
feliciteren **met**	congratulate on	sterven **aan**	die of
gebrek hebben **aan**	be short of	trek/zin hebben **in**	want/fancy
herinneren **aan**[71]	remind	trouwen **met**	marry
huilen **om**	cry at/about	twijfelen **aan**	doubt
kijken **naar**	look at/watch	vragen **om**	ask for
lachen **om**	laugh at	weten **van**	know about
letten **op**	pay attention to	zeggen **tegen**	say to
lijden **aan**	suffer from	zorgen **voor**	care for

For verbs taking *aan* meaning 'to', ☞ *Objects: direct and indirect*, 45.3.

Table 32. Adjectives with prepositions

aardig **tegen**	nice to	lelijk **tegen**	nasty to
benieuwd **naar**	curious about	schadelijk **voor**	harmful to
beroemd **om**	famous for	schuldig **aan**	guilty of
boos/kwaad **op**	angry with	slecht **in**	bad at
gek/dol **op**	mad about	trots **op**	proud of
goed **in**	good at	verbaasd **over**	amazed at
jaloers **op**	jealous of	verliefd **op**	in love with

---

71 Also *zich herinneren aan* 'to remember'.

Note the following:

(i) Words with similar meanings often take the same preposition, e.g. *kwaad* **op** 'angry with' and *woedend* **op** 'furious with'.

(ii) Derived words usually take the same preposition as the word from which they are derived, e.g. *denken* **aan** 'to think of' → *de gedachte* **aan** 'the thought of', *afhangen* **van** 'to depend on' → *afhankelijk* **van** 'dependent on'.

 Many of the common prepositions may also *follow* the noun in contexts where the speaker wishes to emphasise an action, e.g *ik liep het huis* **in/uit** 'I walked into/out of the room', *hij werkte de hele nacht* **door** 'he worked the whole night through'.

 When *het/hem* 'it' and *zij/ze* 'them' refer to non-humans they do not occur with prepositions. Instead, they are replaced by **er**, which follows the verb, and the preposition is added later, e.g. *wat weet jij* **ervan**? (NOT **✗** *van het*) 'what do you know about it?', *ik denk* **er** *niet* **aan** 'I do not think about it/them', *hij liep* **er** *vlak* **langs** 'he walked right past it' (☞ *Er*, 21.1(c)). *Dit* 'this' and *dat* 'that' are replaced by *hier* and *daar* respectively, e.g. *ik heb het* **hiermee** *gesneden* 'I cut it with this', **daarover** *wil ik niet praten* 'I do not want to talk about that (☞ *Demonstrative pronouns*,).' In questions, *wat* 'what' is replaced by *waar*, e.g. **waarover** *wil jij niet praten?* 'what don't you want to talk about?', **waarmee** *kan ik schrijven?* 'what can I write with?' (☞ *Question words*, 60.4(b)) and the relative pronouns *die* and *dat* are also replaced by *waar*, e.g. *de film* **waarover** *ik praat* 'the film that/which I'm talking about' (☞ *Relative Pronouns*, 62.2(b)).[72]

<h1>54   Present participles</h1>

In English, the present participle is the form of the verb ending in '-ing' which is used in a number of different grammatical constructions, e.g. 'I am WORK**ING**', 'he was PLAY**ING**'. In most cases, these do not correspond to present participles in Dutch but to simple verb forms, infinitives etc. depending on the construction in question (☞ *-ING constructions* for details). However, present participles may also be used as adjectives, e.g. 'the WORK**ING** man', and adverbs, e.g. 'he laughed MENAC**ING**LY', which is also the case in Dutch.

54.1   FORMATION: Present participles in Dutch are formed by adding -*d* to the infinitive (or -*de* if the infinitive has only one syllable)

*werken – werken***d**	work(ing)	*hopen – hopen***d**	hope(ing)
*lachen – lachen***d**	laugh(ing)	*gaan – gaan***de**	go(ing)
*opvallen – opvallen***d**	strike(ing)	*staan – staan***de**	stand(ing)

54.2   USE of present participles

(a) Present participles are often used as adjectives[73]

de film was **spannend**	the film was exciting
zijn verhaal was **overtuigend**	his story was convincing
die jurk is zeer **uitdagend**	that dress is very daring

---

72 Note the alternative word order *daar* *wil ik niet* **over** *praten*, **waar** *wil jij niet* **over** *praten?*, **waar** *kan ik* **mee** *schrijven?*, *de film* **waar** *ik* **over** *praat* (Compare *Er*, 21.1(c)).

73 And, like adjectives, they may also be used as nouns, e.g. *de stervende* 'the dying person', *het opvallende* 'the striking thing', *iets spannends* 'something exciting (☞ *Adjectives used as nouns*).

If used before a noun they take the same endings as ordinary adjectives (☞ *Adjectives*, 2.1):

een spannende film	an exciting film
een overtuigend verhaal	a convincing story
het huilende kind	the crying child

(b) And as adverbs

*de jongen viel **lachend** op de grond*	the boy fell to the ground laughing
*de tandarts lachte **dreigend***	the dentist laughed menacingly
*Geert kookt **verbazend** goed*	Geert cooks surprisingly well

Note that, with verbs of position such as *staan* 'to stand', *zitten* 'to sit', *liggen* 'to lie' etc., Dutch uses an infinitive with *te* rather than a present participle, e.g. *hij stond **te lachen*** 'he stood laughing', *ik zat **te lezen*** 'I sat reading' (☞ *-ING constructions*, 31.3).

 English-speaking students of Dutch must note that only present participles functioning as ADJECTIVES and ADVERBS may be translated using present participles in Dutch and not those which are verb forms (except, occasionally, in the literary language, ☞). Thus 'my boss is annoying' can be translated using a present participle (*mijn baas is **vervelend***) while 'my boss is working' cannot (*mijn baas werkt/is aan het werken*, NOT ✗ *mijn baas is **werkend***). A useful test to establish whether a participle is an adjective or not involves placing *very* before the participle. If the sentence is grammatical, the participle is an adjective: e.g. 'my boss is **very** annoying' (ADJ.) BUT NOT ✗ 'my boss is **very** working' (VERB); 'the film was moving/the film was **very** moving' (ADJ.), 'the curtains were moving/BUT NOT ✗ the curtains were **very** moving' (VERB).

In written Dutch, and especially in the literary language, present participles may be used to translate English verb forms in '-ing' when beginning a sentence or following a comma, e.g. '**putting** the money into his jacket pocket, he left the house quietly': *het geld in zijn jaszak **stoppend**, ging hij zachtjes uit het huis*; '"pleased to meet you", he said, **shaking** my hand enthusiastically': *'leuk je eens te ontmoeten', zei hij, mijn hand enthousiast **schuddend**.*

55 Present tense

Generally speaking, the present tense in Dutch and English is used to refer to present time, e.g. 'I FEEL well', although, in some contexts, it may refer to the future or even to the past (☞ 55(b–c)). Most verbs in Dutch are regular in the present tense, with the exception of *hebben* 'to have', *zijn* 'to be', *zullen* 'will', *komen* 'to come' and the modal verbs *kunnen* 'to be able', *mogen* 'to be allowed', *moeten* 'to have to / must' and *willen* 'to want' (☞ *Irregular verbs*, 33.1 and *Modal verbs*, 40.1).

55.1 Formation of the present tense in Dutch

(a) The present tense is formed using the verb stem (i.e. the infinitive minus *-en*) plus the following endings given in bold

Table 33. The present tense of werken *'to work'*

SUBJECT	VERB STEM + ENDING
ik	werk
jij u (sing. and pl.) hij/zij/het	werk – **t**
wij/jullie/zij	werk – **en**

Note that English progressives with BE + -'ing' have no direct equivalent in Dutch:

ik werk I work   OR
I am working

When adding present tense endings one must observe the regular Dutch spelling rules (☞ *Spelling*).

Table 34. The present tense with spelling changes

INFINITIVE		STEM	PRESENT		
			ik	jij/u/hij etc.	wij etc.
hopen	'to hope'	hoop	hoop	hoopt	hopen
raden	'to guess'	raad	raad	raadt	raden
haten	'to hate'	haat	haat	haat*	haten
leven	'to live'	leef	leef	leeft	leven
lezen	'to read'	lees	lees	leest	lezen
wassen	'to wash'	was	was	wast	wassen
gaan	'to go'	ga	ga	gaat	gaan

*Verb stems ending in -*t* do not add another *t*.

(b) When *jij* (or the unstressed form *je*) follows the verb, the ending -*t* is dropped

hoop jij dat hij komt? do you hope that he comes?
lees je die krant? are you reading that newspaper?

The *t* is not dropped, however, if it is part of the verb stem:

haat jij hem? do you hate him?

(c) If the verb has a separable prefix such as *op-*, *in-*, *uit-*, *mee-* etc., the prefix goes to the end of the clause (☞ *Separable verbs*, 64.2)

hij belt me iedere dag OP he rings me up every day
gaan jullie niet meer UIT*?* don't you go out any more?

55.2 USE: The present tense in Dutch is used in much the same way as in English (yet ☞ 📖 below)

(a) It refers to present time, to general time (e.g. in statements like 'the world is round') and to habitual actions

ik schrijf een boek I am writing a book
zij begrijpen de vraag niet they do not understand the question
de aarde draait om de zon the earth revolves around the sun
Jan speelt iedere avond voetbal Jan plays football every evening

(b) It is used, though more frequently than in English, to refer to the future

de trein vertrekt morgen om vijf uur the train leaves tomorrow at five
ik laat jou vanavond de foto's zien I'll show you the photos tonight
duurt het lang? will it take long?

(c) It is also used informally to bring dramatic effect to the narration of past events

*ik **kom** binnen, **zie** hem op de grond*   I come in, see him lying on the ground
*liggen en **bel** direct een ambulance*   and phone for an ambulance
    immediately

 Note that the present in Dutch is also used to translate English perfects in expressions with 'for', 'since' and 'how long', e.g. 'I **have lived / been living** here **for** five years' *ik **woon** hier al vijf jaar*, 'he **has worked / been working** with his brother **since** April' *hij **werkt** sinds april met zijn broer*, '**how long have** you **known** Jan?' *hoe lang **kent** u Jan al?*, meaning literally 'I live there already five years', 'he works since April with his brother', 'how long do you know Jan already?'

56   Professions

In English, the names of many professions are formed by adding the ending '-er' to a particular verb, e.g. a person who teaches is a TEACH**ER**, a person who sings is a SING**ER** etc. In Dutch, they are usually formed by taking the infinitive form of the verb and replacing *-en* with *-er*, e.g. *bakken* 'to bake' → *bakk**er**: Ik ben bakker* 'I am a baker' (☞ *Articles*, 8.1(a) for the omission of *een* 'a'):

schrijven → *schrijv**er***   writer   *werken* → *werk**er***   worker
spelen → *spel**er***   player   *uitgeven* → *uitgev**er***   publisher

 Some names of professions are derived from nouns, e.g. fiets**er** 'cyclist' and some have endings other than *-er*, e.g. *ler**aar*** 'teacher', *handel**aar*** 'merchant/dealer', *kunst**enaar*** 'artist', *winkel**ier*** 'shopkeeper', *tuin**ier*** 'gardener' and many words of French/Latin origin, e.g. *stud**ent*, 'student', *pian**ist*** 'pianist', *souffl**eur*** 'prompter', *organis**ator*** 'organiser', *mus**icus*** 'musician'.

 Nouns referring specifically to females have a special set of endings (☞ *Female endings*).

57   Progressive forms

In English, every tense has a progressive, otherwise known as 'continuous', equivalent which is formed using the verb 'to be' plus a present participle in '-ing', e.g. 'I work – I AM WORKING', 'he cried – he WAS CRYING'. By contrast, Dutch does not have special progressive verb forms and distinctions such as 'I work' versus 'I am working' etc. are either not made at all or are expressed using some other construction:

57.1   Dutch usually uses ordinary (i.e. non-progressive) tenses to translate English progressive forms

*ik **spreek** heel goed Nederlands*   I speak very good Dutch
*ik **spreek** Nederlands op dit moment*   I am speaking Dutch at the moment

57.2 In contexts where the speaker feels the need to stress that an action is progressive, the following constructions can be used

(a) *aan het* (often abbreviated to *aan 't*) INFINITIVE *zijn*

*wat **ben** jij nu **aan het doen**?*	what are you doing now?
*ik **was** de hele dag **aan het werken***	I was working all day
*wacht even! – ik **ben aan 't denken***	wait a minute! – I'm thinking

(b) *bezig zijn te* INFINITIVE (literally 'to be busy . . .'), or *bezig zijn met* INFINITIVE if the verb is on its own

*ze **is bezig** een workaholic **te worden***	she is becoming a workaholic
*we **waren** nog **bezig met organiseren***	we were still (busy) organising

(c) Dutch often specifies the position a person is in when carrying out a particular action. Verbs such as *staan* 'to stand', *zitten* 'to sit', *liggen* 'to lie' and *lopen* 'to walk' are used with *te* + infinitive to render a progressive where English would simply use the verb 'to be'

*ik **stond** op mijn vriend **te wachten***	I was (standing) waiting for my friend
*mijn zoon **zit** naar de tv **te kijken***	my son is (sitting) watching TV
*jij **lag** de hele nacht **te snurken***	you were (lying) snoring all night
*Kees **liep te zingen***	Kees was (walking along) singing

58 Pronunciation

This chapter provides a brief summary of standard Dutch pronunciation. It is intended as a rough guide only and does not take regional and other types of variation into account. 58.1 and 58.2 deal with the consonants and vowels of Dutch and, where possible, a comparison is made with those of standard (RP) English. It should be noted, however, that these comparisons are only approximate as there is virtually no sound in Dutch which is identical to an English sound. The transcriptions of the Dutch examples, given in curly brackets, are also approximate. For the benefit of students familiar with the International Phonetic Alphabet, phonetic symbols are provided in square brackets for each sound and the Dutch examples are transcribed phonetically in 📖 below. Finally, 58.3 outlines the main rules for Dutch word stress.

58.1 CONSONANTS

(a) The following Dutch consonants are pronounced roughly as in English

p,t, k,	*f, s, z,*	*m, n, ng,*	*h, l, c*
pot {**p**ot}	*feest* {**f**eyst}	*man* {**m**an}	*ham* {**h**am}
tien {**t**een}	*spot* {**s**pot}	*niet* {**n**eet}	*lam* {**l**am}
kat {**k**at}	*zien* {**z**een}	*zing* {zi**ng**}	*col* {**k**ol}*

*Note that *c* is pronounced like 's' before *i* and *e*, e.g. *cent* {**s**ent}.

(b) The following Dutch consonants differ in their pronunciation from those of English

Table 35. Pronunciation of Dutch consonants

Spelling	Description	Example
b	like Eng. *b* [b] but pronounced *p* at the end of words, [p]	heb {hep}
d	like Eng. *d* [d] but pronounced *t* at the end of words, [t]	bad {bat}
ch	like Scottish *ch* in *loch*, German *ch* in *Bach* {kh}, [x]	recht {rekht}
sch	pronounced as two separate sounds, *s* plus *ch* {kh}, [sx]	schip {skhip}
g	like Dutch *ch* {kh}, [x] (never like Eng. *g*)	god {khot}
j	like Eng. *y*, [j]	ja {yaah}
v	like Eng. *f* but softer, [f]	vat {fat}
w	• before vowels, like Eng. *v* but softer, with the top teeth almost but not quite touching the lower lip [ʋ] • after vowels, like Eng. *w* [w]	wat {vat} nauw {nouw}
r	pronounced either as a roll with the tip of the tongue behind the teeth as in Italian *Roma*, [r], or as a gargling sound at the back of the mouth as in French *Renee*, German *Ralf*, [ʁ].	ring {rring}
sj	like Eng. *sh*, [ʃ]	tasje {tashuh}
tj	like Eng. *tch*, [tʃ]	katje {katchuh}
-en	pronounced *uh* at the end of words (n is silent), [ə]	zitten {zituh}
-tie	pronounced *tsee* at the end of words, [tsiː]	actie {aktsee}

Notes on consonants

p, t, k   As in French, Spanish and Italian, *p*, *t*, *k* in Dutch sound softer than in English: i.e. similar to English *b*, *d*, *g*. This is because they are pronounced without aspiration (i.e. without the puff of air which usually follows English *p*, *t*, *k*).

d   In a few common words *d* is often pronounced {y} or {w} between vowels, e.g. *goede* {khooyuh}, *houden* {houwuh}.

g   This is usually pronounced with a hard {kh}. However, in words borrowed from French, e.g. *genie* 'genius', *g* is pronounced in the French way before *i* and *e* (i.e. like the *j* in French *Jacques* or the *s* in English *pleasure*), [ʒ].

lk, lm, rg,   These combinations of consonants are often broken up by inserting *e*
rk, rm   (pronounced {uh}) between them, e.g. *film* {filuhm}, *melk* {meluhk}.

58.2 VOWELS: Most vowels in Dutch differ in their pronunciation from those of English

Table 36. Pronunciation of Dutch vowels (and diphthongs)[74]

Spelling	Description	Example
a	like *a* in Eng. *car* but shorter and more clipped. The lips are slightly rounded so that it is between Eng. *a* and *o*,[ɑ]	man {man}
aa (a)	like Eng. *a* in *at* but longer, with the lips spread {aah}, [aː]	maan {maahn}
e	• like Eng. *e in bed* [ɛ] • when unstressed and at the end of words, *e* is pronounced like Dutch *u* {uh} (see below), [e]	bed {bet} tante {tantuh}
ee (e)	like Eng. *ey* in *they*, [eːʲ]	zee {zey}
o	like Eng. *o* in *port* but shorter and more clipped, [ɔ]	vol {fol}
oo (o)	like northern English *oh* or German *o* in *Ohm* with a slight movement towards {w}, [oːʷ]	zoon {zohn}
i	• like Eng. *i* in *hit* [ɪ] • the grammatical ending *-ig* is pronounced {uhkh}, [əx]	ik {ik} zestig {zestuhkh}
ie	like Eng. *ee* in *three*, [iː]	drie {drree}
u	like Eng. *u in curl* but shorter and more clipped {uh},[ʉ]	hun {huhn}
uu (u)	like French *u* in *une*, German *ü* in *für*. The sound can be made by producing an *ee*, as in English, *three* and rounding the lips, [yː]	Ruud {rruut}
oe	like Eng. *oo in school* but slightly shorter, [uː]	doen {doon}
eu	like Eng. *ur* in *curl*, but with rounded lips. Similar to German *ö* as in Köln, [øː].	neus {nurs}
ij/ei	• like the vowel in Eng. *air* plus *y*, [ɛɪ] • the ending *-lijk* is pronounced {luhk}, [lək]	bij {baiy}, ei {aiy} lelijk {leyluhk}
au/ou	like *ou* in Eng. *house* [ɑʊ]	oud {out}, nauw {nouw}
ui	a combination of *a*, as in Eng. *cat* with *uu* as in Dutch *Ruud*, [œʏ]	uit {auut}

Notes on vowels and diphthongs

ee, oo   These are long vowels with a *slight* off-glide towards {y} and {w} respectively.

aai, ooi   These combinations of vowels are pronounced **aah+i** [aːi] and **oh+i** [oːi] respectively, e.g. *saai* {**saahi**}, *mooi* {**mohi**}.

---

74 A diphthong consists of two different vowels within the same syllable, e.g. *ou in **oud** 'old'.

58.3 Stress

(a) Dutch words are usually stressed on the first syllable (the stressed vowels are given in bold print)

*v**a**der*	father	*schr**ij**fster*	authoress
*t**e**kening*	drawing	*sch**oo**nheid*	beauty

Note that compound words are usually stressed on the first word of the compound (on the appropriate syllable), e.g. *b**oe**kwinkel* 'bookshop', *v**a**derfiguur* 'father figure', *sch**oon**heidsinstituut* 'beauty parlour'.

(b) Words with the inseparable prefixes *be-, er-, ge-, her-, ont-* and *ver-* are stressed immediately after the prefix

*gespr**e**k*	talk	*bet**aa**lbaar*	payable
*herh**a**len*	to repeat	*ontw**i**kkelen*	to develop

(c) Separable prefixes are always stressed (☞ *Separable verbs*)

***mee**komen*	go with/along	***uit**gangspunt*	starting point
***op**bellen*	ring up	***af**leveren*	deliver

(d) In words of French/Latin origin, stress is usually placed on the ultimate or penultimate syllable

*stati**on***	station	*prof**e**ssor*	professor
*parapl**u***	umbrella	*sec**o**nde*	second

(e) The following endings (mostly of French origin) are usually stressed

*-**e**nt/-**a**nt*	*-**e**s(se)*	*-(t)**eur***	*-**ie***	*-**ei***	*-**a**tie/-**i**tie*
*-**oo**r*	*-**in***	*-**ie**r*	*-**ie**k*	*-**ij**(n)*	*-**e**ntie/-**a**ntie*
*-**a**ge*	*-tr**i**ce*	*-**a**tor*	*-**i**sme*	*-**aa**t*	*-**e**ren*[75]

e.g. *stud**e**nt* 'student', *tuin**ie**r* 'gardener', *lerar**e**s* 'female teacher', *vriend**in*** 'girlfriend', *slager**ij*** 'butcher's', *kon**ij**n* 'rabbit', *gen**ie*** 'genius', *result**aa**t* 'result', *organis**a**tor* 'organiser', *adver**t**entie* 'advertisement', *bag**a**ge* 'luggage', *bag**a**gebureau* 'luggage office'.

 PHONETIC TRANSCRIPTIONS: 58.1(a) *pot* [pɔt], *tien* [ti:n], *kat* [kɑt], *feest* [fe:ʲst], *spot* [spɔt], *zien* [zi:n], *man* [mɑn], *niet* [ni:t], *ding* [dɪŋ], *ham* [hɑm], *lam* [lɑm], *kol* [kɔl], *cent* [sɛnt]. TABLE 35: *heb* [hɛp], *bad* [bɑt], *recht* [rɛxt] or [ʁɛxt], *schip* [sxɪp], *god* [xɔt], *ja* [ja:], *tasje* ['tɑʃə], *katje* ['kɑtʃə], *vat* [fɑt], *wat* [ʋɑt], *nauw* [nɑuw], *ring* [rɪŋ] or [ʁɪŋ], *zitten* ['zɪtə], *actie* ['ɑktsi:]. Notes: *goede* [xu:jə], *houden* [hɑuwə], *genie* [ʒɛ'ni:], *film* [fɪləm], *melk* [mɛlək]. TABLE 36: *man* [mɑn], *maan* [ma:n], *bed* [bɛt], *tante* ['tɑntə], *zee* [ze:ʲ], *vol* [fɔɫ], *zoon* [zo:ʷn], *ik* [ɪk], *zestig* ['zɛstəx], *drie* [dri:] or [dʁi:], *hun* [hʉn], *Ruud* [ry:t] or [ʁy:t], *doen* [du:n], *neus* [nø:s], *bij* [bɛɪ], *ei* [ɛɪ], *lelijk* ['le:ʲlək], *oud* [ɑʊt], *uit* [œʏt]. Notes: *saai* [sa:ɪ], *mooi* [mo:ɪ].

59 PUT: Dutch equivalents

The translation of the English word 'put' into Dutch may cause difficulties for English speakers as it is used very generally in English while, in Dutch, more specific verbs are

---

75 Yet only as an ending with verbs of French origin, e.g. *stud**er**en* 'to study', *telefon**er**en* 'to phone', *felicit**er**en* 'to congratulate' (Contrast e.g. *her**i**nneren* 'to remember', *l**e**veren* 'to deliver').

needed depending on the nature of the object, the position of the object and the size of the space into which the object is put:

59.1 *ZETTEN* is used if the object is put down vertically. This often corresponds to English 'stand' and 'set'

ik **zette** *de fles op de grond*	I put/stood the bottle on the ground
zij **zette** *het boek weer op de plank*	she put the book back on the shelf

Note that *zetten* is also used in the sense of 'write down', e.g. **zet** *het maar op mijn rekening* 'just put it on my bill'.

59.2 *LEGGEN* is used if the object is put down horizontally. This often corresponds to English 'lay'

hij **legde** *zijn hoofd op haar schouder*	he put/laid his head on her shoulder
ik zal het boek op uw tafel **leggen**	I'll put the book on(to) your table

59.3 *STOPPEN* is used if the object is put into a small space

hij **stopte** *de envelop in een la*	he put the envelope into a drawer
ik **stop** *het boek in mijn tas*	I am putting the book into my bag

Note that *doen* may also be used in this context (☞ 59.4), e.g. *hij* **deed** *de envelop in een la, ik* **doe** *het boek in mijn tas.*

59.4 *DOEN* is a more general word and is used in most contexts other than those described in 59.1 and 59.2 above

ik **doe** *geen zout op mijn eten*	I do not put salt on my food
hij **deed** *te veel melk in zijn koffie*	he put too much milk in his coffee

 If in doubt, it is advisable to find an English synonym for 'put' and then translate it into Dutch, e.g. 'I'll put an advert in the newspaper' (= 'place'): *ik* **plaats** *een advertentie in de krant*; 'can you put it into Dutch?'(= 'translate'): *kunt u het in het Nederlands* **vertalen***?*

60 Question words: WHO?, WHAT?, WHERE? etc.

The most common question words in English, WHO?, WHOSE?, WHICH?, WHAT?, HOW?, WHERE, WHEN? and WHY?, have the following Dutch equivalents:

60.1 WHO(M)? is usually translated by *wie?*

wie *komt vanavond?*	who is coming this evening?
wie *heb jij gezien?*	who(m) did you see?
aan **wie** *heeft Frits bloemen gegeven?*	who(m) did Frits give flowers to?

Note that *wie* is always used to refer to persons, even where English would use *which*:

wie *van hen is getrouwd?*	which of them is married?
met **wie** *van hen heeft hij gewerkt?*	which of them did he work with?

60.2 WHOSE? is usually translated by *van wie?*, literally 'of whom' (☞also 📖)

van wie *zijn deze sokken?*	whose socks are these?
van wie *kwam het idee?*	whose idea was it?

60.3 WHICH?/WHAT? before nouns is translated by *welke?* (*welk?* before singular neuters)

welke *tomaten zijn goedkoper?*	which/what tomatoes are cheaper?
welke *computer gebruikt u?*	which/what computer do you use?
van ***welk*** *spoor vertrekt de trein?*	which/what platform does the train leave from?

Welke? can also stand in for nouns that have been omitted and usually translates English 'which one', e.g. *De computer:* ***welke*** *gebruikt u?* 'The computer: which one do you use?', *Geef mij het kopje –* ***Welke***? 'Give me the cup – Which one?'

60.4 WHAT?

(a) WHAT? is usually translated by *wat?* (unless it precedes a noun and means 'which?', ☞ 60.3)

wat *zei jij?*	what did you say?
wat *doet uw man?*	what does your husband do?
wat *voor een hond is dat?*	what sort of dog is that?

Note the set phrase ***hoe*** *heet u?* 'what are you called?' (*literally* 'how are you called?')

(b) When *wat* occurs with a preposition it is replaced by *waar* and the preposition is added at the end, e.g. NOT ✗ *van wat?* but *waarvan?* (☞ *Prepositions,* 📖):

waarvan *droom jij?*	what do you dream of?
waarover *heb jij het?*[76]	what are you talking about?

60.5 HOW? is translated by *hoe?*, HOW LONG? by *hoe lang?* and HOW MANY? by *hoeveel?*

hoe *gaat het met jou?*	how are you?
hoe lang *duurt de film?*	how long does the film last?
hoeveel *kost het?*	how much does it cost?

60.6 WHERE? is translated by *waar?*

waar *kan ik postzegels kopen?*	where can I buy stamps?

Note that *waar . . . naartoe?* (or *waar . . . heen?*) 'where . . . to?' and *waar . . . vandaan?* 'where . . . from?' occur obligatorily with verbs of motion:

waar *kan ik* ***heen***?	where can I go (to)?
waar *gaat/fietst/vliegt hij* ***naartoe***?	where is he going/cycling/flying to?
waar *komen zij* ***vandaan***?	where do they come from?

---

76 Note that it is very common to split *waar* and the preposition, e.g. ***waar*** *droom jij* ***van***?, ***waar*** *heb je het* ***over***?

60.7 WHEN? is translated by *wanneer?*

> **wanneer** *komt hij terug?*   when is he coming back?

60.8 WHY? is usually translated by *waarom?*[77]

> **waarom** *kom jij niet mee?*   why don't you come too?

 In formal written Dutch, *wiens?* is sometimes used for male subjects and, more rarely, *wier?* for female subjects, e.g. **wiens** *auto is dat?* 'whose car is that?' In spoken Dutch, the colloquial forms *wie z'n?* (male) and *wie d'r?* (female) may be used, e.g. **wie z'n** *auto is dat?* 'whose car is that?', **wie d'r** *kousen zijn dat?* 'whose stockings are those?'

 The question words listed above may also function like conjunctions (i.e. they link clauses together) when no direct question is involved. In these cases, they send the following verb to the end of the clause (☞ *Word order*, 78.1(b)), e.g. *ik weet* **wat** *hij in Amsterdam gedaan heeft* 'I know what he did in Amsterdam', *vertel mij* **hoe** *jij het doet* 'tell me how you do it', *hij zei niet* **waarom** *hij gegaan is* 'he didn't say why he left'.

61   Reflexive verbs

A reflexive verb is a verb whose object refers back to its subject, e.g. 'I$_{[Subj.]}$ wash MYSELF$_{[Obj.]}$'. The objects of reflexive verbs are known as reflexive pronouns, e.g. English 'myself', 'yourself', 'himself' etc., Dutch *me, je, zich* etc. (☞ 61.1). In Dutch, some verbs are always reflexive, e.g. *hij geneert* **zich** 'he is embarrassed', while others may occur either reflexively or with some other object, e.g. *ik kleed* **me** *aan* 'I dress myself' vs. *ik kleed* **mijn kinderen** *aan* 'I dress my children'. Reflexive verbs are more numerous in Dutch than in English and, as it is often difficult to predict which type of verb may be reflexive in Dutch (e.g. **zich** *herinneren* 'to remember' is reflexive in Dutch but not in English), each one must simply be learned on an ad hoc basis. Some examples of commonly used Dutch reflexive verbs are given in 61.2.

61.1   Dutch reflexive pronouns

(a) The reflexive pronouns in Dutch are as follows

Table 37. Reflexive pronouns with the verb zich wassen *'to wash oneself'*

SUBJECT+VERB		REFLEXIVE PRONOUN	
ik	was	me	I wash myself
jij	wast	je (informal)	you wash yourself
u	wast	u* (polite)	you wash yourself
hij/zij/het	wast	zich	he/she/it washes himself/herself/itself
wij	wassen	ons	we wash ourselves
jullie	wassen	je (informal)	you wash yourselves
u	wast	u* (polite)	you wash yourselves
zij	wassen	zich	they wash themselves

*The reflexive pronoun *u* is often replaced by *zich*, especially after the verb form *u heeft* 'you have', and to avoid the occurrence of two *u*'s together, e.g. *wilt u* **zich** *aankleden?* (preferred to *wilt u u aankleden?*) 'Do you want to get dressed?'

---

77 *hoezo* is usually used on its own to mean 'why/what do you mean?/why do you ask?' etc.

(b) USE: Reflexive pronouns always follow the subject and verb

JIJ HOEFT *je niet te generen*	you don't have to feel embarrassed
HEEFT HIJ **zich** *vandaag gewassen?*[78]	has he washed (himself) today?
vanmorgen WILDE IK **me** *niet scheren*	I didn't want to shave this morning

Note that the reflexive pronoun is always present in Dutch while, in English, it may be omitted with some verbs:

ik heb **me** *nog niet gewassen*	I haven't washed (myself) yet
wij verschuilden **ons** *onder het bed*	we hid (ourselves) under the bed

61.2 Some common reflexive verbs in Dutch

Table 38. Verbs that are always reflexive

zich afvragen	ask oneself	zich herstellen	recover
zich bevinden	find oneself	zich schamen voor	be ashamed of
zich gedragen	behave	zich vergissen in	be mistaken
zich generen	be embarrassed	zich verheugen op	look forward to
zich haasten	hurry	zich verslapen	oversleep
zich herinneren	remember	zich voorstellen	imagine

Table 39. Verbs that can be used either reflexively or with other direct objects

zich aankleden	get dressed	zich verbazen	be amazed
zich amuseren	enjoy oneself	zich verdedigen	defend oneself
zich bewegen	move	zich verkleden	change clothes
zich ergeren	get angry	zich verontschuldigen	excuse oneself/apologise
zich opwinden	get excited	zich verschuilen	hide (oneself)
zich scheren	shave (oneself)	zich vervelen	to be bored
zich snijden	cut oneself	zich voelen	feel
zich uitkleden	undress (oneself)	zich wassen	wash (oneself)

61.3 EMPHATIC FORMS: Verbs of the type given in Table 39 above may occur with special emphatic forms of the reflexive pronouns ending in *-zelf* if the speaker wishes to stress the reflexive meaning or make some contrast

*me**zelf***	myself	*ons**zelf***	ourselves
*je**zelf***	yourself	*je**zelf***	yourselves
*zich**zelf***	himself/herself/itself	*zich**zelf***	themselves

ik sneed **me** *met dat mes*   I cut myself with that knife

---

78 Reflexive verbs always take *hebben* in the perfect and pluperfect.

BUT

> *ik sneed niet* DE KAAS *maar **mezelf**!*   I didn't cut the cheese, I cut myself!

Note, however, that the emphatic forms with *-zelf* cannot be used with true reflexive verbs (i.e. those of the type given in Table 38), e.g. *ik vraag **me*** (never ✗ *mezelf*) *af* 'I ask myself/wonder', *hij bevond **zich*** (never ✗ *zichzelf*) *in een moeilijke situatie* 'he found himself in a difficult situation'.

 The emphatic forms *mezelf, jezelf, zichzelf* and *onszelf* can also be used with certain verbs that are not usually reflexive: i.e. some verbs taking a preposition, e.g. *hij praat heel graag* OVER ***zichzelf*** 'he really likes talking about himself', *ik dacht* BIJ ***mezelf*** 'I thought to myself', plus a few other verbs e.g. *wees **jezelf**!* 'be yourself!', *ik ken **mezelf*** 'I know myself'. Otherwise ***zelf*** (without *me-, je-* etc.) is used with non-reflexive verbs (☞*Zelf*).

 Note that *elkaar* is used to render English 'each other', e.g. *we zien **elkaar*** *elke dag* 'we see each other every day', *ze zien **elkaar*** *in de winkel* 'they (will) see each other in the shop'.

62   Relative pronouns: WHO, WHICH, THAT etc.

A relative pronoun is a pronoun that refers back to a noun already mentioned in the sentence. In English, the form of the relative pronoun depends on whether the noun refers to a person or thing, e.g. 'the man WHO came to dinner', 'the girl WHO(M) I saw' versus 'the problem WHICH/THAT must be solved'. In Dutch, it depends on the grammatical gender and number of the noun (☞ 62.1) or on whether the relative pronoun occurs with a preposition (☞ 62.2). In addition, it should be noted that all relative pronouns in Dutch send the following verb to the end of the clause (☞ *Word order*, 78.1(b, ii)).

62.1   *Dat* is used with singular neuter nouns and *die* with all other nouns (i.e. all plurals and nouns of common gender)

> HET *huis **dat** ik gisteren zag*   the house that I saw yesterday
> DE *fiets **die** nu kapot is*   the bike that is now broken
> DE *kinderen **die** tegenover mij wonen*   the children who live opposite me

Note that relative pronouns (and sometimes the following verb) may be omitted in English but never in Dutch:

> *het huis **dat** ik gisteren zag*   the house I saw yesterday
> *de kinderen **die** op de straat spelen*   the children playing in the street
> *de brief **die** aan mij gestuurd werd*   the letter sent to me

Literally 'the house that I saw yesterday', 'the children who play / are playing in the street', 'the letter which was sent to me'.

62.2   When used with prepositions, the relative pronouns are *wie* and *waar*

(a)   *wie* is used to refer to people and is placed after the prepositon[79]

> *de man* OVER ***wie** ik praat*   the man (who/m) I'm talking about
> *de vrouw* VAN ***wie** hij vroeger hield*   the woman he used to love
> *het kind* VOOR ***wie** ik een kado kocht*   the child (who/m) I bought a present for

---

79 In spoken Dutch, *waar* can also be used here.

(b) *waar* is used to refer to things and is placed BEFORE the preposition

de computer **waar**OVER *ik praat*	the computer (that) I'm talking about
de film **waar**VAN *hij vroeger hield*	the film (that) he used to love

Note that it is very common to split such constructions and place the preposition immediately before the verb, e.g. *de computer* **waar** *ik* **over** PRAAT, *de film* **waar** *hij vroeger* **van** HIELD.

Table 40. Summary of relative pronouns

	Noun	Relative pronoun
Singular neuter	het kind	**dat**
Singular common + **all plurals**	de man de kinderen	**die**
Preposition + person	voor het kind voor de kinderen	voor **wie**
Preposition + thing	voor het huis voor de huizen	**waar**voor

62.3 Other relative pronouns in Dutch

(a) *Wat* is used when no specific noun has been mentioned. It is used after words such as *iets* 'something', *niets* 'nothing', *veel* 'many' and after whole clauses

er is IETS **wat** *ik moet vragen*	there is something (that) I must ask
HIJ KWAM OP TIJD, **wat** *ik goed vond*	he came on time, which I liked

(b) *Van wie*, referring to persons, and *waarvan*, referring to things, translate English *whose*[80]

de man **van wie** *de vrouw ziek is*	the man whose wife is ill
de fiets **waarvan** *de band lek was*	the bike whose tyre was flat

 Sentences of the type 'HE WHO works hard earns a lot of money' etc. are translated by using *wie* 'who(ever)' in Dutch, e.g. **wie** *hard werkt verdient veel geld*.

63 SAME: Dutch equivalents

Depending on the context in which it occurs, the English word 'same' has two main equivalents in Dutch:

63.1 *Dezelfde* occurs before nouns of common gender and before all plural nouns. It can also stand in for nouns that have been omitted

is dat **dezelfde** AUTO *als die van Jan?*	is that the same car as Jan's?
ja, het is **dezelfde**	yes, it's the same one
ik houd van **dezelfde** BOEKEN *als jij*	I like the same books as you

---

80 The more formal *wiens* (masculine only) may be used in written Dutch and the more colloquial *die z'n* (masculine) and *die d'r* (feminine) are often used in spoken Dutch.

63.2 *Hetzelfde* is used (i) before singular neuter nouns (and when they are omitted), (ii) to mean 'the same thing' when no particular noun is referred to:

(i) *is dat **hetzelfde** HUIS?*   is that the same house?
   *ja, het is **hetzelfde***   yes, it's the same one

(ii) *hij zegt altijd **hetzelfde***   he always says the same (thing)

 Note that the translation of 'it' and 'they' is always *het* before *dezelfde* and *hetzelfde*, e.g. ***het** is dezelfde auto* 'it is the same car', ***het** zijn dezelfde huizen* 'they are the same houses'.

64   Separable verbs

Dutch has a number of verbs which are derived from other verbs by adding a wide range of prefixes, most of which may also function independently as prepositions, e.g. *door-* 'through', *om-* 'around', *op-* 'up', *in-* 'in', *uit-* 'out' etc. (☞ **Table 41** below for a list of common separable verbs). These are called 'separable prefixes' because they are sometimes separated from the verb in certain grammatical constructions (contrast the inseparable prefixes *be-*, *her-*, *ont-*, *ver-*, *ge-* and *er-* which are never separated from the verb, ☞ *Inseparable verbs*). When using separable verbs in Dutch, one must bear the following points in mind:

64.1 Separable prefixes are always stressed (indicated here by underlining)

*kun jij het bandje **om**draaien?*   can you turn the tape over?
*ik moet hem **op**bellen*   I have to ring him up
*zij zullen niet **uit**gaan*   they will not go out
*wil jij **mee**komen?*   do you want to come along?

64.2 In the imperative, and the present and simple past tenses, the prefix is sent to the end of the clause (☞)

draai** het bandje **om   turn the tape over
*ik **bel** hem nu **op***   I'm ringing him up now
*zij **gaan** niet **uit***   they are not going out
*jij **kwam** niet **mee***   you did not come along

64.3 In the past participle the prefix precedes *ge-* (☞ *Perfect tense*, 48.2(b))

*hij heeft het **om**ge**draaid***   he has turned it around
*ik heb hem **op**ge**beld***   I have phoned him
*zij zijn niet **uit**ge**gaan***   they have not gone out
*jij bent niet **mee**ge**komen***   you did not come along

64.4 If the infinitive is used with *te* (☞ *Infinitives and use of* (om) . . . *te*) the prefix precedes *te* and is written separately

*ik probeer hem **op** te **bellen***   I'm trying to ring him up
*het is te laat om **uit** te **gaan*** it's too late to go out
*jij hoeft niet **mee** te **komen***   you don't need to come along

Note that this is also the case when a VERB immediately prededes the infinitive, e.g. *ik weet dat jij **uit** WIL **gaan*** 'I know that you want to go out', *jij zal niet **mee** KUNNEN **komen*** 'you will not be able to come along'.

Table 41. Common separable verbs

aankomen	arrive	**na**komen	come after
aannemen	accept	**om**draaien	turn round
achterhouden	hold back	**om**kijken	look round
achterlopen	lag behind	**onder**houden	keep under
afspringen	jump off	**onder**sneeuwen	be snowed under
afstappen	step off	**op**houden	hold up
bijspringen	stand by/help	**op**kijken	look up
bijzetten	put next to/by	**over**geven	hand over
binnenblijven	stay in	**over**kijken	look over/through
binnenkomen	come in	**tegen**stemmen	vote against
doorbreken	break through	**tegen**werken	work against
doorlezen	read through	**toe**knikken	nod to (people)
ingaan	go in/enter	**toe**roepen	call out to (people)
inlaten	let in	**uit**gaan	go out
meekomen	come with (people)	**uit**kijken	look out
meespelen	play with (people)	**voor**gaan	go first/lead
nabetalen	pay afterwards	**voor**hebben	have before oneself

Note that some of the prefixes listed in Table 41 above can also be inseparable depending on the verb with which they occur. In these cases, the prefix is unstressed and is never separated from the verb (underlining indicates stress):

achter<u>volgen</u>	pursue	**over**<u>denken</u>	think over/consider
door<u>kruisen</u>	cross/traverse	**onder**<u>nemen</u>	undertake
om<u>helzen</u>	embrace	**voor**<u>zien</u>	foresee

This is particularly the case with *onder*, *over*, *door* and *om*.

*ik **om**helsde hem* (NOT ✗ *helsde hem **om***)   I embraced him
*ik heb het al **over**dacht*   I've already thought it over
    (NOT ✗ *over**gedacht***)

 Note that this does not always mean sending the prefix to the end of the whole sentence, as sentences can often consist of more than one clause (i.e. a combination of subject and verb), e.g. [I rang you up yesterday]_{Clause 1} when [you were working]_{Clause 2}, *ik **belde** jou gisteren **op**, toen jij aan het werk was* NOT ✗ *ik **belde** jou gisteren, toen jij aan het werk was, **op***.

65 Spelling

Generally speaking, Dutch words are spelled as they are pronounced (☞ *Pronunciation*). There are, however, certain systematic spelling changes which must be taken into account. These changes affect Dutch words when particular types of ending are added, e.g. *maan – manen* 'moon – moons', *man – mannen* 'man – men' (compare English *thin – thinner, fat – fatter* etc.). The general principles governing the Dutch spelling changes are outlined in 65.1–65.3 below:

65.1 Changes involving stressed vowels: In closed syllables (i.e. those ending in a consonant), there is a written distinction between the long vowels *aa, ee, oo, uu* and the short vowels *a, e, o, u*. When these syllables become open, by adding a vowel after the final consonant, the following spelling changes occur[81]

(a) Words with the long vowels *aa, ee, oo* and *uu* drop one vowel

maan – manen	moon – moons	*breed – breder*	broad – broader
poot – poten	paw – paws	*muur – muren*	wall – walls

Note that this is not necessary if two or more consonants follow the long vowels, e.g. *woord – woorden* 'word – words', *breed – breedst* 'broad – broadest'.

(b) Words with the short vowels *a, e, i, o* and *u* double the following consonant to keep the vowels short

man – mannen	man – men	*dik – dikker*	fat – fatter
pot – potten	pot – pots	*bus – bussen*	bus – buses

Note that this is not necessary if two or more consonants follow the short vowels, e.g. *hand – handen* 'hand – hands', *dik – dikst* 'fat – fattest'.

Table 42. Spelling changes with vowels

		Final consonant	Consonant+vowel	
long	aa	raam	ra-men	window/s
	ee	been	be-nen	leg/s
	oo	ik hoop	wij ho-pen	I/we hope
	uu	ik stuur	wij stu-ren	I/we send
short	a	ram	ram-m-en	ram/s
	e	pen	pen-n-en	pen/s
	i	ik zit	wij zit-t-en	I/we sit
	o	ik hop	wij hop-p-en	I/we hop
	u	dun	dun-n-er	thin/ner

65.2 FINAL VOWELS: At the end of words, *aa, oo* and *uu* are written as single vowels. As soon as *-n* or two or more consonants are added, however, the vowels are doubled

ik ga – wij gaan	I go – we go	*foto – fotootje*	photo – small photo
ik sta – wij staan	I stand – we stand	*oma – omaatje*	grandma – granny

---

81 The syllables become 'open' (i.e. end in a vowel) as the following consonant begins the next syllable, e.g. *maan/ma-nen, poot/po-ten*. If there are two consonants, however, the syllable division comes between them, e.g. *man-nen, han-den*.

65.3 Changes involving *f/v* and *s/z*: *f* and *s* occur at the end of words and before consonants while *v* and *z* occur in the middle of words before vowels

(a) After a long vowel, a diphthong (written as two vowels) or *l/m/n/r*, *v* and *z* become *f* and *s* respectively at the END of words and BEFORE CONSONANTS

*leven – ik lee**f***	to live – I live	*reizen – ik rei**s***	to travel – I travel
*verven – gever**f**d*	to paint – painted	*lezen – hij lee**s**t*	to read – he reads

(b) Conversely, *f* and *s* after a long vowel, a diphthong or *l/m/n/r* become *v* and *z* respectively when followed by a VOWEL

*brief – brie**v**en*	letter – letters	*huis – hui**z**en*	house – houses
*kalf – kal**v**eren*	calf – calves	*vies – vie**z**er*	dirty – dirtier

 Note that (i) these spelling changes only apply within a word. Thus, the addition of a second word to form a compound does not affect the spelling of the first, e.g. *sp**ee**l* 'game' – *sp**ee**lautomaat* 'slot machine', *aut**o*** 'car' – *aut**o**snelweg* 'motorway'. The same applies to the addition of the adjective-forming ending *-achtig* '-like', e.g. *b**oo**machtig* 'tree-like', *ka**t**achtig* 'cat-like'; (ii) there are a few words which do not undergo the spelling changes involving *v/f* and *z/s*, e.g. *kous – kou**s**en* 'stocking(s)', *wens – wen**s**en* 'wish(es)', *kies – kie**s**e* 'delicate' (+ adjective ending) and words ending in *-graaf* (Eng. -'graph'), e.g. *fotograaf – fotogra**f**en* 'photographer(s)', *paragraaf – paragra**f**en* 'paragraph(s)'.

 DUTCH SPELLING REFORM: There has recently been a reform of some aspects of Dutch spelling which foreign learners need to be aware of. Roughly speaking, the five main areas of change are: (i) *k*, *y* and *ae* in many words of Latin/French origin have been changed to *c*, *i* and *e* respectively, e.g. *produkt* → *product*, *insekt* → *insect*, *dioxyde* → *dioxide*, *praeses* → *preses* 'chairman'; (ii) In compound words, the linking element *-e-* has been replaced by *-en-* in cases where the first element of the compound is a noun with a plural form in *-en*, e.g. *pann**e**koek* → *pann**en**koek* 'pancake', *per**e**-boom* → *per**en**boom* 'pear tree' (☞ *Compound words*,); (iii) In compound words, a hyphen is used instead of a diaeresis to indicate the separate pronunciation of two similar vowels, e.g. *naäpen* → *na-apen* 'to ape' (☞ *Accents*, 1.2); (iv) Geographical names do not drop their hyphen when derived, e.g. *Zuidafrikaans* → *Zuid-Afrikaans* 'South African' (derived from *Zuid-Afrika*); (v) Words borrowed from English now observe the Dutch spelling rules given in 65.1–65.3 above, e.g. *scoren* 'to score a goal' – *ik sc**oo**r, hij sc**oo**rt* 'I score, he scores'.[82]

66 SUCH (A): Dutch equivalents

English 'such' and 'such a' have two main equivalents in Dutch when they appear before nouns:

66.1 *Zo'n* (or, less commonly, *zulk een*) translate English 'such a'

***zo'n** auto heb ik ook*	I have such a car, too
*ze hebben **zo'n** groot huis*	they have such a big house
*het was **zo'n** saaie lezing*	it was such a boring lecture

Note that *zo'n* is a more commonly used abbreviation of *zo een*.

---

82 The new spellings are listed in the *Van Dale* monolingual dictionaries (*Groot woordenboek der Nederlandse taal*, 1995 and the *Handwoordenboek Hedendags Nederlands*, 1996), the *Van Dale* Dutch–English and English–Dutch dictionaries (1988, 1996) and in the *Woordenlijst Nederlandse taal/het 'groene boekje'* (Den Haag/Antwerpen: SDU/Standaard, 1995). The general rules of the spelling reform are set out in P. A. J. Wels, *De spelling meester: handleiding voor de praktijk en interpunctie van het Nederlands* (Utrecht: Lemma, 1996).

66.2 *Zulk(e)* translates English *such*. It occurs before all plural nouns and before nouns which do not occur with *een* 'a'

zulk *brood vind ik smakeloos*	I find such bread tasteless
ik had **zulke** *schoonheid nooit gezien*	I had never seen such beauty
ik begrijp **zulke** *mensen niet*	I do not understand such people

Note that *zulk* appears before singular neuter nouns and *zulke* elsewhere (i.e. before common gender nouns and all plurals).

67 Superlatives

The superlative is the form of the adjective used to denote an extreme or unsurpassed level, e.g. 'the tallest tree', 'the fastest car'. In English, superlatives are formed either by adding '-est' to the adjective, e.g. 'smallEST', 'cleverEST', or, if the adjective has more than two syllables, by placing the word 'most' in front of it, e.g. 'MOST interesting', 'MOST intelligent'. The formation and use of superlatives in Dutch are as follows (☞ also *Comparatives*):

67.1 Formation of superlatives

(a) Dutch superlatives are usually formed with *-st* (or *-t* if the adjective already ends in *-s*) irrespective of the length of the adjective. Note that no spelling changes are needed here

*mooi-***st**	nicest/prettiest	*interessant-***st**	most interesting
*laag-***st**	lowest	*moeilijk-***st**	most difficult
*duur-***st**	most expensive	*vers-***t**	freshest

Note also the existence of a special emphatic form of the superlative beginning with *aller-*, e.g. **aller**mooist 'prettiest of all'.

(b) For ease of pronunciation, adjectives ending in *-st* and *-sch* do not form their superlatives with *-st* but with *meest* 'most'

meest *juist*	most just/fair	**meest** *logisch*	most logical
meest *typisch*	most typical	**meest** *romantisch*	most romantic

Note that some adjectives in *-s* may also follow this pattern, e.g. *wijs-***t** or **meest** *wijs* 'wisest'.

67.2 When superlatives are used before nouns they take the same endings as ordinary adjectives (☞ *Adjectives*)

*de goedkoopst***e** *wijn*	the cheapest wine
*de allerlaagst***e** *prijzen*	the lowest prices of all
*de meest typisch***e** *gerechten*	the most typical dishes

They can also stand in for nouns that have been omitted:

*dit huis is het grootst***e**	this house is the biggest (one)
*de wijn? – ik koop de goedkoopst***e**	the wine? – I'll get the cheapest (one)
*zijn die de meest typisch***e***?*	are those the most typical (ones)?

67.3 When used in a more general way at the end of clauses (i.e. neither preceding nor standing in for a particular noun), superlatives occur with *het*

*wanneer is de buurman **het luidst**?*	when is the neighbour (the) loudest?
*waar zijn de huizen **het mooist**?*	where are the houses (the) nicest?
*Jan werkt **het hardst***	Jan works (the) hardest

Note that, in this type of construction, *het* is obligatory in Dutch while *the* may be omitted in English.

67.4 Superlatives may also be used as nouns in constructions of the type *het leukste is . . .* 'the nicest thing is . . .', *het moeilijkste is . . .* 'the most difficult thing is . . .' etc. (☞ *Adjectives used as nouns*, 4.2)

 Irregular superlatives: *goed – **best*** 'good – best', *kwaad – **ergst*** 'bad – worst', *graag – **liefst*** 'gladly – like . . . best' (☞ *Graag*, 26.2), *veel – **meest*** 'much – most', *weinig – **minst*** 'few – fewest/least'. Note the use of *minst* '(the) least', e.g. *de **minst** belangrijke vergadering* 'the least important meeting', *Kees drinkt het **minst*** 'Kees drinks the least' (☞ also *Comparatives*,).

 When specifying one member of a group, Dutch usually uses the preposition *van* while English uses 'in' (or sometimes 'of'), e.g. *zij is de beste student **van** de klas* 'she's the best student in the class', *dit is de mooiste kamer **van** het huis* 'this is the nicest room in the house', *het is het grootste gebouw **van** de wereld* 'it's the biggest building in the world'.

68 THEN: Dutch equivalents

The English word 'then', referring to time, has two main equivalents in Dutch:

68.1 *Dan* is used with verbs in the present (and imperative), the future/future perfect and the conditional/conditional perfect

KOM *eerst naar huis en **dan** ETEN we*	come home first and then we'll eat
*ik ZAL eerst Jan BEZOEKEN en **dan** jou*	I will visit Jan first and then you
*ik ZOU het KOPEN en **dan** later verkopen*	I would buy it and then sell it later

68.2 *Toen* is used with verbs in the SIMPLE PAST and the PERFECT/PLUPERFECT. It translates English 'then' and 'at the/that time'

***toen** VERHUISDE hij naar Amsterdam*	then he moved to Amsterdam
*en wat HEB jij **toen** GEZEGD?*	and what did you say then?
*ik HAD hem **toen** niet HERKEND*	I had not recognised him then

Note that *toen* meaning 'then' must not be confused with *toen* meaning 'when', the latter of which sends the verb to the end of the clause (☞ *WHEN: Dutch equivalents*, 77.2).

69 Time

In English and Dutch, there are two ways of telling the time. The more formal way uses the twenty-four hour clock expressed in terms of numbers, e.g. *het is **vier uur vijfentwintig*** 'it is four twenty-five', *de trein vertrekt om **achttien uur vijfenveertig*** 'the train leaves at eighteen forty-five', while the less formal and more common way uses the twelve hour clock, together with expressions such as **half** 'half past', **kwart voor** 'a quarter to', **'s morgens** 'in the morning' etc. This chapter deals with the more common way of telling the time in Dutch, as it is here that certain notable differences from English arise (☞ especially 69.1(b) and 69.1(e)). In addition, 69.2 lists some common expressions of time which may be useful to the foreign learner.

69.1 Telling the time in Dutch

(a) 'o'clock' = *uur* meaning 'hour'

het is ÉÉN **uur**[83]

(b) 'half past' = *half* plus the COMING hour

het is **half** TWEE

Thus, Dutch *half* means 'half to' or 'half before' rather than 'half past'.

(c) 'a quarter to/past' = *kwart voor/over*

het is **kwart voor** ZEVEN   *het is* **kwart over** TIEN

(d) *Voor* and *over* are also used with the minutes from a quarter to the hour to a quarter past the hour

het is VIJF **voor** ACHT   *het is* TIEN **over** ZES

(e) The minutes from a quarter past the hour to a quarter to the hour are expressed in relation to the HALF hour

het is VIJF **voor half drie**   *het is* TIEN **over half drie**

Note that *twintig voor/over* 'twenty to/past' is also possible, yet *vijfentwintig voor/over* 'twenty-five to/past' is rare.

69.2 Some useful expressions of time

hoe laat is het?	what time is it?
hoe laat . . .	at what time
om *twee uur* **precies**	at two o'clock exactly
(*om*) **een uur of** *twee*	(at) about two o'clock
tegen *half drie*	(at) around half past two
drie uur **'s morgens** (or **'s ochtends**)	three o'clock in the morning

---

83 For the use of accents, ☞ *Accents*, 1.1.

's middags / 's avonds / 's nachts	in the afternoon / evening / at night
op het **hele** / **halve** *uur*	on the hour / half hour
over *drie minuten*	in three minutes' (time)
over *een* **kwartier** / *een* **half** *uur*	in a quarter of an hour / half an hour
ik bleef drie **uur*** / **jaar*** / *dagen* / *weken*	I stayed for 3 hours / years / days / weeks
een uur / dag / week **geleden**	an hour / day / week ago
drie **keer per** *uur / dag / week / maand*	three times an hour / day / week / month
deze / **vorige** / **volgende** *week*	this / last / next week
dit / **vorig** / **volgend** *jaar*	this / last / next year
vandaag / **vanmorgen** / **vanavond**	today / this morning / this evening
gisteren / **eergisteren**	yesterday / the day before yesterday
morgen / **overmorgen**	tomorrow / the day after tomorrow

*Uur 'hour(s)' and *jaar* 'year(s)' always appear in the singular after numbers.

70 Toch

The word *toch*, which is more common in spoken than in written Dutch, is difficult to translate into English as it has a number of different meanings depending on the context in which it occurs. Generally speaking four main functions may be identified:[84]

70.1 It renders English 'yet', 'anyway', 'nevertheless', 'after all'

ik ben moe maar ik kom **toch**	I'm tired but I'll come nevertheless
maar hij is **toch** *haar vader*	but he is her father after all

70.2 It is used to make a question out of a statement

u bent **toch** *de man van Anita?*	you're Anita's husband, aren't you?
maar hij is **toch** *een vriend van jou?*	but he's a friend of yours, isn't he?

70.3 It renders '-ever' in questions with 'whoever', 'whatever', 'however' etc.

wie kan het **toch** *zijn?*	whoever can it be?
wat wil jij **toch**?	whatever / what on earth do you want?

70.4 It lends emphasis to requests

kom **toch**!	do come!
vertel het me **toch**!	go on, tell me!

71 UNDERSTAND: begrijpen or verstaan?

Generally speaking, there are two ways of translating English 'to understand' into Dutch:

---

84 Note that *toch* follows the same word order rules as *niet* 'not' (☞ *Niet*).

71.1 *Begrijpen* is used to mean 'to understand' in the sense of 'to comprehend'

zijn vrouw **begrijpt** *hem niet*	his wife does not understand him
sorry, ik **begrijp** *u niet – mijn*	sorry, I don't understand (you) – my
Nederlands is niet zo goed	Dutch is not so good
je **begrijpt** *er niets van*	you don't understand at all

71.2 *Verstaan* means 'to understand' what you have heard in the sense of 'to catch what was said'

hij is moeilijk te **verstaan** *want*	he is difficult to understand because
hij spreekt heel onduidelijk	he speaks very unclearly
sorry, ik **versta** *u niet – de muziek*	sorry, I don't understand (you) – the
is te luid	music is too loud

72 USED TO: Dutch equivalents

In English, the phrase 'used to' is used very frequently to refer to habitual actions in the past or to circumstances which no longer exist, e.g. 'we USED TO go to the cinema once a week', 'he USED TO be a school teacher'. In Dutch, there are two ways of rendering English 'used to':

72.1 The very formal way uses *plegen* with *te* + infinitive to express habitual actions

mijn moeder **placht** TE ZEGGEN	my mother used to say
zij **plachten** *hun oom* TE BEZOEKEN	they used to visit their uncle
hij **placht** *haar altijd* TE VOLGEN	he always used to follow her

72.2 It is much more common, however, simply to use either the past or perfect tenses together with words such as *vroeger* 'formerly', *vaak* 'often', *gewoonlijk* 'usually' etc. (☞ *Past tense* and *Perfect tense*)

ik HEB **vroeger** *in Brugge* GEWOOND	I used to live in Bruges
hij HEEFT *mij* **vroeger** *nooit* BEZOCHT	he never used to visit me
zij GINGEN **vaak** *zwemmen*	they (often) used to go swimming
ik BELDE *hem* **gewoonlijk** *elke dag* OP	I used to ring him up every day

Note that the past and perfect are also used to translate English 'would' when referring to habitual actions in the past, e.g. *als kind* **ging** *hij vaak zwemmen* 'as a child he would often go swimming'.

73 Verbs: summary of tenses

A verb is a word which indicates the performance or occurrence of an action or the existence of a condition, e.g. 'he WORKS', 'it GREW', 'you WERE ill'. In English and Dutch, it is that part of speech which occurs with a subject (usually a personal pronoun) and changes its form to show person, number and tense, e.g. Dutch *wij* **werk-en**, *het* **groei-de**, *jij* **was** *ziek*. This chapter provides an overview of the different verb forms for each tense in Dutch, taking the regular verbs *werken* 'to work' and *groeien* 'to grow', as examples. Note that the tenses listed below are dealt with in more detail in the separate entries for each one. Irregular and strong verbs are dealt with under the heading *Irregular verbs*.

Table 43. Summary of verb tenses

TENSE	SUBJECT	*WERKEN*	*GROEIEN*
Present	ik	werk	groei
	jij/u/hij/zij/het	werk-t (werk jij)	groei-t (groei jij)
	wij/jullie/zij	werk-en	groei-en
Simple past	ik/jij/u/hij/zij/het	werk-te	groei-de
	wij/jullie/zij	werk-ten	groei-den
Perfect	ik	heb ge-werk-t	ben ge-groei-d
	jij/u	hebt ge-werk-t	bent ge-groei-d
	hij/zij/het/(u)	heeft ge-werk-t	is ge-groei-d
	wij/jullie/zij	hebben ge-werk-t	zijn ge-groei-d
Pluperfect	ik/jij/u/hij/zij/het	had ge-werk-t	was ge-groei-d
	wij/jullie/zij	hadden ge-werk-t	waren ge-groei-d
Future	ik/jij/u/hij/zij/het	zal werken	zal groeien
	wij/jullie/zij	zullen werken	zullen groeien
Future perfect	ik/jij/u/hij/zij/het	zal gewerkt hebben	zal gegroeid zijn
	wij/jullie/zij	zullen gewerkt hebben	zullen gegroeied zijn
Conditional	ik/jij/u/hij/zij/het	zou werken	zou groeien
	wij/jullie/zij	zouden werken	zouden groeien
Conditional perfect	ik/jij/u/hij/zij/het	zou gewerkt hebben (had gewerkt)	zou gegroeid zijn (was gegroeid)
	wij/jullie/zij	zouden gewerkt hebben (hadden gewerkt)	zouden gegroeied zijn (waren gegroeid)

74 Verbs derived from other words

In English, verbs may be derived from nouns, e.g. 'hammer' – 'TO HAMMER', adjectives, e.g. 'hard' – 'TO HARDEN', and other verbs, e.g. 'to do' – 'TO UNDO', either by adding prefixes, e.g. 'UNdo', endings, e.g. 'hardEN', or simply by using other parts of speech as verbs without changing their form, e.g. 'HAMMER'. In Dutch, verbs are derived from nouns, adjectives and verbs by adding prefixes and/or endings, e.g. *hameren* 'to hammer', **her-***lezen* 'to re-read', yet, as there is usually no simple one-to-one correspondence between the Dutch and English prefixes and endings, it is difficult to set out hard and fast rules for verb derivation in Dutch. On the whole, each verb must be learnt individually, although it may be helpful to foreign learners to identify the most common ways of deriving verbs in Dutch. The following are given as a rough guide only:

74.1 Verbs are derived from nouns by adding -en and -eren with the appropriate spelling changes (☞ *Spelling*)

(a) -en is added to most nouns

*kam**men***	to comb	*bel**len***	to ring a bell
*wat**eren***	to water	*tennis**sen***	to play tennis
*fiet**sen***	to cycle	*voetbal**len***	to play football

(b) -eren is added to nouns of Latin and Greek origin

*telefoon – telefon**eren***	telephone – to telephone
*telegraaf – telegraf**eren***	telegraph – to telegraph
*urine – urin**eren***	urine – to urinate

Note that verbs derived from nouns are always regular, e.g. *ik tennis**te** / heb **ge**tennist*, *ik voetbal**de** / heb **ge**voetbald*, *ik telefoneer**de** / heb **ge**telefoneerd* (☞ *Past tense* and *Perfect tense*).

74.2 The inseparable prefixes be-, her-, ont-, ver-, ge- and er- are used to derive verbs from nouns, adjectives and, in particular, from other verbs (for details ☞ *Inseparable verbs*)

*pak – **ver**pakken*	package – to package
*schrijven – **her**schrijven*	to write – to rewrite
*nemen – **ont**nemen*	to take – to take away

74.3 In addition, verbs may be derived from other verbs by using a wide range of separable prefixes which are usually prepositions that can occur as independent words (for details ☞ *Separable verbs*)

*komen – **aan**komen*	to come – to arrive
*kijken – **om**kijken*	to look – to look around
*gaan – **uit**gaan*	to go – to go out

75 Verbs of position: *staan, liggen* and *zitten*[85]

The Dutch verbs *staan* 'to stand', *liggen* 'to lie' and *zitten* 'to sit' are often used in contexts where, in English, one would simply use the verb 'to be'. They are particularly common in constructions with *er* (☞ *Er*, 21.1) and with *te* + infinitive (☞ *Infinitives and use of (om) . . . te*, 30.2(a)).

75.1 *Staan* is used with objects in a vertical position

*de wijnfles **stond** op tafel*	the wine bottle was/stood on the table
*er **staan** twee boeken op de plank*	there are two books on the shelf

Note that *staan* is also used to mean 'to be written (down)', e.g. *het **staat** op uw rekening* 'it is (written down) on your bill'.

---

85 Compare the verbs *zetten, leggen* and *stoppen* meaning 'to put' (☞ *PUT*, 59.1–59.3).

75.2 *Liggen* is used with objects in a horizontal position. It is also used with place names and buildings to mean 'to be situated'

*de krant **ligt** op tafel*	the newspaper is (lying) on the table
*er **liggen** twee boeken op het bed*	there are two books on the bed
*het huis **ligt** bij het park*	the house is (situated) near the park

75.3 *Zitten* is often used with objects inside a small space

*de sleutels **zitten** in zijn jaszak*	the keys are in his jacket pocket
*er **zit** geen geld in mijn portemonnaie*	there's no money in my purse

76 Wel

The word *wel*, which is more common in spoken than in written Dutch, has two main functions: (i) contradictory, (ii) emphatic. In both cases, it follows the same word order rules as *niet* 'not' (☞ *Niet*):

76.1 It is used as the opposite of *niet* and renders emphatic 'do' (or emphatic 'be') in English

vind jij mijn jurk niet leuk?	don't you like my dress?
*ik vind hem **wel** leuk*	I DO like it
kom jij niet mee? –	aren't you coming with us?
*ik kom **wel** mee*	I AM coming

76.2 It is used for general emphasis

*dat weet ik **wel**!*	I KNOW (that)!
*ik zal het **wel** proberen*	I WILL try it
*ik kan **wel** voor mezelf zorgen (hoor)*	I CAN look after myself (you know)
*kun je het doen? – **jawel**!*	can you do it? YES, certainly!

77 WHEN: Dutch equivalents

The English word 'when' has three main equivalents in Dutch: *wanneer, toen* and (as an alternative to *wanneer*) *als*. Note that these three words send the following verb to the end of the clause when used as conjunctions (☞ *Conjunctions*,17.2).

77.1 *Wanneer*

(a) *Wanneer* is used when asking a question

***wanneer** komt de volgende trein?*	when does the next train leave?
***wanneer** heb jij het gestuurd?*	when did you send it?
***wanneer** was hij ziek?*	when was he ill?

(b) It is also used as a conjunction before verbs in the present, the future/future perfect, the conditional/conditional perfect and the perfect

ik doe het **wanneer** *ik klaar* BEN	I'll do it when I'm ready
ik weet niet **wanneer** *ik* GAAN ZOU	I don't know when I would go
ik zal het u zeggen **wanneer** *hij* AANGEKOMEN IS	I'll tell you when he has arrived

(c) It translates English 'whenever' in all tenses

wanneer *hij naar Amsterdam* GING	whenever he went to Amsterdam
wanneer *ik hem* ZAG, *was hij dronken*	whenever I saw him he was drunk
kom **wanneer** *je* WIL	come whenever you want

Note also *telkens wanneer* and *telkens als*, meaning 'whenever'.

77.2 *Toen* is used as a conjunction before verbs in the SIMPLE PAST and PLUPERFECT

toen *hij naar Amsterdam* GING	when he went to Amsterdam
toen *ik hem* ZAG, *was hij dronken*	when I saw him he was drunk
toen *zij het huis* GEKOCHT HADDEN	when they had bought the house

Note that *toen* meaning 'when' must not be confused with *toen* meaning 'then', the latter of which does not send the verb to the end (☞ *THEN: Dutch equivalents*, 68.2).

77.3 *Als* may be used as an alternative to *wanneer* when it is a conjunction (☞ 77.1(b–c))[86]

ik doe het **als** *ik klaar* BEN	I'll do it when I'm ready
als *hij naar Amsterdam* GING	whenever he went to Amsterdam

Note that *als* also means 'if'. Thus, a sentence such as *ik doe het* **als** *ik klaar ben* could mean 'I'll do it when I'm ready' or 'I'll do it if I'm ready.'

78 Word order

Dutch is similar to English in that the basic word order is SUBJECT–VERB–OBJECT, e.g. [**de student**]$_{Subj.}$ [**leest**]$_{Verb}$ [**het boek**]$_{Obj.}$ 'the student reads the book'. As sentences become more complex, however, the word order of Dutch begins to differ, sometimes quite radically, from that of English. This chapter deals with those differences between Dutch and English word order that may cause problems for English learners of Dutch. Before doing so, however, it is necessary to explain two important concepts that play a major role in determining the position of the verb in Dutch sentences:

(i) FINITE vs. NON-FINITE VERB FORMS: Finite verbs may change their form to show person, number and tense, e.g. *ik* **werk** 'I work', *hij* **werk-t** 'he works', *wij* **werk-en** 'we work', *hij* **werk-te** 'he worked' etc., while non-finite forms, i.e. infinitives and participles, remain constant, e.g. *ik zal/wij zullen* **werken** 'I/we will work', *ik heb/hij heeft/zij hebben* **gewerkt** 'I have/he has/they have worked'.

---

86 Yet *als* cannot replace *wanneer* followed by a conditional/conditional perfect, e.g. *ik weet niet* **wanneer**/✗*als ik GAAN ZOU* 'I don't know when I would go'.

(ii) SUBORDINATE vs. MAIN CLAUSES: A clause is that part of the sentence which contains one finite verb, usually with a subject. Thus the sentence *Jan* HEEFT *een boek geschreven* 'Jan has written a book' consists of one clause while [*Jan* HEEFT *een boek geschreven*] *en* [*ik* HEB *het gelezen*] 'Jan has written a book and I have read it' contains two.[87] A subordinate clause is introduced by a subordinating conjunction, e.g. **als** 'if', **dat** 'that', **omdat** 'because', **toen** 'when' (☞ *Conjunctions*, 17.2) while a main clause is not, e.g. [*ik* WEET]$_{\text{Main}}$ **dat** [*Jan een boek geschreven* HEEFT]$_{\text{Subordinate}}$.[88]

78.1 THE POSITION OF THE FINITE VERB

(a) In basic main clauses, the finite verb is always the SECOND idea

(i) It usually follows the subject

[*ik*]$_1$ [**ga**]$_2$ *naar Rome*	I'm going to Rome
[*mijn moeder*]$_1$ [**is**]$_2$ *lerares*	my mother is a teacher
[*de oude man*]$_1$ [**kwam**]$_2$ *thuis*	the old man came home

(ii) If an expression of time, place or manner is placed at the beginning of the clause (e.g. for special emphasis, ☞ 78.9), the subject and verb are inverted so that the verb remains in second position

[*over een week*]$_1$ [**ga**]$_2$ *ik naar Rome*	I'm going to Rome in a week's time
[*op school*]$_1$ [**werkt**]$_2$ *Theo hard*	at school Theo works hard
[*dronken*]$_1$ [**kwam**]$_2$ *de oude man thuis*	the old man came home drunk

(b) The finite verb goes to the END of the clause[89]

(i) In subordinate clauses (i.e. after subordinating conjunctions, ☞ *Conjunctions*, 17.2 for a list of the most common ones)

ik weet DAT *hij ziek* **is**	I know that he is ill
hij vroeg mij OF *ik geld* **had**	he asked me whether I had money
TOEN *hij mij* **zag**, *lachte hij*	when he saw me he laughed

(ii) After relative pronouns (☞ *Relative pronouns*)

de man DIE *met mijn broer* **werkt**	the man who works with my brother
het boek DAT *ik gisteravond* **las**	the book that I read last night
de stoel WAAR*op de dame* **zit**	the chair on which the lady is sitting

(c) The finite verb comes at the BEGINNING of the clause

(i) In 'yes-no' questions and imperative clauses

wil *jij een kopje koffie?*	do you want a cup of coffee?
gaat *u met de trein?*	are you going by train?
geef *mij dat boek!*	give me that book!

---

87 Note that constructions with (*om*) . . . *te* + infinitive also constitute one clause, e.g. [*ik* **belde** *jou gisteren op*]$_1$ [*om jou iets* **te vragen**]$_2$ 'I rang you up yesterday to ask you something'.

88 Main clauses may be introduced by co-ordinating conjunctions, e.g. [*ik belde jou op*]$_{\text{Main}}$**maar** [*jij was niet thuis*]$_{\text{Main}}$ 'I rang you up **but** you were not at home'. (☞ *Conjunctions*, 17.1).

89 ☞ also 📖 for more complex sentences.

(ii) In main clauses preceded by a subordinate clause or by a construction with *om . . . te* + infinitive (☞ *Infinitives,* 📖)

TOEN *hij mij* ZAG, ***lachte*** *hij*	when he saw me he laughed
ZODRA *ik klaar* BEN, ***kom*** *ik even langs*	as soon as I'm ready I'll come along
OM *eerlijk* TE ZIJN, ***ben*** *ik er tegen*	to be honest, I'm against it

Table 44. The position of the finite verb

Basic			hij	**gaat**		morgen	naar R.	
Subordinate	omdat	hij				morgen	naar R.	**gaat**
Inverted	morgen		**gaat**	hij			naar R.	
After subordinate	als hij kan,		**gaat**	hij	morgen	naar R.	
Question			**gaat**	hij	morgen	naar R?	

78.2 THE POSITION OF THE NON-FINITE VERB (i.e. infinitives and past participles)

(a) Infinitives and past participles appear at the end of a clause[89]

het zal morgen weer ***regenen***	it will rain again tomorrow
ik moet vanavond thuis ***blijven***	I must stay at home tonight
jij hebt mijn wijn ***gedronken***	you have drunk my wine
de jongen was in de stad ***geweest***	the boy had been in town

Note that this rule is often broken in spoken Dutch, e.g. *ik heb een reis* ***gemaakt*** *naar Ierland* 'I travelled to Ireland.'

(b) Unless the finite verb has been sent to the end (☞ 78.1b)

hij zegt DAT *het morgen* REGENEN ***zal***	he says that it will rain tomorrow
OMDAT *ik vandaag thuis* BLIJVEN ***moet***	because I must stay at home today
TOEN *je mijn wijn* GEDRONKEN ***hebt***	when you drank my wine
de jongen DIE *in de stad* GEWEEST ***was***	the boy who had been in town

Note, however, that some speakers prefer to place the finite verb immediately before the infinitive/participle:

hij zegt DAT *het morgen* ***zal*** REGENEN
OMDAT *ik vandaag thuis* ***moet*** BLIJVEN
TOEN *jij mijn wijn* ***hebt*** GEDRONKEN
de jongen DIE *in de stad* ***was*** GEWEEST

This is particularly common with modal verbs:

OMDAT *ik vandaag thuis* ***moet*** BLIJVEN
hij zegt DAT *hij naar Amsterdam* ***wil*** VERHUIZEN

(c) In tenses with a past participle AND an infinitive, the relative order of these is flexible

ik zal het ***gezien*** HEBBEN/HEBBEN ***gezien***	I will have seen it

Table 45. The relative position of finite and non-finite verbs

| Basic | | | hij | zal | naar R. | | gaan | |
| | | | hij | is | naar R. | | gegaan | |

| Subordinate | omdat | hij | | | naar R. | | gaan | zal |
| | omdat | hij | | | naar R. | | gegaan | is |

| OR | omdat | hij | | | naar R. | zal | gaan | |
| | omdat | hij | | | naar R. | is | gegaan | |

> *ik zou **gekomen** ZIJN/ ZIJN **gekomen**   * I would have come
> *het moet **gezien** WORDEN/ WORDEN   * it must be seen
>   ***gezien***

And note the subordinate word order, e.g. *dat ik het **zal** hebben gezien / dat ik het gezien **zal** hebben, dat het **moet** worden gezien/ dat het gezien **moet** worden* etc.

(d) In sentences with two infinitives, one of which is a modal (☞*Modal verbs*), THE MODAL INFINITIVE ALWAYS PRECEDES THE NON-MODAL INFINITIVE[90]

> *ik **heb** het niet **kunnen** VINDEN   * I could not find it
> *hij **had** mijn wijn **willen** DRINKEN   * he had wanted to drink my wine
> *ik **zal** het morgen **moeten** DOEN   * I will have to do it tomorrow

And note the subordinate word order:

> *de pen* DIE *ik niet **heb** kunnen vinden*   the pen that I could not find
> ALS *hij mijn wijn **had** willen drinken*   if he had wanted to drink my wine
> OF *ik het morgen **zal** moeten doen*   whether I'll have to do it tomorrow

Table 46. The relative position of modal and non-modal infinitives

| Basic | | hij | heeft | naar R. | | moeten | gaan |
| Subordinate | omdat | hij | | naar R. | heeft | moeten | gaan |

78.3 For verbs with separable prefixes, ☞ *Separable verbs*

78.4 (a) In sentences with expressions of time and/or manner and/or place, the basic order is TIME – MANNER – PLACE

Table 47. Expressions of time, manner and place

Subject + verb	TIME (when?)	MANNER (how?)	PLACE (where?)
1. ik ga	morgen	met de trein	naar Utrecht
2. hij kwam	vrijdag	heel moe	thuis
3. ik ging	vroeger	graag	naar de stad
4. wij rijden	vaak	samen	naar ons werk
5. Jan zat	de hele dag	huilend	in de tuin

---

90 This also applies to other verbs which, like the modals, occur with a bare infinitive (☞ *Blijven, Laten*, 35.2 and *Infinitives*, 30.1(d)).

As we see from the English translations of sentences 1–5 above, English has the reverse word order, i.e. PLACE, MANNER, TIME:

1. I'm going to Amsterdam by train tomorrow.
2. He came home very tired on Friday.
3. I used to like going to town. (*Literally*: I went earlier willingly to town.)
4. We often drive to work together.
5. Jan sat in the garden crying all day.

(b) Expressions of time usually precede phrases beginning with a preposition

*zij praat **altijd** OVER zichzelf*	she always talks about herself
*ik heb het **gisteren** VAN Jan gekregen*	I got it from Jan yesterday
*ik werk **nooit** MET een computer*	I never work with a computer

(c) They may also precede a direct object

*zij heeft **altijd** PROBLEMEN*	she always has problems
*ik maak **om twee uur** THEE*	I make tea at two o'clock
*ik kijk **vanavond** TV*	I'm watching TV this evening
*ik bezoek **vandaag** EEN KENNIS*	I'm visiting an acquaintance today

If, however, the direct object is (i) a pronoun or (ii) a noun preceded by a possessive *mijn, jouw, zijn* etc. or by *de/het*, the expression of time usually follows:

*ik bezoek HEM **vandaag***	I'm visiting him today
*hij bezoekt ZIJN moeder **nooit***	he never visits his mother
*zij schreef DE brief **op dinsdag***	she wrote the letter on Tuesday

78.5 For the relative position of direct and indirect objects, ☞ *Objects: direct and indirect*

78.6 For the position of reflexive pronouns ☞ *Reflexive verbs*

78.7 For the position of *er,* ☞ *Er*

78.8 For the position of *niet, nog niet, nooit, ook, ook niet* and *wel,* ☞ *Niet*

78.9 Deviations from the usual word order

(a) Certain elements may be placed at the beginning of the clause if special emphasis is required

Table 48. Word order used for emphasis

EXPRESSIONS OF TIME	**morgen** werk ik de hele dag	**tomorrow** I'm working all day
NOUNS	**die film** heb ik al gezien	I've already seen **that film**
DEMONSTRATIVES	**dat** kun jij niet doen!	you can't do **that**!
INDEFINITE PRONOUNS	**niets** heb ik gezegd	I didn't say **anything**
(less commonly) PERSONAL OBJECT PRONOUNS	**hem** vind ik niet aardig maar **haar** wel	I don't like **him** but I do like **her**

(b) Expressions of time are commonly placed at the beginning of the clause, even where no special emphasis is required

's zondags ga ik naar de kerk	on Sundays I go to church
om half elf kwam hij thuis	he came home at half past ten
om twee uur vertrekt de trein	the train leaves at two o'clock

 Placing a verb at the end of a subordinate clause often causes problems for foreign learners, particularly where another clause immediately follows. In such cases, students are often tempted to place the verb at the end of the whole *sentence* rather than at the end of the appropriate clause. This must be avoided, e.g. *ik weet dat hij thuis **blijft**, omdat hij geen geld heeft* 'I know that he is staying at home because he has no money' (NOT ✗ *ik weet dat hij thuis, omdat hij geen geld heeft **blijft***); *ik belde jou gisteren **op**, toen jij aan het werk was* 'I rang you up yesterday when you were working' (NOT ✗ *ik belde jou gisteren, toen jij aan het werk was **op***), *ik wil hem morgen **opbellen** om hem iets te vragen* 'I want to ring him up tomorrow to ask him something' (NOT ✗ *ik wil hem morgen om hem iets te vragen **opbellen***). Note, however, that the verb is often placed after relative clauses (i.e. those beginning with a relative pronoun), e.g. *ik wil de film* DIE *vanavond in de bioscoop draait,* **zien** 'I want to see the film that is on at the cinema tonight' (although *ik wil de film* **zien** DIE *vanavond in de bioscoop draait* is also possible). This is due to the fact that relative clauses are seen as immediately connected to the preceding noun and are therefore not as independent as other types of clause.

79   *Zelf*: MYSELF, YOURSELF etc.

The Dutch word *zelf* renders English 'myself', 'yourself', 'himself' etc. when the speaker wishes to emphasise the person carrying out the action described by the verb. Generally speaking, *zelf* follows the same word order rules as *niet, nooit* etc. (☞ *Niet*):

*moet ik alles **zelf** doen?*	do I have to do everything myself?
*dat heb jij **zelf** gezegd*	you said that yourself
*hij kookt **zelf***	he does his own cooking

Note that *zelf* can only be used with verbs that are not reflexive, otherwise the reflexive pronouns ***me, je, zich*** etc. must be used (☞ *Reflexive verbs*). In addition, some reflexive and non-reflexive verbs may occur with the emphatic forms **mezelf, jezelf, zichzelf** etc. (☞ *Reflexive verbs*, 61.3 and ▱).

80   *Zou*

Zou (plural *zouden*), the past tense form of *zullen* 'will', is often difficult to translate into English as it has a number of different functions depending on the particular grammatical construction in which it occurs. Some common ones are:

80.1   Zou(den) is most commonly used in the conditional to render English 'would' (☞ *Conditional and conditional perfect tenses, Hypothetical sentences with als: IF*)

*dat **zou** hij nooit doen*	he would never do that
*wij **zouden** liever koffie drinken*	we would prefer to drink coffee
*ik **zou** het gekocht hebben*	I would have bought it

80.2 *Zou(den)* also translates English 'should'

(a) when it means 'would'

ik **zou** heel dankbaar zijn	I should/would be very grateful
zij **zouden** het leuk vinden	they should/would like that

(b) when used in negative questions where a judgement is implied

zou jij nu niet eens naar bed gaan?	shouldn't you be going to bed now?

Otherwise 'should' is usually translated using *moeten* 'to have to' / 'must' (☞ *Modal verbs*, 📖 📖).

80.3 *Zou(den)* renders English 'was/were going to' (in the sense of 'was/were meant to')

ik **zou** hem gisteren opbellen, maar	I was going to / was meant to ring
ik had geen tijd	him yesterday but I didn't have time

80.4 It is also used to mean 'to be said to' / 'to be alleged to'

zij **zouden** ruzie gehad hebben	they are said to have had a row
hij **zou** zijn vrouw vermoord hebben	he is alleged to have murdered his wife

80.5 *Zou(den)* sometimes renders 'I wonder if'

zou hij ziek zijn?	I wonder if he's ill
zouden zij getrouwd zijn?	I wonder if they are married

Exercises

1 Accents

The following Dutch sentences are translations of the English ones below but without any accents. Add accents where you think appropriate:
1 Zij is zo jong, slechts drieentwintig.
2 Ik hoop dat ik kan komen.
3 Zij zijn geevacueerd.
4 Jij kunt het zelf doen.
5 Ik heb geen idee.
6 Hij vindt mij wel aardig.
7 Wil je twee koekjes bij de koffie? – Nee, ik wil maar een koekje.

1 She's <u>so</u> young, just twenty-three.[1]
2 I <u>hope</u> I can come.
3 They have been evacuated.
4 You can do it <u>yourself.</u>
5 I have <u>no</u> idea.
6 He <u>does</u> like me.
7 Do you want two biscuits with the coffee? No, only one biscuit.

2 Adjectives

A

1 (i) *Explain how and / or why the following adjectives have or have not changed their spelling after the addition of* -*e*:
1 groot – grote
2 grootst – grootste
3 nat – natte
4 hard – harde
5 braaf – brave
6 laf – laffe

(ii) *Read the following sentences and explain why some of the adjectives in capitals have an* -*e* *ending while others do not:*

---

1 Underlining indicates stress.

1 Nederlands is een heel MOEILIJKE taal.
2 Linda neemt een HEET bad.
3 Ik eet de GROTERE appel.
4 Dit is mijn JONGSTE kind.

2 *Read the following sentences and explain why none of the adjectives in capitals have an* -*e* *ending:*
1 Ik heb geen GOED boek gevonden.
2 Het huis heeft ALUMINIUM deuren en ramen.
3 Zij wachtte bij de GESLOTEN deur.
4 Hij zit bij het NATIONAAL Ballet.

B

Add -*e* *to the following adjectives where appropriate, taking care to change the spelling where necessary:*
1
1 De gek_ oud_ man.
2 Een stout_ meisje.
3 Leeg_ flessen.
4 Jans zwart_ overhemd.
5 Mijn vroeger_ werk.
6 Rood_ neuzen.
7 Een overwerkt_ leraar.
8 Jouw vreselijk_ stem.

2
1 Geen beter_ koffie.
2 Een kleiner_ kopje.
3 Dat gebroken_ schoteltje.
4 Wijs_ mannen.
5 Die lila_ rok.
6 Vurig_ liefde.
7 Het doof_ kind.
8 Een laag_ prijs.
9 Dit ingewikkeld_ leven.
10 Zijn link_ been.

✍ **1** *Write a short text in Dutch describing someone's appearance. Include at least five of the* *articles of clothing listed below and five different colours used as adjectives, e.g.* HIJ DRAAGT EEN BLAUWE TRUI *etc.*

DE BROEK = trousers
DE STROPDAS – tie
DE TRUI = pullover
DE JAS = jacket/coat
HET OVERHEMD = shirt
HET ONDERBROEKJE
    = underpants
DE SCHOENEN = shoes

WIT = white
BLAUW – blue
GEEL = yellow
GRIJS = grey
ROOD = red
ORANJE = orange
PAARS = purple

2 *Write a short text in Dutch describing any scene or situation. Include as many adjectives as you can, some (but not all) of which require endings, e.g.* EEN DROEVIG OUD *MANNETJE STOND VOOR DE* GESLOTEN *DEUR VAN HET* GROTE, INDRUKWEKKENDE *HUIS etc.*

☺☺ **Dialogue**

Insert the correct forms of the adjectives in brackets into the gaps below:

In een café

Ober: Meneer, mevrouw?
Max: Een __ (alcoholvrij) biertje, alstublieft.
Hanna: Voor mij een __ (wit) wijn.
Ober: Het spijt me, mevrouw. We hebben alleen __ (rood) wijn.
Hanna: Heeft u dan __ (vers) sinaasappelsap?
Ober: Nee, het spijt me. Dat hebben we ook niet.
Hanna: Dan neem ik een __ (zwart) koffie.
———————
Hanna: Bah! Die koffie is __ (afschuwelijk)! Hij is veel te __ (sterk).
Max: Geef het maar aan mij. Ik houd wel van __ (sterk) koffie. Ober! Heeft u __ (warm) melk voor de koffie? En __ (bruin) suiker?
Hanna: En een __ (groot) pot thee voor mij?
Ober: Het spijt me, mevrouw. Ik kan u alleen een __ (klein) kopje thee geven. En we hebben alleen __ (wit) suiker.
Hanna: Nou, goed dan. Zijn dat __ (zoet) koekjes?
Ober: Waar?
Hanna: Naast dat __ (groot, rond) gebak aan de __ (recht) kant.

Ober: O ja. Dat zijn onze __ (zelfgebakken) boterkoekjes.
Hanna: Dan neem ik twee van de __ (groter) en twee van de (kleiner).
Max: Het is vrij __ (koud) hier. Ik geloof dat het van de __ (openstaande) deur komt. Kunt u hem dichtdoen, alstublieft?
Ober: Nee, dat is niet __ (mogelijk). {*De ober gaat weg*}.
Max: Wat een __ (onvriendelijk) ober.
———————
Hanna: Bah! __ (slap) thee en __ (hard) koekjes. Wat __ (vervelend)!
Max: Ja, en mijn bier is ook niet zo __ (lekker). En ze hebben mij ook nog een __ (vuil) glas gegeven.
Hanna: Waar is de rekening? Dat is de __ (duurst) koffie die ik ooit gedronken heb!
Max: Hier komen we nooit meer terug. Wat een __ (slecht) café, zeg!

3 Adjectives derived from other words

A

Translate the following sentences into English, paying particular attention to the derived adjectives in bold print:
1 Het verhaal was **eindeloos**. *eind* = end
2 Zij is heel **succesvol**. *succes* = success
3 De film was heel **grappig**. *grap* = joke, fun
4 Het was **onvoorstelbaar**. *zich voorstellen* = to imagine
5 Hij heeft **visachtig**e ogen. *vis* = fish

B

1 *Form adjectives from the following words by matching each one with the appropriate ending and translate your answers into English:*
1 Amerikaan   Endings -(e)lijk, -ig, -baar, -s
2 nevel
3 bereiken
4 vader

2 *Form as many adjectives as you can from the words below using the endings* -(e)**lijk**, -**ig**, -**baar**, -**s**,

-vol, -(e)loos, -achtig, -vormig, -matig,
-zaam and the prefix **on-** *where appropriate and*
give the English translation of each one:
EXAMPLE: gevoel 'feeling'
ANSWERS: (i) **gevoelig** 'sensitive';
(ii) **gevoelloos** 'unfeeling, insensitive'

1	haar	7	gevaar
2	zon	8	groen
3	land	9	Utrecht
4	Oostenrijk	10	hart
5	herkennen	11	god
6	lezen	12	zwijgen

4 Adjectives used as nouns

A

1 *Translate the following words into English*:
1 De schuwe
2 De kleinen
3 Het moeilijke
4 Iets beters

2 *Translate the following sentences into English*:
1 Welke jongen bedoel jij? – De luie.
2 Ken jij de overledene?
3 Het vervelende is dat ik geen geld heb.
4 Het beste is dat hij rijk is.
5 Het huis is niets bijzonders.

B

1 *Derive the appropriate nouns from the following adjectives in capitals and then translate each one into English*:
1. Iets GROTER
2. Mijn NIEUW
3. De ZWART
4. Het LAATST

2 *Derive the appropriate nouns from the following adjectives in capitals and then translate each sentence into English*:
1 Zie je die LANG met de baard?
2 Het STOM is dat ik mijn sleutel vergeten ben.
3 Vertel me eens iets INTERESSANT.
4 Neem iets WARMER mee.

5 Adverbs

A

Translate the following pairs of sentences into English:
1 Jij bent langzaam. – Jij eet langzaam.
2 Het liedje is goed. – Geert zingt goed.
3 Hij is verschrikkelijk. – Hij is verschrikkelijk stout.
4 Het was een ongelofelijke situatie. – Het was een ongelofelijk moeilijke situatie.

B

Add the missing adverbs:

1 Jij praat te __.	QUICKLY
2 Hij tekent heel __.	BADLY
3 __ gedaan!	WELL
4 Mijn zoon is een __ bekwame student.	POTENTIALLY

6 ALL: Dutch equivalents

A

Translate the following sentences into English and explain the reasons for the choice of each form in bold print:
1 Wie gaat naar de bioscoop? – Wij gaan **allemaal**.
2 **Allen** kunnen deze oefening doen.
3 **Alle** sollicitanten moeten om elf uur aankomen.
4 **Al** de beste plaatsen waren bezet.
5 **Alles** is mogelijk.

B

*Insert **alle**, **allen**, **allemaal**, **al** or **alles*** *into the gaps below where appropriate*:
1 Ik weet __ en jij weet niets.
2 Hij heeft __ die boeken gelezen.
3 Wie komt vanavond? Jan, Kees of Piet? Ze komen __.
4 __ lege flessen moeten teruggegeven worden.
5 Tegenwoordig spreken __ Engels.

7 Apostrophes

A

Explain why some of the forms below have apostrophes while others do not:

1 Anita's nieuwe huis.
2 Jaaps vrienden.
3 Mariekes man.
4 Dat is Frans' fiets.
5 De jongens.
6 Mijn foto's.
7 Goedenavond dames!
8 J.M.'s ski's.

B

Fill in the gaps below with apostrophes where appropriate:

1 Dit is Erica_s jurk.
2 Dat is Jan_s broek.
3 Ik ben met Jos_ vrouw uitgegaan.
4 Hij heeft twee BMW_s.
5 De meisje_s spelen in de tuin.

8 Articles: usage

A

1 *Explain the presence or the absence of **een** in the following sentences*:

1 Mijn broer is arts.
2 Zij was een heel goede lerares.
3 Mijn man is Nederlander.
4 Zij praat met een Duitser.

2 *Explain the presence or the absence of the articles **de** and **het** in the following sentences*:

1 Veel mensen zijn bang voor de dood.
2 Voor mij is het werk heel belangrijk.
3 Ik kom op 7 juni en mijn man komt op de 10e.
4 Hij speelt altijd piano na het avondeten.
5 De hond en de kat vechten in de tuin.

B

1 *Insert **een** where appropriate*:
1 Ik ben __ loodgieter.
2 Jan Wolkers is __ goede schrijver.
3 Bent u __ Amsterdammer?
5 Linda wil __ heel beroemde actrice worden.

2 (i) *Insert **een** where appropriate*:
1 Mijn jongste zoon wordt __ manager.
2 Hij moet __ student blijven.
3 Als __ student was hij heel naïef.
4 Ga niet zonder __ hoed uit.

(ii) *Fill in the gaps below with **de** or **het** where appropriate*:
1 __ leven is soms heel moeilijk.
2 Speel je __ piano of __ orgel?
3 Kom een keer op __ koffie!
4 In __ winter moet je iets warms aantrekken.
5 De lege fles staat nog steeds op __ tafel.
6 Hij schrijft in __ Nederlands.

9 Blijven

A

Translate the following sentences into English:
1
1 Ik blijf wachten tot hij komt
2 De kinderen blijven spelen.
3 Blijven jullie daar wonen?

2
1 Ans bleef de hele dag op haar vriend wachten.
2 Linda en haar vriendin bleven tot twee uur 's morgens praten.
3 Ik wil vanmorgen in bed blijven liggen.
4 Blijf hard werken!
5 Tijdens het onweer is het kind blijven huilen.

B

*Rewrite the following sentences using **blijven** to express a continuous or repeated action*:

1

1 Ik bel hem op.
2 Zij schrijven mij brieven.
3 Bens hond blaft.

2

1 Gisteren keken de jongens de hele nacht tv.
2 Ik wil bij dit bedrijf werken.
3 Jan stuurt zijn ex-vriendin bloemen hoewel zij het niet leuk vindt.
4 Lees maar!

10 BOTH: Dutch equivalents

A

Translate the following sentences into English and explain the reasons for the choice of each form in bold print:

1 Wie gaat naar de bioscoop? Wij gaan **allebei**.
2 Mijn zoons studeren **allebei** scheikunde.
3 **Beiden** willen leraar worden.
4 **Beide** oefeningen waren makkelijk maar zij waren **allebei** te lang.
5 Zijn jullie **allebei** stom?

B

*Insert **beide**, **beiden** or **allebei** into the gaps below where appropriate*:

1 Jaap vindt __ meisjes erg mooi.
2 Woont Geert nog steeds bij zijn moeder? Ja, __ wonen in Utrecht.
3 Wij willen __ verhuizen.
4 Duits en Nederlands zijn __ moeilijk.
5 Wil je de rode jurk of de blauwe? __.

11 Capital letters

Add capital letters where necessary:

1 kom woensdag eens langs!
2 linda heeft een duitse man.
3 piet studeert engels.
4 kunt u deze brief in het nederlands vertalen?

5 's morgens bezorgt jan de krant aan meneer kramer.
6 wanneer is jouw verjaardag? op twintig februari.
7 ik praatte met mevrouw dijkstra op dinsdag 3 maart.
8 's maandags ontmoeten de studenten mevrouw kok, hun lerares ijslands.

12 Colloquial Dutch

Rewrite the following sentences using a more colloquial style:

1 Zijn vrouw heeft hem verlaten.
2 Ik had het nooit gedacht.
3 Komt hij met de moeder van Annika?
4 Je hebt een heel aardige dochter.
5 Neem een koekje!
6 - Heb je een asbak? – Ik moet kijken.

13 Commas

A

Translate the following sentences into English and explain the presence or absence of commas in each one:

1 Toen Kees aankwam, was hij erg moe.
2 Hij is echter een heel succesvolle advocaat.
3 De studenten die hard werken, zullen de hoogste cijfers krijgen.
4 Ik ga niet, tenzij Jan met ons meekomt.
5 De werkeloosheid is met 15, 3 percent zeer laag.

B

Fill in the gaps below with commas where appropriate:

1 Ik ga vanavond niet uit __ omdat ik geen geld heb.
2 Piet had altijd al gedacht __ dat zijn vader te streng was.
3 De film __ die deze week in de bioscoop draait __ is heel goed.
4 Saskia's man __ die nu zo kaal als een biljartbal is __ heeft een andere vrouw.

5 Toen de katten de hond zagen __ renden zij weg.

14 Comparatives

A

Explain how and why the following adjectives have or have not changed their spelling after the addition of the comparative ending:
1 breed – breder
2 zuur – zuurder
3 nat – natter
4 braaf – braver

B

1 *Form comparatives from the following Dutch adjectives:*

1 laag	7 succesvol
2 zwaar	8 puur
3 doof	9 belangrijk
4 wit	10 geel
5 vies	11 oppervlakkig
6 los	12 helder

2 *Replace the adjectives in capitals with the correct comparative form WHERE POSSIBLE and translate each sentence into English:*
 1 Het boek is GOED dan de film.
 2 Ja, maar ik lees niet graag. Ik ga GRAAG naar de bioscoop.
 3 Hij eet VEEL dan ik.
 4 Hij heeft WEINIG geld dan zij.
 5 De GROTE sjaal is veel GOEDKOOP dan de KLEINE.
 6 Het OUDE huis is GROOT dan het NIEUWE.
 7 Ik vind zijn VROEGER films GRAPPIG.
 8 Ik ben even INTELLIGENT als jij.
 9 Wijn wordt steeds DUUR.
 10 Hoe RIJK ik word, hoe GELUKKIG ik ben.

C

1 *Write a short text in Dutch comparing the appearance and/or characteristics of any two people*
you know using plenty of comparatives, e.g. MIJN VADER IS **GROTER** EN **DUNNER** DAN MIJN MOEDER etc.

2 *Write a short text in Dutch comparing any two scenes or situations using as many comparatives and different comparative constructions as you can, e.g.* STUDENTEN HEBBEN **MINDER** GELD **DAN** VROEGER EN HET WORDT **STEEDS MOEILIJKER** OM EEN **BETERE** BAAN TE VINDEN etc.

15 Compound words

A

Translate the following sentences into English and explain why some of the compounds in bold print contain a connecting element:
1 Linda is **huisvrouw**.
  huis = 'house', vrouw = 'wife'
2 Jaap is **dierenarts**.
  dier = 'animal', arts = 'doctor'
3 Jan werkt in een **bloemenwinkel**.
  bloem = 'flower', winkel = 'shop'
4 Anne is **winkelbediende**.
  winkel = 'shop', bediende = 'assistant'
5 Wij zijn allemaal tegen **kinderarbeid**.
  kind = 'child', arbeid = 'labour'
6 Wij hebben een nieuwe **regeringspartij**.
  regering = 'government', partij = 'party'
7 Doe jouw **veiligheidsgordel** om!
  veiligheid = 'safety', gordel = 'belt'

B

1 *Make compounds out of the following pairs of words and translate your answers into English:*
1 post + kantoor
2 geld + som
3 school + jongen
4 kleren + kast
5 gezondheid + zorg
6 kind + kamer

2 *Form as many compounds as you can from the nouns, verbs and adjectives below and give the English translation of each one:*

inkt	vlek	zwart	fles
wijn	melk	maken	harig

16 Conditional and conditional perfect tenses[2]

A

Translate the following sentences into English:

1
1 Ik zou meer bier drinken.
2 De wijn zou te duur zijn.
3 Het studentenhuis zou geen verwarming hebben.
4 Het kind zou niet zo stout zijn.

2
1 Ik zou de brief niet geschreven hebben.
2 Wij zouden langer in Den Haag gebleven zijn.
3 Ik had meer van jou verwacht.
4 Studeren in Nederland was een goed idee geweest.

B

1 *Put the following sentences into the conditional:*
EXAMPLE: De politieagent vangt de dief.
ANSWER: De politieagent **zou** de dief **vangen**.
1 Frits geeft bloemen aan zijn vrouw.
2 De leraar wordt heel boos.
3 Marc en Ruud spelen voetbal.
4 De trein vertrekt om vier uur.
5 Vinden de studenten de les veel te moeilijk?

2 (i) *Put sentences 1–5 above into the conditional perfect:*
EXAMPLE: De politieagent vangt de dief.
ANSWER: De politieagent **zou** de dief **gevangen hebben**.

(ii) *Rewrite your conditional perfect sentences 1–5 using contracted forms:*
EXAMPLE: De politieagent zou de dief gevangen hebben.

---

2 ☞ also *Hypothetical sentences with **als** and related exercises.*

ANSWER: De politieagent **had** de dief **gevangen**.

C

1 *Write a short text in Dutch explaining what you **would do** if you won a million pounds next week. Try to use as many conditional sentences as you can, e.g.* IK **ZOU** EEN SNELLE AUTO **KOPEN** etc.

2 *Write a short text in Dutch explaining what you **would have done** if you had won a million pounds last year. Try to use as many conditional perfect sentences as you can, e.g.* IK **ZOU** EEN SNELLE AUTO **GEKOCHT HEBBEN** *or* IK **HAD** EEN SNELLE AUTO **GEKOCHT** etc.

17 Conjunctions: AND, BUT, BECAUSE etc.

A

Translate the following sentences into English, paying particular attention to the conjunctions in bold print and their effect on word order:
1 Geert wil een koek bakken **maar** hij heeft geen eieren.
2 **Toen** Frits jong was, luisterde hij altijd naar ABBA.
3 Wil je meekomen **of** werk je vanavond?
4 Piet vraagt Jaap **of** Harald een nieuwe vriendin heeft.
5 **Sinds** ik aankwam, is het weer heel slecht geweest.
6 **Zover** ik weet, is hij nog in Utrecht.

B

1 *Using the conjunctions given in capitals below, join the following sentences together and change the word order where necessary:*
EXAMPLE: Ik kom niet. Ik ben moe.   OMDAT
ANSWER: Ik kom niet **omdat** ik moe **ben**.

1 Hij kwam aan. Het was te laat.   MAAR
2 Wij moeten hard werken. Anders krijgen wij lage cijfers.   WANT

3 Jullie moeten de koffie klaar hebben. Zij
  komen vanavond aan.   ZODRA
4 Ans was studente. Zij ontmoette haar
  eerste vriend.   TOEN
5 Piet is leraar. Zijn vrouw is tandarts.   EN
6 Ik ga niet naar de bruiloft. Jij koopt voor
  mij een nieuwe jurk.   TENZIJ
7 Harald is heel dik. Hij eet niet veel.
         HOEWEL
8 Jij mag een biertje hebben. Jij rijdt niet.
         ZOLANG

2 *Combine the following pairs of clauses using either* **omdat**, **hoewel**, **toen** *or* **terwijl** *where appropriate and change the word order if necessary*:
1 Ik ben heel moe. Ik ging gisteravond vroeg
  naar bed.
2 Zij moet vandaag vroeger opstaan. Zij
  brengt haar dochter naar school.
3 Ik maak het bad schoon. Jij doet de was.
4 Hij zag haar in de bus zitten. Hij ging naar
  zijn werk.
5 Wij moeten met de tram gaan. Mijn auto is
  kapot.
6 Er was een probleem met de computer. Hij
  was splinternieuw.

C

1 *Write a short text in Dutch describing the appearance and/or characteristics of a friend or relative using as many co-ordinating conjunctions as you can, e.g.* HIJ IS RIJK **MAAR** HIJ WOONT IN EEN KLEINE FLAT *etc. Try also including some subordinating conjunctions.*

2 *Write a short text in Dutch describing a scene or situation that you have encountered. Use as many co-ordinating and subordinating conjunctions as you can, both to link clauses and to introduce sentences, e.g.* STEEDS MEER STUDENTEN ZOEKEN EEN BAANTJE **OMDAT** ZIJ NIET GENOEG GELD VOOR HUN STUDIE HEBBEN. **HOEWEL** DE SITUATIE MOEILIJK IS, HEBBEN ZIJ GEEN ANDERE MOGELIJKHEDEN etc.

18 Days and months

A

Translate the following sentences into English:
1 Vrijdags bezoekt Jan zijn vader.
2 Hij komt (op) dinsdag negentien mei.
3 Ik zie jou (op) maandag de eenentwintigste.
4 Annika gaat begin augustus naar
  Amsterdam.

B

Re-write the following sentences using words instead of numerals:
1 Piet is op vrijdag 12/7/1968 geboren.
2 Is jouw verjaardag op de 1e? – Nee, op de 2e.
3 Kom je op 7/8 of op 1/10?
4 Dit jaar gaat zij op de 30e op vakantie.
5 Sinterklaas is op 5/12.

C

Write a diary of what you intend to do for the next year. Include at least ten events along with the date of each one written out in full, e.g. IK GA **OP MAANDAG TIEN AUGUSTUS** NAAR SPANJE EN BLIJF TOT **WOENSDAG DE TWINTIGSTE** etc.

19 Demonstrative pronouns: THIS, THAT etc.

A

Translate the following sentences into English and explain the choice of **dit** *versus* **deze** *and* **dat** *versus* **die**:
1 Deze wijn is te droog.
2 Hoe vind je dit brood?
3 Deze tulpen zijn mooier dan die rozen.
4 Zie je die boom?
5 Dat is niet waar.
6 Dit zijn mijn beste vrienden.

B

1 *Replace the following definite articles* **de** *and* **het** *with the appropriate demonstrative pronoun (i.e. the*

*equivalent of 'this/these' before **hier** 'here' and
'that/those' before **daar** 'there'):*
EXAMPLE: de man hier – de vrouw daar.
ANSWER: **deze** man hier – **die** vrouw daar.
1 De student daar.
2 Het kind daar.
3 De kinderen hier.
4 Het kopje hier.
5 De mensen daar.

2 *Enter the appropriate demonstrative pronouns into
the gaps below:*
1 __ boek is heel interessant.   THIS
2 Hij kwam uit __ richting.   THAT
3 __ wijn is beter dan __ bier.   THIS, THAT
4 __ is de betere wijn.   THIS
5 __ huizen zijn veel groter dan __ flats.
                                    THESE, THOSE
6 __ bakkerij is duur maar __ is goedkoper.
                                   THIS, THAT ONE
7 Ik houd meestal niet van meloenen maar
   __ was lekker.   THAT ONE
8 __ is mijn kantoor en __ zijn de nieuwe
   computers.   THIS, THOSE
9 __ zijn mijn nieuwe oorbellen.   THESE
10 Zet jouw kopje __ op en jouw glas __ op.
                                      THIS, THAT

C

*Imagine that you are in a shop buying food. Ask for
five of the following items using the appropriate
demonstrative pronouns instead of **de** and **het**:*
this/these   HET BROOD = bread
                 DE TOMATEN = tomatoes
                 HET WATER = water
                 DE KOFFIE = coffee
that/those   DE KAAS = cheese
                 DE DRUIVEN = grapes
                 DE KOEKJES = biscuits
                 HET BIER = beer

20 Diminutives

A

Translate the following sentences into English:
1 Het katje speelt met het muisje.

2 Zij heeft twee broertjes.
3 Het meisje spreekt heel zachtjes.
4 Hij is een lief jongetje.
5 Hij heeft een raar autootje.

B

*Derive diminutives from the following nouns and
adverbs:*
1

1	boek	7	fles
2	peer	8	tafel
3	deken	9	oorbel
4	arm	10	riem
5	som	11	haring
6	slaapkamer	12	pen

2

1	mannen	7	zoon
2	vrouwen	8	glas
3	tomaten	9	jongen
4	druiven	10	zacht
5	sla	11	knus
6	paraplu	12	stiekem

C

*Imagine that you are in a shop buying clothes for a
small child. Ask for five of the following garments
using diminutive forms to indicate smallness:*
BROEK = trousers   SOKKEN = socks
JAS = jacket/coat   MUTS = cap
TRUI = pullover   SCHOENEN = shoes
SJAAL = scarf   LAARZEN = boots

21 Er

A

*Translate the following sentences into English and
explain the function of each **er**:*
1 Ik heb hem er twee keer gezien.
2 Waar is de stoel? Ik zit erop.
3 Zij denken er niet meer aan.
4 Er zitten vijf studenten in de klas.
5 In mijn klas heb ik er twintig.

B

1 (i) *Replace the following phrases in bold print with* **er** *and move the prepositions in capitals to the appropriate place*:

EXAMPLE: Ik kijk niet meer NAAR **het programma**.

ANSWER: Ik kijk **er** niet meer **naar**.

1 Ik wacht OP **de trein**.
2 Wij weten helemaal niets VAN **het verhaal**.
3 Wat doe je MET **het mes**?
4 Zij praat nog steeds OVER **haar problemen met mannen**.
5 Ik heb niet genoeg geld VOOR **de bioscoop**.
6 Denk AAN **mijn woorden**!

(ii) *Replace the following words in bold print with* **er** *and change the word order if necessary*:

EXAMPLE: Ik heb twee **boterhammen**.

ANSWER: Ik heb **er** twee.

1 Hoeveel kaartjes heb je meegebracht? – Ik heb vijf **kaartjes** meegebracht.
2 Hoeveel kinderen hebben zij? – Zij hebben geen **kinderen**.
3 Heeft hij veel vrienden? – Nee, hij heeft niet veel **vrienden**.

(iii) *Replace the stressed form* **daar** *'there' with its unstressed equivalent* **er** *and change the word order if necessary*:

EXAMPLE: **Daar** heb ik nooit gewoond.

ANSWER: Ik heb **er** nooit gewoond.

1 **Daar** is hij met zijn vriendin geweest.
2 **Daar** heb ik hem gezien.
3 **Daar** ben ik niet lang gebleven.
4 **Daar** heeft Jaap zijn eerste vrouw ontmoet.

2 *Insert* **er** *into the following sentences where appropriate and change the word order if necessary*:

1 Een oude roestige auto staat voor mijn deur.
2 Vier meisjes spelen op het gras.
3 Was gisteren iemand thuis?
4 Kijk! Een bus komt.
5 Twee politieagenten wachten voor het huis.

6 Wilt u een biertje? – Jawel, ik wil twee, alstublieft!
7 Ben je ooit in Antwerpen geweest? Ja, ik heb zes jaar met een vriend gewoond.
8 Ik houd van Amsterdam. Er zijn veel grachten. – Ja, er zijn ook veel in Utrecht.
9 Houd je van opera? – Nee, ik houd helemaal niet van.
10 Dat vlees ziet goed uit. – Ja, maar er zijn niet veel groenten bij.

22 Female endings

A

Translate the following sentences into English:

1 Erica is schrijfster en haar zus is maatschappelijk werkster.
2 Jaaps vriendin is communiste.
3 Mariekes lerares is Poolse.
4 De Italiaanse is een heel goede kokkin.
5 Mijn moeder is politieagente.

B

Derive the feminine equivalents of the masculine nouns below:

1 werker	7 Zweed
2 kapper	8 Turk
3 verkoper	9 Nederlander
4 specialist	10 wolf
5 hertog	11 leraar
6 keizer	12 dompteur

23 Future and future perfect tenses

A

Translate the following sentences into English:

1

1 Ik zal morgenavond in België zijn.
2 Wij zullen vóór maart verhuizen.
3 De situatie zal moeilijker worden.
4 Het zal erg vermoeiend zijn.

2

1   Het reisbureau zal alles georganiseerd
    hebben.
2   Ik zal hem ontmoet hebben.
3   Zij zullen waarschijnlijk tot het weekend
    gebleven zijn.
4   Wij zullen vóór half acht vertrokken zijn.

B

1 *Put the following sentences into the future tense*:
EXAMPLE: Jaap woont in Amsterdam.
ANSWER: Jaap **zal** in Amsterdam **wonen**.
1   Piet en Geert komen om acht uur aan.
2   Geef jij bloemen aan je buurvrouw?
3   De trein vertrekt vanavond.
4   De kinderen slapen volgende week bij hun
    grootouders.
5   Mijn buurman is al zeventig.

2 (i) *Put sentences 1–5 above into the future perfect
tense*:
EXAMPLE: Jaap woont in Amsterdam.
ANSWER: Jaap **zal** in Amsterdam
gewoond hebben.

(ii) *Take your answers to 23B1 above and show
which of the future sentences can also be expressed
using the present tense without changing their meaning.
In those cases where the present tense is not possible,
explain why.*

C

1 *Write a short text in Dutch explaining what you are
going to do next week. Try to use as many future tense
forms as you can, e.g.* IK **ZAL** OP MAANDAG
BOODSCHAPPEN **DOEN** etc.

2 *Write a short text in Dutch explaining what you
will have done by next year. Try to use as many
future perfect constructions as you can, e.g.* IK **ZAL** EEN
NIEUWE BAAN **GEVONDEN HEBBEN** EN **ZAL**
VERHUISD ZIJN etc.

24 Geen

A

Translate the following sentences into English:
1   Ik ben geen toerist. Ik woon hier.
2   Er is niet één bioscoop in deze stad.
3   Het spijt me, ik heb geen kleingeld.
4   Dat is geen goede foto.
5   Dit zijn geen dure schoenen.

B

Make the following sentences negative:
1   Ik heb een idee.
2   Wil je een biertje?
3   Zij is huisvrouw.
4   Het is een wonder dat hij geld heeft.
5   Jaap en Wim zijn aardige jongens.
6   De student heeft dit jaar één boek gelezen!

25 Gender

A

*Identify which of the following groups of words are
neuter and which groups are of common gender*:
1   man, vrouw, hond, kat, muis.
2   mannetje, vrouwtje, hondje, katje, muisje.
3   eten, drinken, lezen, schrijven.
4   lezing, rekening, vrijheid, mogelijkheid,
    bakker, schrijver, leraar.
5   bewijs, gebied, verkeer, verdriet.

B

1 *Insert **de** or **het** into the gaps below*:

1 __ hond	11 __ bakker
2 __ hondje	12 __ gebak
3 __ leven	13 __ begrip
4 __ wijn	14 __ woordenboek
5 __ zwart	15 __ vriendin
6 __ staal	16 __ vertaling
7 __ man	17 __ verhaal
8 __ vrouw	18 __ grappige
9 __ meisje	19 __ universiteit
10 __ kind	20 __ feminisme

2 *Complete the following sentences*:

1 Woont hij in __ noordoosten? – Nee, in __ noordwesten.
2 Heb jij __ nieuwe huis gezien? – Nee, ik heb __ niet gezien.
3 Hoe laat vertrekt __ trein? – __ vertrekt om twee uur.
4 Waar is __ pen? – Heb jij __ gezien?
5 Hoe was __ film? – __ was heel goed.
6 Ken jij __ meisje van de boekwinkel? – Nee, ik ken __ niet.

26 Graag

A

Translate the following sentences into English:
1 Jan leest heel graag.
2 Frits kijkt liever naar de tv.
3 Gaat hij niet graag naar de bioscoop?
4 Mijn oma luistert het liefst naar de radio.
5 Reist u graag of blijft u liever thuis?

B

*Insert **graag** into the appropriate place in the following sentences and translate each one into English*:
1 Ik wou een taxi bestellen.
2 Mijn man brengt u naar de luchthaven.
3 Waarom ga je niet naar school?
4 Mijn baas werkt.
5 Ik wou weten, hoe hij het doet.

27 Hypothetical sentences with als: IF[3]

A

Translate the following sentences into English:
1
1 Als mijn oma één glas wijn dronk, zou zij dronken worden.

2 Als ik naar Groningen zou gaan, zou ik een paraplu meenemen.
3 Als de studenten harder werkten, zouden zij betere cijfers krijgen.
4 Als wij vanavond zouden opbellen, zou je thuis zijn?

2

1 Als oom Jos naar Amsterdam gegaan was, zou hij de tulpen gezien hebben.
2 Als het weer beter geweest was, had ik tennis gespeeld.
3 Als de les niet zo laat geweest was, zouden meer studenten gekomen zijn.
4 Als jullie vroeger opgebeld hadden, waren wij nog thuis geweest.

B

1 *Rewrite the following phrases as hypothetical sentences referring to what one **would do** in the future and translate each one into English*:
EXAMPLE: Ik hard WERKEN – ik veel geld VERDIENEN.
ANSWER: **Als** ik hard **werkte** (or **zou werken**), **zou** ik meer geld **verdienen**. If I worked hard I would earn more money.

1 Piet 's morgens vroeger wakker WORDEN – hij 's avonds moe ZIJN.
2 Jaap meer tijd HEBBEN – hij meer voetbal SPELEN.
3 Wij vroeger thuis KOMEN – wij naar de televisie KIJKEN.
4 Mevrouw Baayen geld aan haar zoon GEVEN – hij naar de bioscoop GAAN.
5 De studenten dit boek LEZEN – zij veel van de Nederlandse taal WETEN.

2
(i) *Rewrite the phrases 1–5 above as hypothetical sentences referring to what one **would have done** in the past and translate each one into English*:
EXAMPLE: Ik hard WERKEN – ik veel geld VERDIENEN.
ANSWER: **Als** ik hard **gewerkt had, zou** ik meer geld **verdiend hebben**.

---

3 ☞ also *Conditional and conditional perfect tenses* and related exercises.

If I had worked hard I would have earned
a lot of money.

(ii) *Take your answers to 2i above and rewrite them
using contracted forms*:
EXAMPLE: Als ik hard gewerkt had, zou ik
meer geld verdiend hebben.
ANSWER: **Als** ik hard **gewerkt had, had**
ik meer geld **verdiend**.

C

*Do Exercises **16C** on the conditional and conditional
perfect tenses including as many sentences with **als** as
you can, e.g.* ALS IK MILJOEN POND ZU **WON, ZOU**
IK EEN SNELLE AUTO **KOPEN** etc.

28 Imperative

A

Translate the following sentences into English:
1 Ga niet te vaak uit.
2 Wees niet te laat.
3 Brengt u mij een fles wijn.
4 Laten we feesten!
5 NIET PARKEREN.

B

1 *Put the verbs in capitals below into the (general)
imperative*:
1 LATEN me met rust!
2 SLAPEN lekker.
3 ETEN niet zo veel.
4 LEZEN hoofdstuk drie van dit boek.
5 GEVEN me een zoen.

2 *Put the verbs in capitals below into the imperative*:
1 OPBELLEN dit nummer na negen uur.
2 MEEKOMEN morgenavond naar het
feestje.
3 STUREN mij een fax.   (*very polite*)
4 LOPEN rechtdoor tot de hoek van de
straat.   (*very polite*)
5 ZIJN braaf.

C

*Imagine that you are going to meet someone and you
need to give them instructions in Dutch on how to get
there and what to do. Write these down using as many
imperatives as you can, e.g.* KOM OM TWEE UUR
NAAR HET CAFÉ *etc.*

You may want to make use of the following phrases:
DE BUS NEMEN = to take the bus
VÓÓR HET ZIEKENHUIS UITSTAPPEN = to get
off/alight in front of the hospital
RECHTDOOR GAAN TOT . . . = to go straight
ahead until . . .
BIJ DE STOPLICHTEN OVERSTEKEN = to cross
over at the traffic lights
LINKS/RECHTS AFSLAAN = to turn left/right
VÓÓR HET CAFÉ WACHTEN = to wait in front of
the cafe

29 Indefinite pronouns: SOME, ANY, EACH etc.

A

Translate the following sentences into English:
1 Iedereen kent Jaap maar niemand kent zijn
vrouw.
2 Wil je iets drinken? Nee, niets.
3 Ik heb wat vis meegebracht.
4 Sommige talen zijn moeilijker dan andere.
5 Mevrouw van Duin gaat elk jaar naar
Italië.
6 Haar man is zo lui. Hij wil niets doen.

B

*Fill in the gaps below with the appropriate indefinite
pronoun*:
1 Hier, drink __ wijn!   SOME
2 De studenten vinden __ cursussen
interessanter dan __.   SOME, OTHERS
3 __ kijken naar de tv en __ lezen.
SOME, OTHERS
4 Hij doet het __ keer.   EVERY
5 __ kan gedichten schrijven.   ANYONE
6 Heb jij __ gezien?   ANYONE

30 Infinitives and use of (om) . . . te

A

Translate the following sentences into English and explain why **te**, **om . . . te** *or the bare infinitive have been used in each case*:

1 De politieagent stond naar de inbreker te kijken.
2 Hij zag hem in het huis inbreken.
3 Ik werk heel hard om mijn huur te betalen.
4 Zij zaten in de auto zonder met elkaar te praten.
5 Dat is te verwachten.

B

1 (i) *Rewrite the following sentences using* **om . . . te** *plus the infinitive*:

EXAMPLE: Jan werkt hard. Hij betaalt zijn huur.
ANSWER: Jan werkt hard **om** zijn huur **te betalen**.

1 Piet wil geld. Hij gaat naar de bioscoop.
2 Hij gaat boodschappen doen. Hij helpt zijn oma.
3 Ik heb meer bloem nodig. Ik bak deze koekjes.
4 Heb je genoeg geld? Koop je die jurk?
5 Ik moet morgen heel vroeg naar mijn werk gaan. Ik stuur vóór acht uur een fax.

(ii) *Rewrite the following sentences using* **liggen**, **staan** *and* **zitten** *with* **te** *plus the infinitive. Take care to maintain the original tense*:

EXAMPLE: Jan werkte hard. (zitten)
ANSWER: Jan **zat** hard **te werken**.

1 Geert drinkt zijn bier. (zitten)
2 De hond blaft naar de melkboer. (staan)
3 De baby huilt de hele nacht. (liggen)
4 De kinderen keken naar het vliegtuig. (staan)
5 De kat sliep. (liggen)

2 *Fill in the gaps below with* **te** *or* **om . . . te** *only where necessary*:

1 Jantje durft __ zijn leraar __ beledigen.
2 Wie komt er __ __ tennissen?
3 __ zijn vrouw __ ergeren kwam Jaap laat thuis.
4 De kinderen gaan __ morgen __ zwemmen
5 Hij weet heel goed __ vrouwen __ verleiden.
6 Jij hoeft mij __ niet meer op __ bellen.
7 Dat boek is makkelijk __ __ lezen.
8 Ik probeer __ het morgenochtend __ doen.

C

1 *Write a short text in Dutch describing your latest visit to the shops. Use as many infinitive constructions with* **om . . . te** *as you can, e.g.* IK GING NAAR DE SUPERMARKT **OM** BROOD, KAAS EN WIJN **TE** KOPEN etc.

2 *Write a short text in Dutch describing your latest visit to the shops. Use as many different constructions with* **te**, **om . . . te** *and the bare infinitive as you can, e.g.* IK MOEST NAAR DE SUPERMARKT **GAAN**, **OM** BROOD, KAAS EN WIJN **TE KOPEN** MAAR HET BEGON **TE REGENEN** etc.

31 -ING constructions: Dutch equivalents

The following English sentences have been incorrectly translated into Dutch using a present participle (marked by an asterisk) to render '-ing'. Replace these participles with an appropriate alternative construction:

EXAMPLE: Piet stood talking.
　　　　　Piet stond *pratend.
ANSWER: Piet stond **te praten**.

1 I sat watching TV all evening.
2 They heard the neighbours playing loud music.
3 He sees her waiting for the bus every morning.
4 She does it without thinking.
5 He rings me up instead of writing.
6 Who is the man living opposite you?
7 We waited all morning, hoping for a bus to come.

8 Getting off the train, he saw her waiting on the platform.

1 Ik zat de hele avond tv *kijkend.
2 Zij hoorden de buren harde muziek *spelend.
3 Hij ziet haar iedere morgen op de bus *wachtend.
4 Zij doet het zonder *denkend.
5 Hij belt me op in plaats van *schrijvend.
6 Wie is de man tegenover jou *wonend?
7 Wij wachtten de hele morgen, *hopend dat een bus zou komen.
8 De trein *uitstappend, zag hij haar op het perron *wachtend.

32 Inseparable verbs (☞ also Separable verbs)

1 *Make sentences out of the following phrases by inserting the verbs in capitals below into the appropriate places. Use (a) the present tense, (b) the perfect tense:*
EXAMPLE: Piet, het probleem.   BEGRIJPEN
ANSWERS: (a) Piet **begrijpt** het probleem.
        (b) Piet **heeft** het probleem **begrepen**.

1 Hij, het hele verhaal aan zijn vriend.
                      VERTELLEN
2 Ik, hem niet meer.   HERKENNEN
3 De leraar, zijn vraag.   HERHALEN
4 Uw bezoek, ons.   VERRASSEN
5 Jan, de top.   BEREIKEN
6 Mijn broer, zijn eigen foto's. ONTWIKKELEN

2 *Derive as many verbs as you can from the following verbs, nouns and adjectives, using the most common inseparable prefixes* **be-, her-, ont-** *and* **ver-**, *and translate your answers into English:*
1 man   5 hard
2 moeder   6 open
3 kleden   7 lezen
4 spreken   8 dekken

33 Irregular verbs[4]

A

Translate the following sentences into English:
1 Ik schreef aan mijn vriend maar hij las de brief niet.
2 Zij aten kaas en dronken wijn.
3 Zij brachten hem thuis.
4 Het kopje viel op de grond.
5 Ik dacht dat ik het begrepen had.

B

Give the simple past forms (first person singular and plural, **ik** *and* **wij**) *and the past participles of the following verbs. Indicate which verbs take* **zijn** *in the (plu)perfect:*

1

1	hebben	7	komen
2	zijn	8	gaan
3	weten	9	doen
4	denken	10	zullen
5	zeggen	11	vragen
6	zien	12	worden

2

1	blijven	9	slapen
2	kijken	10	vangen
3	verdwijnen	11	eten
4	sluiten	12	nemen
5	zoeken	13	zitten
6	bezoeken	14	vinden
7	kopen	15	staan
8	houden	16	kiezen

C

1 *Write a short text in Dutch describing, in the simple past tense, what you did yesterday evening. Use as many irregular verbs as you can, e.g.* IK **GING** NAAR DE BIOSCOOP *etc.*

2 *Write a short text in Dutch describing, in the simple past tense, what you and a friend did yesterday evening. Use as many irregular verbs in the plural as*

---

4 ☞ also *Past tense* and *Perfect tense* exercises.

you can, e.g. WIJ **GINGEN** NAAR EEN FEESTJE EN **BLEVEN** ER DRIE UUR etc.

34 KNOW: *weten* or *kennen*?

Insert the correct forms of **weten** *or* **kennen** *where appropriate*:

1 Dit brood is lekker. __ u hoeveel het kost?
2 Ik __ die man maar ik __ zijn naam niet.
3 __ je dit boek? Het is heel goed.
4 Ik __ niet hoe hij het doet.
5 Hij __ zeker dat ik boven de veertig ben.
6 Hoe vindt u Amsterdam? Ik __ de stad niet zo goed.
7 __ u het gezegde 'praatjes vullen geen gaatjes'?

35 *Laten*

A

Translate the following sentences into English:

1 Laat mij het doen.
2 Mevrouw de Wit liet haar zoon naar het feestje gaan.
3 Laten we morgen naar Amsterdam gaan.
4 Je moet je koffie niet koud laten worden.
5 Ik wil mijn jurk laten stomen.
6 Jaap liet zijn moeder naar de luchthaven brengen.
7 Piet had zijn computer al een keer laten repareren.

B

Rewrite the following sentences inserting **laten** *to render the meaning 'to have something done' (without changing the original tense)*:
EXAMPLE: Jan repareert zijn horloge.
ANSWER: Jan **laat** zijn horloge **repareren**.

1 Hij brengt zijn auto naar een garage.
2 Wij maken ons huis iedere donderdag schoon.
3 Ik moet deze film ontwikkelen.

4 Hij heeft een bos bloemen aan zijn vrouw verstuurd.
5 Wij hebben een verjaardagsfeestje georganiseerd.

36 Letter writing

A

Translate the following letter into English, taking care to maintain its formal style:

Amsterdam, 20 augustus 1996

Reisbureau AirWays
Postbus 918
1182 GP Amsterdam

Betreft: reis naar Calamar.

Geachte mevrouw/mijnheer,

Vorige week keerde ik terug van een reis die bij u was geboekt naar Calamar in Spanje. Tot mijn spijt moet ik u melden dat deze geheel niet aan de gewekte verwachtingen uit de folder voldeed.

Ten eerste was de hostess niet aanwezig bij mijn aankomst op het vliegveld, zoals wel in uw folder werd beloofd. Daarop moest ik zelf een taxi nemen naar het hotel, wat fl. 100,— kostte. Bij het inchecken in Hotel Sol de Corazon bleek dat er geen éénpersoonskamer meer was en dus moest ik een kamer delen met iemand van het reisgezelschap. Het hotelmanagement verzekerde mij dat uw reisbureau niet genoeg kamers hadden geboekt. Tenslotte klopte de informatie in uw folder ook niet wat betreft de excursies. De hostess organiseerde alleen een trip naar een klooster, maar de beloofde excursie naar Barcelona ging niet door, omdat de bus niet tijdig was geboekt.

Graag zou ik van u willen vernemen wat de oorzaak was van de verkeerde informatie in de folder. Ook de reden voor het verkeerde aantal boekingen in het hotel zou ik graag willen weten. Enige compensatie voor de taxikosten en de afgelaste excursie lijkt mij op zijn plaats.

Ik zie uw antwoord met belangstelling tegemoet.

Hoogachtend,

Paul van Haalen.

Paul van Haalen
Prinsengracht 23
1023 AC Amsterdam.

B

1 *Write a short formal letter in Dutch to the manager of an electrical appliances store explaining that the video recorder which you bought there two months ago no longer works. Ask him/her if it is possible to return it and be given a refund.*

Vocabulary:
DE VIDEORECORDER = video recorder
MOGELIJK ZIJN = to be possible
BIJ U = at your place (house/shop etc.)
IETS TERUGBRENGEN = to return something
KOPEN (KOCHT, GEKOCHT) = to buy
EEN TERUGBETALING GEVEN = to give a refund
. . . MAANDEN GELEDEN = . . . months ago
NIET MEER FUNCTIONEREN = not to work any
    more

2 *Imagine that you are the manager of the travel agency AirWays and have just received the letter set out in 36A above. Write your own reply in Dutch apologising for the mishaps and explaining why these occurred.*

C

1 *Write an informal letter to a friend asking him/her how s/he is and what s/he has been doing over the last few months. Tell him/her your latest news.*

2 *Write a formal letter to the Nederlands Taalbureau, 1101 HV Amsterdam, asking for information about Dutch summer courses for foreign students. Start by introducing yourself and explain why you are interested in such a course.*

37 LIVE: *leven* or *wonen*?

*Insert the correct forms of **leven** or **wonen** where appropriate:*
1 __ je nog steeds bij je ouders?
2 Hij __ niet meer.
3 Wat een mooi huis! Hier __ jullie erg leuk.
4 Wanneer __ Beethoven?
5 Waar __ Bach?
6 Hij __ alleen voor zijn werk.
7 Wij __ vlakbij de Duitse grens.
8 Eén boterham met kaas iedere dag? Daar
    kan ik niet van __!

38 MAY/MIGHT: Dutch equivalents

A

Translate the following sentences into English:
1 Misschien is dat haar vriendje.
2 Hij wil het misschien met ons vieren.
3 Misschien hebben zij het al verkocht.
4 Zij kunnen nu verhuisd zijn.
5 Jij zou het misschien niet kunnen begrijpen.

B

Make the following sentences less definite by adding words to convey the meanings 'may'/'might':
1 Ik heb ongelijk.
2 Hij is vandaag aangekomen.
3 Dat is de melkboer.
4 Hij heeft zijn vrouw verlaten.
5 Jij hebt het al gehoord.

39 MEAN: *betekenen, bedoelen* or *menen*?

*Insert the correct forms of **betekenen**, **bedoelen** or **menen** where appropriate:*
1 Hij werkt vanavond. Dat __ dat hij niet
    mee kan komen naar het feestje.
2 Ik weet nooit wat hij __.
3 Heb je een woordenboek bij je? Ik weet
    niet wat dit woord __.

4 Ja, ik weet wat je __.
5 Hij ruimt zijn kamer op. Dat __ dat hij
   bezoek krijgt.
6 __ u dat u liever thuis zou blijven?
7 Hij zegt dat hij zijn vrouw haat maar hij __
   het niet echt.

40 Modal verbs

A

Translate the following sentences into Dutch:
1
1 Hij wil iedere avond uitgaan.
2 Wij konden de toiletten niet vinden.
3 Mag ik u iets vragen?
4 Zij moesten hun huis verkopen.

2
1 Wie heeft de rekening moeten betalen?
2 Ik had jou niet willen storen.
3 Wij zullen hem vanavond niet mogen
   bezoeken.
4 Zij zouden op dinsdag niet kunnen
   vertrekken.
5 Een kind had het beter kunnen doen.
6 Ik had niet zoveel geld moeten uitgeven
7 Jij moet het gehoord hebben.

B

1 (i) *Using the appropriate present tense forms of the
modal verbs in capitals, make modal constructions out
of the following sentences:*
EXAMPLE: Jaap woont in Amsterdam.
                                    WILLEN
ANSWER: Jaap **wil** in Amsterdam **wonen**.
1 Jan en Ans reserveren een kamer   WILLEN
2 Telefoneer je hier?   MOGEN
3 De trein komt om acht uur aan   MOETEN
4 Geeft u mij een brochure?   KUNNEN
5 Waar spelen de kinderen?   KUNNEN

(ii) *Take your answers to B1 (i) above and put the
modal verbs into the simple past tense:*
EXAMPLE: Jaap wil in Amsterdam wonen.
ANSWER: Jaap **wilde (wou)** in Amsterdam
   wonen.

2 (i) *Take your answers to B1 (i) above and put the
modal verbs into (a) the future tense, (b) the perfect
tense:*[5]
EXAMPLE: Jaap wil in Amsterdam wonen.
ANSWERS:
(a) Jaap **zal** in Amsterdam **willen wonen**.
(b) Jaap **heeft** in Amsterdam **willen wonen**.

(ii) *Rewrite the following sentences to convey the
meanings (a) 'could have', (b) 'should have' and
translate your answers into English:*
EXAMPLE: Jaap speelt voetbal.
ANSWERS:
(a) Jaap **had** voetbal **kunnen spelen**.
   Jaap could have played football.
(b) Jaap **had** voetbal **moeten spelen**.
   Jaap should have played football.
1 Wij gaan vroeger naar bed.
2 Jij blijft langer.
3 Ik neem de eerste trein om half acht.
4 Zij kopen een goedkopere auto.

(iii) *Rewrite the following sentences, replacing the
simple verbs in bold with modal constructions. Take
care to maintain the original tense:*
EXAMPLE: Jaap speelde voetbal. (willen)
ANSWER: Jaap **wilde** voetbal **spelen**.
1 Ik repareerde het niet. (kunnen)
2 Hij gaf haar duizend gulden. (moeten)
3 Ik vertrek morgen. (willen)
4 Mijn zoon rookt niet. (mogen)
5 Ga je vroeg naar bed? (moeten)
6 Zul je vers brood kopen? (kunnen)
7 De studenten hebben de les niet begrepen.
   (kunnen)
8 De jongen is niet naar school gegaan.
   (willen).

41 *Niet*[6]

A

*Translate the following sentences into English and
explain the position of **niet** in each one:*
1 Hij zag de film vanavond niet.

---

5 For further exercises on modals in the perfect
   tense, ☞ *Word order*, 78B 2(iii).
6 ☞ also *Geen* and related exercises.

2 Ik vond de film niet bijzonder spannend.
3 De trein moet niet vóór tien uur 's morgens
   vertrekken.
4 Ik werk vandaag niet.
5 Ik werk niet vandaag maar morgen.

B

1 *Make the following sentences negative*:
1 Ik rook.
2 Hij is dik.
3 Zij lezen veel.
4 Het staat in de kast.
5 Ik kom woensdag.
6 Hij wast de auto.
7 Zij hebben een auto.

2 (i) *Insert the words in capitals into the appropriate place in the following sentences*:
1 Ging jij graag naar school? Ik.   NIET
2 Heb jij geen geld? Ik.   OOK NIET
3 Hij heeft het gedaan.   NOG NIET
4 Ik heb de man van Annika aardig
   gevonden.   NOOIT
5 Hij heeft een woord gezegd.   NOOIT

(ii) *Insert **niet** into the appropriate place in the following sentences (assuming that no special emphasis is required)*:
1 Jan heeft Jaap sinds vorige maand gezien.
2 Piet heeft twee jaar geleden bij zijn ouders
   gewoond.
3 Er zijn vandaag veel mensen in het café
4 Dat is zijn nieuwe auto.
5 Ik had de vleesgerechten kunnen
   aanbevelen.
6 De leraar kent dit jaar de nieuwe
   schoolkinderen en hun ouders zo goed.
7 Hij komt vanavond met zijn vrouw.
8 Roel gebruikt vandaag de computer die hij
   nu op zijn kantoor heeft.

42 Noun plurals

A

1 (i) *Explain how and/or why the following nouns have or have not changed their spelling after the addition of -**en***:
1 paar – paren   5 geloof – geloven
2 paard – paarden   6 stof – stoffen
3 man – mannen   7 huis – huizen
4 hand – handen   8 bus – bussen

(ii) *Explain why the following forms have -**s** plurals*:
1 deken – dekens   4 lepel – lepels
2 schrijver – schrijvers   5 dame – dames
3 tekenaar – tekenaars   6 oma – oma's

B

1 (i) *Add -**en** or -**s** to the following nouns, changing the spelling where necessary*:
1 student   9 steen
2 studente   10 meisje
3 vogel   11 lerares
4 muis   12 boom
5 prijs   13 tuinier
6 leugenaar   14 bezem
7 brief   15 jas
8 muur   16 vlag

(ii) *Give the singular forms of the following plurals*:
1 boeken   5 benen
2 pennen   6 uien
3 ogen   7 neven
4 neuzen   8 flessen

2 *Give the plural forms of the following nouns*:
1 kind   9 ei
2 opa   10 stad
3 film   11 gat
4 video   12 spel
5 cd   13 weg
6 dag   14 mogelijkheid
7 glas   15 leraar
8 rad   16 zoon

C

Write a shopping list in Dutch including as many plural forms as you can, e.g. TWEE KILO **TOMATEN** *etc.*

43 Nouns derived from other words[7]

A

Translate the following pairs of sentences into English and note the relationship between each adjective/verb and derived noun in bold print:

1 Die leraar is **ervaren**. – Die leraar heeft veel **ervaring**.
2 Anne is steeds **moe**. – Anne lijdt aan **moeheid**.
3 De kast is te **breed**. – Wat is de exacte **breedte** van de kast?
4 De politie kan het niet **bewijzen**. – De politie heeft geen enkel **bewijs**.
5 Zij **giechelen** de hele tijd. – Hij vindt hun stomme **gegiechel** vervelend.

B

Derive nouns from the adjectives and verbs below and give the English translation of each one:
EXAMPLE: vriendelijk 'friendly'
ANSWER: **de vriendelijkheid**
'friendliness'

1 werkelijk	7 verschillen
2 waar	8 brommen
3 hopeloos	9 bonzen
4 aansluiten	10 dik
5 lezen	11 wijd
6 bereiken	12 oppervlakkig

44 Numbers

A

Put the following numbers into figures using the Dutch conventions:

1 zevenentwintig
2 honderdeenenvijftig
3 drieduizendachtentachtig
4 negenhonderdduizend
5 vierduizendzeshonderdvijfendertig

---

7 ☞ also *Adjectives used as nouns, Diminutives, Female endings, Professionals* and related exercises.

6 eenendertigste
7 duizendeerste
8 negenentachtigste
9 tiende
10 honderdderde

B

Write the following numbers out in words:

1 59
2 263
3 1132
4 807,5
5 f 75, 93
6 de 3e keer
7 de 45e student
8 zijn 102e verjaardag
9 1/2 van het huis
10 5/6 van het bedrag

45 Objects: direct and indirect

A

Translate the following sentences into English:
1 Ik zal jou de foto's laten zien.
2 Geef het aan mij.
3 Ik wou jou iets over mezelf vertellen.
4 Hij geeft het aan jou, niet aan hen.
5 Ik heb het aan mijn broer geleend.

B

*Complete the following sentences by adding the indirect object given in capitals below. Insert **aan** and/or change the word order where appropriate:*
EXAMPLE: Ik schrijf een brief. MIJN MOEDER
ANSWER: Ik schrijf een brief **aan mijn moeder**.
(OR Ik schrijf **mijn moeder** een brief).
1 Hij stuurt een kaartje. HAAR
2 Ik heb mijn huiswerk gegeven. DE LERAAR
3 Ik heb het gegeven. HEM
4 Dat behoort. MIJN VRIEND
5 Hij legde het probleem uit. DE STUDENT

46 Passive

A

Translate the following sentences into English:

1
1 Het wordt vaak gezegd.
2 De inbreker werd door de politie gearresteerd.
3 De bruiloft is al georganiseerd.
4 Zij waren al drie keer door hun ouders gewaarschuwd.

2
1 Er werd niets gedaan.
2 Er zal niet meer gevochten worden.
3 Aan mij zijn deze boeken gegeven.
4 Over haar wordt vaak gepraat.

B

1 *Put the following sentences into (a) the present passive, (b) the simple past passive:*
EXAMPLE: Jaap ziet Anne.
ANSWERS:
(a) **Anne wordt door Jaap gezien**.
(present passive)
(b) **Anne werd door Jaap gezien**.
(past passive)
1 De studenten lezen deze boeken.
2 Mijn vader bouwt dit huis.
3 De docent bekritiseert de essays.
4 Iemand doet het.
5 Een goede monteur repareert de auto.
6 Iemand maakt deze koekjes voor ons.

2 (i) *Put sentences 1–6 above into (a) the perfect passive, (b) the pluperfect passive:*
EXAMPLE: Jaap ziet Anne.
ANSWERS:
(a) Anne **is** door Jaap **gezien**.
(perfect passive)
(b) Anne **was** door Jaap **gezien**.
(pluperfect passive)

(ii) *Put the following sentences into the passive, taking care to maintain the original tense:*
EXAMPLE: Een deskundige zal het doen.
(future tense)

ANSWER: **Het zal door een deskundige gedaan worden**. (future passive)
1 Hij zal het feest organiseren.
2 De leraar zal de jongens bestraffen.
3 Veel mensen zullen het boek kopen.
4 Alleen ik zou het doen.
5 Alleen de advocaat zou de brieven lezen.

(iii) *Rewrite the following passive sentences using non-passive constructions to express the same meaning:*
1 Hier wordt Engels gesproken.
2 In Enschede kan Duits geld gebruikt worden.
3 Mijn auto is gestolen.

47 Past tense (simple past)[8]

A

1 *Explain the choice of -te versus -de with the following verbs:*
1 maken – maakte   5 groeien – groeide
2 praten – praatte   6 leggen – legde
3 blaffen – blafte   7 geloven – geloofde
4 missen – miste   8 verbazen – verbaasde

2 *Explain why the past tense has been used in the following sentences instead of the (more commonly used) perfect:*
1 De oude man knipoogte, knikte met het hoofd en glimlachte.
2 Toen ik in Amsterdam woonde en werkte.
3 Toen hij mij opbelde.
4 Zij zei dat zij ongelukkig was.
5 Ik kon en wilde het niet doen.

B

Put the verbs below into the appropriate form of the simple past tense:

1
1 ik werken   7 ik spellen
2 hij tanken   8 jij spelen
3 het kosten   9 wij wassen
4 wij voelen   10 u koken
5 ik schreeuwen   11 jullie wonen
6 hij mompelen   12 wij leven

8 ☞ also *Irregular verbs* and related exercises.

2

1 ik heten	9 wij verhuizen
2 wij haten	10 jullie verven
3 hij zich haasten	11 ik tekenen
4 wij branden	12 hij hervatten
5 ik feliciteren	13 jij aanknopen
6 hij opletten	14 ik afleveren
7 jullie uitvissen	15 hij meelachen
8 wij organiseren	16 u bedoelen

C

1 *Write a short text in Dutch explaining what you did yesterday. Use as many simple past forms as possible,* e.g. IK **LUISTERDE** NAAR DE RADIO etc.

2

Write a short report in Dutch on something that happened in the news yesterday. Try to use as many different types of verb in the simple past tense as you can (i.e. regular verbs, irregular verbs, separable verbs), e.g. DE MINISTER-PRESIDENT **VERMELDDE** GISTEREN DAT HIJ VAN PLAN **WAS** DE INKOMSTENBELASTING TE VERHOGEN. HIJ **LEGDE** UIT DAT etc.

☺☺ **Dialogue**

Fill in the gaps below with the appropriate forms of the past tense:

Max vertelt Geert van zijn sollicitatiegesprek

Geert: Dag, Max. Je hebt toch gisteren je sollicitatiegesprek voor de nieuwe baan gehad? Vertel eens. Hoe was het?

Max: O, het __ (gaan) niet bijzonder goed, __ (vinden) ik. Ten eerste __ (opstaan) ik te laat. Ik __ (zijn) heel moe, omdat ik me zorgen __ (maken) en ik __ (slapen) al een paar nachten niet goed.

Geert: Maar je __ (hoeven) je toch geen zorgen te maken. Je __ (hebben) heel goede kansen, __ (denken) ik.

Max: Ja, maar ik __ (slapen) ook niet goed, omdat de baby vrij veel __ (huilen) en mij vaak wakker __ (maken). Dus ik __ (aankomen) laat en ook heel moe bij het bedrijf.

Geert: __ (zijn) ze boos?

Max: Nee, ik __ (uitleggen) dat ik een kleine baby heb en ze __ (begrijpen) het. Ze __ (lijken) mij heel vriendelijk. Maar ik __ (zijn) boos op mezelf.

Geert: En het gesprek zelf?

Max: Ik __ (kunnen) niet goed inschatten, hoe ze me __ (vinden). De baas __ (stellen) heel moeilijke vragen, die ik zo goed als ik __ (kunnen) __ (beantwoorden) maar hij __ (glimlachen) nauwelijks, wat ik erg ontmoedigend __ (vinden). Ik __ (proberen) me op zijn collega te concentreren want hij __ (lijken) me aardiger. Het hele gesprek __ (duren) een uur en toen __ (moeten) ik nog een half uur met de andere sollicitanten in een wachtkamer zitten. Dat __ (maken) me nog onzekerder want ik __ (horen) ze over hun ervaringen praten, die allemaal heel positief __ (zijn). Ik __ (voelen) me erg slecht. Toen __ (binnenkomen) de secretaresse en __ (zeggen) dat ze ons binnen drie dagen met de beslissing op zou bellen.

48 Perfect tense[9]

A

1 *Explain why some of the following past participles are formed with **ge . . . t** while others have* **ge . . . d** *or no **ge**- prefix at all:*

1 maken – gemaakt	6 verhuizen – verhuisd
2 missen – gemist	7 herhalen – herhaald
3 blaffen – geblaft	8 ontmoeten – ontmoet
4 wonen – gewoond	9 redden – gered
5 leven – geleefd	

2 *Translate the following sentences into English and explain why some of them are formed using **zijn**:*

1 Ik ben naar huis gegaan.
2 Mijn opa is vorig jaar gestorven.
3 Wat ben jij gegroeid!

---

9 For irregular past participles, ☞ *Irregular verbs* and related exercises.

4 Zijn jullie naar Luik gefietst? – Ja, wij hebben vier uur gefietst.

B

*Put the following sentences into the perfect tense (using the correct form of **hebben** plus the past participle):*
EXAMPLE: Jan werkt de hele dag.
ANSWER: Jan **heeft** de hele dag **gewerkt**.
1 (i)
  1 Ik maak een jurk.
  2 Hoe spel je dat?
  3 Hij speelt heel goed gitaar.
  4 Wij wonen in Amsterdam.
  5 Zij organiseren het feestje.
  6 Zij praten niet meer met elkaar.
  7 Wat bedoelt u?
  8 Hij redt de jongen.
  9 Jij verrast me.
 10 Hoor je dat?

(ii) *Fill in the gaps below using the correct form of **hebben** or **zijn** where appropriate:*
 1 Geert __ een lange brief geschreven.
 2 Wij __ vanavond thuis gebleven.
 3 Jullie __ nooit veel geld gehad.
 4 Het __ al gebeurd.
 5 Hij __ nog niet met het werk begonnen.
 6 __ jullie naar Maastricht gevlogen? – Ja, wij __ met KLM gevlogen.

2 *Put the following sentences into the perfect tense:*
 1 Ik vrees het.
 2 Wij verven de slaapkamer.
 3 Hij gaat iedere dag met de bus naar zijn werk.
 4 De kinderen letten in de les nooit op.
 5 Zij komen om vier uur aan.
 6 Ik ben nooit ziek.
 7 De trein vertrekt al.
 8 Wij ontmoeten haar in het café.
 9 Weet je hoe haar man heet? – Ja, maar ik vergeet het.
 10 Rijd je naar Groningen? – Ja ik rijd in mijn nieuwe auto.

C

1 *Write an informal letter to a friend in Dutch explaining what you have done during the last year.*

Use as many perfect tense forms as possible, e.g. IK **HEB** DIT JAAR HEEL VEEL **GESTUDEERD** etc.

2 *Write an informal letter to a friend in Dutch explaining what you have done during the last year. Try to use as many different types of verb in the perfect tense as you can (i.e. regular verbs, irregular verbs, separable verbs), e.g.* IK **HEB** DIT JAAR HEEL HARD **GEWERKT** OMDAT IK EEN NIEUWE BAAN **GEKREGEN HEB**. IK **BEN** BEGIN JANUARI **BEGONNEN** etc.

☺☺ Dialogue
Fill in the gaps below with the appropriate forms of the perfect tense:

Wim vertelt Max van zijn reis

Max: Hallo, Wim! Jou __ ik al heel lang niet __ (zien). Waar __ je __ (zijn)? Je __ toch niet in het ziekenhuis __ (liggen)?

Wim: Hoi, Max! Nee hoor, ik __ eerst een maand in Engeland __ (rondreizen) en daarna __ ik nog een reis __ (maken) naar Ierland. Vorige week __ ik weer __ (terugkomen).

Max: Wat leuk! Welke plaatsen __ je allemaal __ (bezoeken)?

Wim: Oh, te veel om op te noemen. Eerst __ ik naar Londen __ (gaan) waar ik in een sjiek hotel __ __ (overnachten). In die week __ ik vaak __ (uitgaan): naar theaters, musea en de pub, natuurlijk!

Max: __ je ook __ (eten) in het hotel?

Wim: Ja, één keer, want vaker __ ik het niet __ (kunnen) __ (betalen) door de hoge koers van het pond.

Max: Wat __ je nog meer __ (doen)?

Wim: Ik __ naar Schotland __ (vliegen) en __ __ (rondlopen) in de Highlands. Op een rondleiding in Glasgow __ ik een leuk meisje __ (ontmoeten). Zij __ me toen __ (uitnodigen) om naar Ierland te komen met haar. Zij __ daar namelijk tien jaar __ (wonen) en __ me __ (rondleiden) door het prachtige land!

Max: Hoe lang __ je daar __ (blijven)?

Wim: Ik __ vier dagen daar __ (blijven) en toen __ ik op het vliegtuig __ (stappen)

naar Amsterdam. We __ __ (beloven)
elkaar te schrijven.
Max: Dus je __ het wel leuk __ (hebben)?
Wim: Ja, ik __ heel erg __ (genieten).

49 Personal pronouns: I, YOU, HE etc.

A

1 *Translate the following sentences into English:*
1 Kunt u mij helpen?
2 Zij ziet hem iedere dag.
3 Hij geeft haar bloemen.
4 Ben jij klaar?
5 Wonen jullie niet meer bij hen?
6 Zij waren met ons op vakantie.
7 Wij komen met jou mee.
8 Zij is ouder dan hij en ik vind haar
vriendelijker dan hem.

2 *Translate the following sentences into English,
underlining the pronouns which need to be emphasised.
Explain why some of the pronouns in bold print are
stressed while others are unstressed:*
1 Heb **je** mijn oorbellen gezien?
2 Ik kan mijn oorbellen niet vinden. Heb **jij
ze** gezien?
3 **Die** heb ik niet gezien maar hier zijn wat
andere.
4 Zijn ouders? Hij zei dat hij **ze** haatte. – En
wat zeiden **zij**?
5 **We** gaan naar de stad.
6 Jullie kunnen thuis blijven maar **wij** gaan
naar de stad.
7 Hij vertelde **me** dat hij van **mij** hield en
van geen andere vrouw.

B

1 (i) *Fill in the gaps below with the appropriate
stressed personal pronouns:*
1 Wanneer komt Piet? – __ komt om acht
uur.
2 Wat doet Linda? – __ is studente.
3 Waar komt u vandaan? – __ kom uit
Engeland.

4 Waar wonen uw ouders? – __ wonen in
Amerika.
5 Hoe heet jij? – Hanna. En __?
6 Heb jij met Theo gepraat? – Ja, __ heb __
net opgebeld.
7 Heb jij Annika gezien? – Ja, maar __ heb
niet met __ gepraat.
8 Wanneer komt Theo jou ophalen? – __
komt __ om acht uur ophalen.
9 Hoe gaat het met u? – Goed. En met __?
10 Kan een van jullie Jan en Erica opbellen?
– Nee, dat kunnen __ niet doen want __
hebben __ hun nummer niet gegeven.

(ii)
1 Wil __ niet meer met __ werken?
                    YOU (informal sg.), ME
2 Denkt __ dat __ gelukkig zijn?
                    YOU (polite sg.), THEY
3 __ kunnen __ morgen bezoeken   WE, THEM
4 __ zal __ mijn adres geven   I, THEM
5 __ wil met __ praten
                    SHE, YOU (informal sg.)

(iii) *Take your answers to B1 (i) and (ii) above and
replace the stressed pronouns with the corresponding
unstressed forms where possible. Only give the
unstressed forms which are used both in speech AND
in writing.*

2 (i) *Fill in the gaps below with the correct personal
pronouns. Use the forms appropriate to spoken/less
formal written Dutch (i.e. unstressed pronouns as the
norm, stressed pronouns where a contrast/emphasis is
required):*
1 Ga __ naar de vergadering? – Nee, ga __ ?
                    YOU, YOU (both informal sg.)
2 Ik vind __ aardig. – Ik vind __ ook aardig.
                    YOU, YOU (both informal sg.)
3 Ik wil met __ praten. – Met __?
                    YOU (informal sg.), ME
4 __ kunnen langer blijven maar __ gaan
naar huis.   YOU (informal pl.), WE
5 Ik ga met __, __ en __.
                    YOU (informal sg.), HIM, HER
6 Kunt __ __ morgen opbellen?
                    YOU (polite sg.), ME
7 __ zijn vorig jaar naar Spanje gegaan. – O,
__ waren er ook.   WE, WE

8 Wat hebben __ gezegd? – __ hebben niets
gezegd. Hun advocaat heeft voor __
gepraat.' THEY, THEY, THEM

(ii) *Insert the correct translation of 'it', 'they' and 'them' into the gaps below*:

1 Deze wijn is uitstekend. – Ja, __ was erg
duur. IT
2 Is het raam open? – Nee, ik heb __
dichtgedaan. IT
3 Wat staat in de brief? – Ik heb __ nog niet
gelezen. IT
4 Ik heb koekjes gebakken en __ zijn lekker.
THEY
5 __ zijn heel goede appels. THEY
6 Hoe was de film? __ was heel goed. IT
7 __ is een oude film maar ik ken __ niet.
IT, IT
8 Wat doe je met die kussens? – Ik zit __ op.
THEM

☺☺ **Dialogue**
Fill in the gaps below with the appropriate personal pronouns. Use unstressed pronouns as the norm and stressed forms only where necessary:

Hanna ontmoet haar vriendin Erica op straat

Hanna: Dag, Erica. Hoe gaat het met __?
Erica: Goed. En met __ ?
Hanna: Ook goed. Waar ga __ naartoe?
Erica: Naar de markt. En __?
Hanna: __ ga ook naar de markt. __ kunnen
er samen naar toe gaan.
Erica: Ok! Maar __ moeten even op Linda
wachten. __ heb __ gisteren gezegd dat __
vandaag naar de markt wou en __ zei dat
__ ook mee wou gaan.
Hanna: Goed. Waar moeten __ op __
wachten?
Erica: Bij de bushalte.
Hanna: O, gaan __ met de bus?
Erica: Ja. __ weet niet zeker wanneer __ komt,
maar __ kunnen __ op wachten en als het
te laat wordt, gaan __ gewoon lopen. __ is
niet zo ver.
Hanna: Goed. Hoe gaat het trouwens met
Linda's man?
Erica: Veel beter. Ik heb __ gisteren gezien en

__ heeft __ verteld dat __ twee weken
geleden naar drie verschillende artsen
gegaan is maar __ wisten niet wat __ had.
Maar een week later voelde __ zich sowieso
veel beter.
Hanna: O, daar is Linda. Hallo ......

50 Pluperfect tense

A

Translate the following sentences into English:
1 Ik had met mijn baas getelefoneerd.
2 De voorstelling was om half acht
begonnen.
3 Wij hadden een taxi besteld.
4 Onze buurman was al drie keer verhuisd.
5 Wij waren al aangekomen.

B

*Go to Exercises **48B** above (Perfect tense) and put all the sentences in **B1** and **B2** into the pluperfect*:
EXAMPLE: **B1** (i) Jan werkt de hele dag.
ANSWER: Jan **had** de hele dag
gewerkt.

EXAMPLE: **B1** (ii) Geert __ een lange brief
geschreven.
ANSWER: Geert **had** een lange
brief **geschreven**.

EXAMPLE: **B2** ik vrees het.
ANSWER: ik **had** het **gevreesd**.

51 Possession

A

Translate the following sentences into English:
1 Dat is de baas van mijn man.
2 Hier is ons huis. Het hare staat er
tegenover.
3 Onze kamer is groot maar die van Jaap is
nog groter.
4 Mijn auto staat in de garage. Mag ik de
jouwe even nemen?

B

1 *Make possessive sentences out of the following phrases:*

EXAMPLE: Jaap – de handschoenen.

ANSWERS: Jaap**s** handschoenen *or* de handschoenen **van** Jaap.

1 Meneer Zuidema – de zoon.
2 Mevrouw de Wit – de bloemen.
3 Geert – de hond – de spitse tanden.
4 De oude man – het geld.
5 De kinderen – het speelgoed.
6 Ik – de nieuwe jas.
7 Jij – de vrouw.
8 Frits – de vrienden.

2 (i) *Fill in the gaps below with the appropriate translation of 'mine', 'yours', 'his' etc.:*

1 Van wie is dit bier? Het is van __.   MINE
2 En die wijn? – Dat is de __.
                      YOURS (informal sg.)
3 Zijn die spullen van __?
                      YOURS (informal sg.)
4 Mijn jurk is mooier dan de __.   HERS
5 Als de jouwe kapot is, neem dan maar de __.   MINE

(ii) *Answer the questions below by translating the sentences in capitals. Take particular care with the translation of 'it' and 'they':*

EXAMPLE: Is dat jouw computer?
                         NO, IT IS HIS

ANSWERS: Nee, **het** is **de zijne**. OR
          Nee, **hij** is van **hem**.

1 Is dat Geerts kamer?   NO, IT IS MINE.
2 Is dat het adres van de huisbaas?
                       NO, IT IS OURS.
3 Zijn deze boeken van hem?
                  NO, THEY ARE HERS.
4 Van wie zijn deze flessen?
           THEY ARE YOURS (informal pl.).
5 Van wie is dit potlood?
          IT IS NOT MINE. MINE IS RED.
6 Zijn mijn voeten groter dan zijn voeten?
          YES, YOURS (informal sg.)
          ARE BIGGER THAN HIS.

52 Possessive pronouns

A

Translate the following sentences into English:
1 Drink je koffie op!
2 Zij heeft problemen met haar baas.
3 Hij heeft zijn vrienden en zijn familie uitgenodigd.
4 Wat doen jullie in je vrije tijd?
5 Is dit mijn boek of jouw boek?

B

1 *Fill in the gaps below with the appropriate Dutch possessive pronouns:*
1 __ buurvrouw komt met __ zoon.   MY, HER
2 De studenten hebben __ huiswerk niet gedaan.   THEIR
3 Dit is __ vriend Max en __ vrouw Anita.
                      OUR, HIS
4 Hier is __ nieuwe adres.   OUR
5 Hoe gaat het met __ moeder?
                  YOUR (polite sg.)
6 Hoe gaat het met __ kinderen?
               YOUR (informal pl.)
7 Hebben jullie problemen met __ auto?
               YOUR (informal pl.)
8 Heeft u __ arm gebroken? Nee, __ pols.
               YOUR, MY

2 *Fill in the gaps below with either the stressed or the unstressed form of the second person singular pronoun where appropriate:*
1 Knoop __ jas dicht!   YOUR (informal sg.)
2 __ jas is niet zo warm als die van mij.
               YOUR (informal sg.)
3 Let op __ hoofd!   YOUR (informal sg.)
4 Dat is __ probleem, niet het mijne.
               YOUR (informal sg.)

53 Prepositions

A

Translate the following sentences into English and note that there is often no direct one-to-one correspondence between English and Dutch prepositions:

1 Wat doe jij in het weekend?
2 Hij was boos op mij want ik had om een sigaret gevraagd.
3 Op het feest praatte ik met veel mensen over de Europese Unie.
4 Weten zij van het ongeluk?
5 Je kunt op die arts rekenen want hij zorgt voor zijn patiënten.
6 Zij is verliefd op haar baas en wil met hem trouwen.
7 Waar is de krant? Zit jij erop?[10]
8 Dit potlood is stomp. Ik kan er niet mee schrijven.

B

1 *Insert the appropriate Dutch prepositions into the gaps below and translate each sentence into English*:

1 De krant ligt __ de grond.
2 Ik wacht __ jou.
3 Mijn zoon speelt __ de buurjongen.
4 Mijn man praat __ de buurman.
5 Woont hij __ zijn ouders?
6 Ik werk __ C&A.
7 Studeert zij __ de universiteit of zit zij nog __ school?
8 Zij gaan __ Amerika.

2 *Fill in the gaps below with the correct translations of the prepositions in capitals*:

1 We hebben elkaar __ drie uur __ de kapper ontmoet.   AT
2 Ga je __ de bus of __ de trein?   BY
3 Ik kom __ Engeland. Waar kom jij __?
                                             FROM
4 Ik bleef __ een dag in Jerez en ging toen __ een week naar Cadiz.   FOR
5 De les begint __ tien minuten.   IN
6 Ze heeft twee klokken: één __ de plank en één __ de muur.   ON
7 Ik schrijf __ mijn vriend die __ Duitsland verhuisd is.   TO
8 Wat doe je __ Kerstmis?   AT

---

10 ☞ *Er* and related exercises.

☺☺ **Dialogue**

☺☺ **Dialogue**
Fill in the gaps below with the appropriate prepositions:

In het park

Max: Dag, Geert!
Geert: Hoi, Max!
Max: Wat doe jij hier?
Geert: Ik wacht __ mijn vriendin. En jij?
Max: Ik ben __ de weg __ mijn werk. Ik loop altijd __ het park omdat de weg korter is.
Geert: Maar het is vrij laat. Wat zijn je werktijden?
Max: __ tien __ half zes. Oh, hartelijk gefeliciteerd __ je verjaardag, trouwens.
Geert: Ja, bedankt! Mijn vriendin zou me __ negen uur ontmoeten maar nu is het al __ half tien. Ik wacht dus meer dan een half uur. En uitgerekend __ mijn verjaardag!
Max: Sinds wanneer heb je een vriendin? Daar wist ik niets __.
Geert: __ februari. Je hebt al __ haar __ de telefoon gepraat.
Max: Oh, je bedoelt de vrouw die __ Scheveningen komt. Ik heb ook een foto __ haar gezien. __ mij heeft ze geen gebrek __ charme. Wat leuk __ je!
Geert: Ja, maar __ het feit dat ze erg mooi is, ga ik, denk ik, niet __ haar trouwen. Ze komt altijd te laat __ onze afspraakjes. Ik kan niet __ haar rekenen!

54 Present participles

A

Translate the following sentences into English:

1 Mijn werk is heel vermoeiend.
2 Ik heb een vliegende schotel gezien.
3 Het is een erg ontroerende film.
4 Hij schudde zuchtend het hoofd.
5 Hij reed zingend naar zijn werk

B

Give the present participles of the verbs below:

1 spelen   2 groeien

3 dromen   6 doen
4 slapen   7 gaan
5 inkomen   8 uitgaan

55 Present tense[11]

A

1 *Explain how and / or why the following verbs have or have not changed their spelling in the present tense*:
1 wonen – ik woon   4 gaan – ik ga
2 worden – ik word   5 geloven – ik geloof
3 wassen – ik was   6 lezen – ik lees

2 *Translate the following sentences into English and note the different uses of the present tense*:
1 Woon jij in Amsterdam?
2 Hij geeft haar iedere dag bloemen.
3 Hij komt morgen aan.
4 Ik werk al zes maanden aan dit boek.
5 Hoe lang ben je al getrouwd?

B

1 (i) *Put the verbs below into the appropriate form of the present tense*:
1 ik werken   7 ik spellen
2 jij tanken   8 jij spelen
3 het kosten   9 hij wassen
4 voelen jij?   10 koken jij?
5 ik schreeuwen   11 jullie wonen
6 hij mompelen   12 hij leven

(ii) *Replace the subjects in bold print with those in brackets and change the verb form if necessary*:
1 **Wij** dromen van een groot huis op het land. (Mijn vader).
2 **Ik** geef hem honderd gulden per week. (De huurders).
3 Gaat **u** naar de stad? (Jij).
4 **Ik** laat de kat uit. (Mijn man).
5 Praat **hij** met de buurman? (Theo en Annika).
6 **Hij** leest de krant niet meer (De studenten).

---

11 For irregular present forms, ☞ *Irregular verbs*, 33.1.

2 (i) *Put the verbs below into the appropriate form of the present tense*:
1 ik heten   9 hij verhuizen
2 wij haten   10 jij verven
3 hij zich haasten 11 ik tekenen
4 u zenden   12 hij hervatten
5 ik feliciteren   13 jij aanknopen
6 jij opletten   14 ik afleveren
7 hij uitvinden   15 wij meelachen
8 organiseren jij? 16 u bedoelen

(ii) *IRREGULAR VERBS: Replace the subjects in bold print with those in brackets and change the verb form if necessary*:
1 **Wij** komen om vier uur aan. (Mijn broer).
2 **Ik** ben te moe. (De kinderen).
3 Zal **hij** een kamer nodig hebben? (Meneer en mevrouw van Lenthe).
4 **Wij** hebben geen tijd. (Mijn man).
5 **Wim** is een goede vriend van Theo (Jij).

C

1 *Write a short text in Dutch describing your daily routine. Use as many present tense forms as possible, e.g.* IK **MAAK** EEN POT THEE EN **LEES** DE KRANT etc.

2 *Write a short text in Dutch describing your daily routine. Use as many different types of verb in the present tense as possible (e.g. regular verbs, irregular verbs, separable verbs), e.g.* IK **STA** OM ACHT UUR **OP**, **MAAK** EEN POT THEE etc.

☺☺ Dialogue

Fill in the gaps below with the appropriate forms of the present tense:

Max telefoneert met zijn vriend Geert

Geert: Geert Vismans.
Max: Dag, Geert, met Max. Hoe __ (gaan) het met je?
Geert: Dag, Max. Heel goed. __ (komen) je vanavond langs?
Max: Nee. Ik __ (kunnen) niet. Daarom __ (opbellen) ik je. Ik __ (moeten) thuisblijven want Hanna __ (zijn) ziek. Ze __ griep en __ (liggen) in bed. De kinderen __ (hebben) tot acht uur hun muziekles en dan __ (ophalen) ik ze.

Geert: Wat jammer! Misschien __ (kunnen) we volgende week naar een voetbalwedstrijd gaan. Ajax __ (spelen) tegen PSV. Ik __ (weten) niet precies op welke dag ze __ (spelen) maar mijn collega Piet __ (weten) het zeker. Ik __ (vragen) hem morgen en dan __ (opbellen) ik je.

Max: Fijn! Dan __ (doen) we dat. Je __ (weten) dat ik heel graag naar het voetbal __ (gaan). Ik __ (hopen) dat wij nog kaartjes __ (krijgen).

Geert: O ja. Je __ (hoeven) je geen zorgen te maken. Okee, Max, tot volgende week. __ (doen) je de groeten aan Hanna voor me?

Max: Ja, zal ik doen. Dag, Geert.

56 Professions

From the verbs and nouns below, derive the names of the corresponding professions and give the English translation of each one:

1 onderwijzen
2 schrijven
3 schoonmaken
4 fiets
5 voetbal
6 vis
7 leren
8 organiseren
9 examineren
10 fluit
11 gitaar
12 tuin

57 Progressive forms

A

Translate the following sentences into English using progressive forms where appropriate:

1 Ik keek naar de tv toen hij binnenkwam.
2 Waaraan denk je?
3 Wat doe je vanavond? – Ik ga naar de bioscoop.
4 Ik word moe van al dit werk.
5 Het ontbijt is klaar! – Ja, ik kom!

B

Rewrite the following sentences, stressing the progressive aspect:
EXAMPLE: Ik werk nog.

ANSWER: **Ik ben nog aan het werken.**

1 Hij wast zijn auto.
2 Zij verhuizen.
3 Lees jij nog?
4 Zij wacht op de bus.
5 Wacht even! Wij eten nog.

58 Pronunciation

A

Say whether the following pairs of Dutch words rhyme:

1 laat – maat
2 kaas – jas
3 mij – zei
4 fijn – been
5 tien – steen
6 koud – gauw
7 koud – uit
8 muis – huis
9 duur – doen
10 doe – deur
11 zoon – boom
12 wijk – lelijk

B

1 (i) *Pronounce the following pairs of words and ask either your teacher or a Dutch native speaker to correct your pronunciation. If possible, record yourself on tape:*

1 pit – dit
2 heb – hebben
3 oud – oude
4 pek – pech
5 sok – schok
6 ga – ja
7 sjaal – tja
8 vol – wol
9 rood – door
10 relatie – geven
11 kap – kaap
12 pen – peen
13 pot – poot
14 zin – zien
15 zender – pittig
16 Rus – reus
17 moer – muur
18 blijven – bleven
19 trouw – trui
20 draai – gooi

(ii) *Show where the main stress falls on each of the words below by underlining the stressed vowel:*

1 regenen
2 knipogen
3 herkennen
4 opgeven
5 onderwijzeres
6 meespelen
7 verhongeren
8 leraar
9 kokkin
10 afstappen
11 kruidenier
12 organiseren
13 kinderen
14 diamant
15 instituut
16 lopen
17 hardlopen
18 studententijd
19 beweging
20 muziekkritiek

2 *The following sounds usually present problems for English speakers of Dutch. Pronounce each sentence five times and ask your teacher or a Dutch native speaker to correct you. If possible, record yourself on tape:*

1 *g/ch*: Iedere da**g** s**ch**rikken de s**ch**oonmakers van de **g**ekke vo**g**el.

2 *r*: **R**einie**r r**eed **R**oos in zijn **r**ode auto **r**ond.

3 *a* vs. *aa*: V**a**nd**aa**g g**aa**t de m**a**n n**aa**r de st**a**d.

4 *u*: Je k**u**nt r**u**stig met h**u**n z**u**s in de b**u**s zitten.

5 *eu*: De kl**eu**r van de d**eu**r is r**eu**ze!

6 *uu*: R**uu**d d**u**wde de d**u**re deur tegen de m**uu**r.

7 *ij*: H**ij** z**ei** tegen m**ij** dat z**ij** kl**ei**n l**ij**kt.

8 *ui*: In de t**ui**n achter het h**ui**s zit een m**ui**s.

59 PUT: Dutch equivalents

1 *Insert the appropriate Dutch equivalent of English* **put** *into the gaps below and translate each sentence into English. Use the present tense throughout:*

1 Hij __ altijd ketchup op zijn pataat.
2 Ik __ de kleren in de wasautomaat.
3 Zij __ het kopje op het schoteltje.
4 Hij __ melk in zijn koffie.
5 Hij __ de brief in de brievenbus.

2 *Insert the appropriate Dutch equivalent of English* **put** *into the gaps below and translate each sentence into English. Take care to use the appropriate tense forms:*

1 __ de papieren op mijn bureau, alsjeblieft.
2 Ik heb het op de lijst __.
3 Kun je de koekjes op het bord __?
4 Ik heb het kaartje in mijn jaszak __.
5 Heb je de baby in bed __?

60 Question words: WHO?, WHAT?, WHERE? etc.

A

Translate the following sentences into English:
1 Op welke verdieping is de herenkleding?
2 Met wie spreekt hij?
3 Van wie is dat geld?
4 Wat wil hij?
5 Waaraan denk jij?
6 Hoe werkt die automaat?

B

Fill in the gaps below with the correct translation of the question words in capitals:
1 __ boek heb jij nodig en __? WHICH?, WHEN?
2 Geef mij de fles. – __ fles? WHICH?
3 __ van die auto's is van hem? WHICH (ONE)?
4 __ van jouw vrienden heeft kinderen? WHICH (ONE)?
5 __ is de melk? WHERE?
6 __ voor bier heb jij thuis? WHAT?
7 __ gaat de film over? WHAT?
8 __ speel jij mee? WHAT?

C

Imagine that you are preparing to interview someone. Make a list of questions in Dutch which you could ask. Include as many question words as possible, e.g. HOE HEET U? WAAR KOMT U VANDAAN? *etc.*

61 Reflexive verbs

A

*Translate the following sentences into English and explain why some of the reflexive pronouns in bold print end in -**zelf** while others do not:*
1 Ik verheug **me** op vanavond.
2 Wij vroegen **ons** af of het de moeite waard was.
3 Wij weten heel weinig van **onszelf**.
4 Zij waste de baby en toen **zichzelf**.
5 Jij denkt altijd aan **jezelf**.

B

1 *Replace the subjects in bold print with those given in brackets and change the reflexive pronouns and verb forms where necessary:*
EXAMPLE: **Ik** was me. (mijn broer)
ANSWER: **Mijn broer wast zich**.
1 **Zij** kleden zich uit. (ik)
2 **Mijn vader** ergert zich te veel (jij)
3 **De kinderen** vervelen zich. (wij)
4 **Ik** herinner me het verhaal niet zo goed. (Geert en Ruud)
5 **Ik** had heimwee, maar ik heb me snel aangepast aan het land. (mijn zusje, zij)

2 *Insert the appropriate reflexive pronouns into the gaps below:*
1 Je moet __ schamen!
2 Sorry, hoor, ik heb __ vergist.
3 Hij haast __ naar de deur.
4 Hebben jullie __ op het feest geamuseerd?
5 Zij hebben __ heel slecht gedragen.
6 Waarom bent u laat? Heeft u __ verslapen?
7 Wij voelen __ hier thuis.
8 Stel __ voor dat je erg rijk bent.
9 Was je kleren en dan __ !
10 Hij moest eerst zijn vrouw en toen __ verdedigen.

62 Relative pronouns

A

Translate the following sentences into English and explain the choice of relative pronoun in each case:
1 Ik ontmoet een vriend **die** met mij werkt.
2 Ik wil geen kind **dat** steeds huilt.
3 Dit is de buurman van **wie** ik de auto repareer.
4 Dat is Jan, met **wie** ik voetbal speel.
5 Dit is de computer **waar** ik mee werk.

B

1 (i) *Rewrite the following sentences using relative pronouns to refer to the nouns in captials below.*

Remember that these pronouns send the verb to the end of the clause:
EXAMPLE: De MAN wacht op de bus.
ANSWER: De man **die** op de bus **wacht**.
1 Mijn VRIEND studeert Engels.
2 De KOFFIE is koud.
3 Het HUIS staat leeg.
4 Het MEISJE woont tegenover mij.
5 De MEISJES spelen met hun poppen.

(ii) *Make relative constructions out of the phrases in capitals below, changing the word order where necessary:*
EXAMPLE: De man wacht OP DE BUS.
ANSWER: De bus **waarop** de man wacht (*or* De bus **waar** de man **op** wacht).
1 Mijn broer denkt AAN HET PROBLEEM.
2 Ik kijk NAAR HET PROGRAMMA.
3 De sleutels zitten IN DE JASZAK.
4 De jongen speelt MET DE BAL.

2 (i) *Rewrite the following sentences using relative pronouns to refer to the nouns in capitals below. Remember that these pronouns send the verb to the end of the clause:*
EXAMPLE: Ik heb het BOEK gelezen.
ANSWER: Het boek **dat** ik gelezen **heb**.
1 Ik heb de WIJN gedronken.
2 De jongens hebben het RAAM gebroken.
3 Hij gaat met het MEISJE naar school.
4 Ik heb vorige week KLEREN gekocht.
5 Het brood is heel goedkoop van de BAKKER.
6 Mijn zoon is bang voor de LERAAR.
7 Mijn dochter zit in de KLAS.
8 Hij wil niet op de STOEL zitten.

(ii) *Fill in the gaps below with the appropriate relative pronoun and translate each sentence into English:*
1 Ik kom zo. Ik moet eerst telefoneren, __ niet lang duurt.
2 Hij is voor zijn examens geslaagd, __ heel goed voor hem is.
3 De slager had niets __ ik wou.

63 SAME: Dutch equivalents

*Insert **dezelfde** or **hetzelfde** into the gaps below where appropriate*:

1 Ik heb __ broek als jij.
2 Het leven is niet meer __.
3 Zijn dat __ bloemen?
4 Is dat __ winkel? Ja, het is __.
5 Hij ging om acht uur en ik deed __.
6 Zij wonen in __ gebouw maar niet in __ flat.

64 Separable verbs

1 *Make sentences out of the following phrases by inserting the verbs in capitals below into the appropriate places. Use the present tense throughout*:
EXAMPLE: Jan, zijn broer.   OPBELLEN
ANSWER: Jan **belt** zijn broer **op**.

1 De trein, om acht uur.   AANKOMEN
2 De muizen, van de kat.   WEGLOPEN
3 Geert, liever.   THUISBLIJVEN
4 Ik, het geld, aan mijn vriend.   TERUGGEVEN
5 Wanneer, hij, de wasautomaat?
          AFLEVEREN
6 Hij, zijn nieuwe vriendin, aan zijn moeder.
          VOORSTELLEN
7 Annika, haar baan.   OPGEVEN
8 Jan, de kat.   UITLATEN

2 (i) *Take your answers to 1 above and put each verb into the perfect tense*:
EXAMPLE: Jan belt zijn broer op.
ANSWER: Jan **heeft** zijn broer **opgebeld**.

(ii) *Rewrite the following sentences by introducing each one with **ik heb geen tijd** followed by an **om . . . te** construction*:
EXAMPLE: Ik bel jou op.
ANSWER: **Ik heb geen tijd om** jou **op te bellen**.

1 Ik kom binnen.
2 Ik ga 's avonds uit.
3 Ik speel met hem mee.
4 Ik lees het hele boek door.
5 Ik ga naar mijn kantoor terug.

(iii) *Derive as many verbs as you can from the following verbs using separable prefixes and translate your answers into English*:

1 ademen   3 denken
2 werken   4 spreken

65 Spelling

A

1 *Explain how and/or why the following adjectives have or have not changed their spelling after the addition of the ending -**e***:

1 groot – grote   4 hard – harde
2 grootst – grootste   5 braaf – brave
3 nat – natte   6 laf – laffe

2 *Explain how and/or why the following nouns have or have not changed their spelling after the addition of the plural ending -**en***:

1 prijs – prijzen   3 bel – bellen
2 vis – vissen   4 wortel – wortelen

B

1 (i) *Add the plural ending -**en** to the following nouns and change the spelling where necessary*:

1 smak   9 graaf
2 smaak   10 neef
3 woord   11 rij
4 neus   12 baas
5 temperatuur   13 das
6 kop   14 vel
7 soep   15 middel
8 ui   16 ster

(ii) *Add the comparative ending -**er** to the following adjectives and change the spelling where necessary*:

1 hoog   5 los
2 oud   6 braaf
3 laag   7 laf
4 boos   8 wijs

2 (i) *Give the singular form of the following plural nouns and change the spelling where necessary*:

1 benen   5 sokken
2 beelden   6 dozen
3 tomaten   7 muizen
4 druiven   8 ogen

(ii) *Give the first person singular* (ik) *form of the following verbs and change the spelling where necessary*:

1 kopen	5 spelen
2 haten	6 spellen
3 zich haasten	7 vrezen
4 geloven	8 wassen

66 SUCH (A): Dutch equivalents

Insert **zo'n** *or* **zulk(e)** *into the gaps below where appropriate and translate each sentence into English*:
1 __ grote man heb ik nooit gezien.
2 __ muziek heb ik nooit gehoord.
3 Hij praat nooit over __ dingen.
4 Ik wou graag __ hoed.
5 Zij wil met __ mensen niets te maken hebben.
6 Het is __ mooie dag.
7 Ik ben niet in __ verhalen geïnteresseerd.
8 Hij vindt __ eten te scherp.

67 Superlatives

A

Translate the following sentences into English:
1 Hij heeft de grootste auto maar ik heb de snelste.
2 Deze aardbeien zijn goed maar die zijn de allerbeste.
3 Zij was de meest cynische van de groep.
4 Kees drinkt het meest.
5 Wanneer was hij het gelukkigst?

B

1 *Give the superlative forms of the following Dutch adjectives*:

1 hoog	7 succesvol
2 zwaar	8 praktisch
3 vies	9 belangrijk
4 goed	10 echt
5 wit	11 oppervlakkig
6 wijs	12 tragisch

2 (i) *Complete the following sentences using superlatives*:
EXAMPLE: Hanna is de __ vrouw die ik ken. (mooi).
ANSWER: Hanna is de **mooiste** vrouw die ik ken.
1 Dat was de __ film die ik ooit gezien heb. (spannend).
2 Dit is het __ restaurant van de stad. (fijn).
3 Het zijn de __ kinderen van die groep. (braaf).
4 Haar man praat steeds het __. (hard).

(ii) *Complete the following sentences using superlatives preceded by* **de** *or* **het** *where appropriate*:
EXAMPLE: Jan is **groot** maar ik ben __ __.
ANSWER: Jan is **groot** maar ik ben **de grootste**.
1 Mijn kinderen zijn allebei **lui** maar mijn zoon is __ __.
2 De koffie is **lekker**. Ja, dit merk is __ __.
3 Dit café is **goedkoop** maar dat van gisteren was __ __.
4 Mijn collega's zijn allemaal **aardig** maar mevrouw Dijkstra is __ __.
5 Jan werkt **weinig** maar zijn vriend Geert werkt __ __.
6 Het is **goed** dat jij vanavond komt. Ja, maar __ __ is dat ik overnachten kan.

68 THEN: Dutch equivalents

Insert **dan** *or* **toen** *into the gaps below where appropriate and translate each sentence into English*:
1 Hij gaat naar Frankrijk en __ naar Spanje.
2 Ik had __ geen geld.
3 __ zag ik hem op de grond liggen.
4 Als dat gebeurt, wat doe je __?
5 Wat heeft hij __ gedaan?
6 Ik had hem __ niet aardig gevonden.
7 Hij nam haar bij de hand. – En __?
8 Bel mij eerst op en __ haal ik jou op.
9 Wij zullen elkaar eerst in de stad ontmoeten en __ samen naar het café gaan.
10 Zij wachtten vijf minuten en __ kwam de bus.

69 Time

A

Translate the following sentences into English:
1 Het is tien voor twaalf.
2 Komt hij om half vier of om half vijf?
3 Hij komt over twee uur aan.
4 De trein is al vertrokken. Het is fijf over tien.
5 Hoe laat is het? – Het is vijf over half elf.
6 Ik wacht tot tien voor half twaalf.

B

1 *Write out the following times in Dutch:*

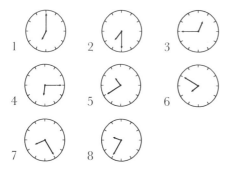

2 *Replace the numbers/phrases in brackets with the appropriate Dutch equivalent:*
1 De film begint (at 8.00 precisely).
2 Zij belde mij (at about 9) op.
3 Zij kwamen (around 2.30 a.m.) thuis.
4 Zij gingen (10 minutes ago) uit.
5 De bus komt (on the hour) en de tram komt (on the half hour).
6 Hij komt mij (in a quarter of an hour) ophalen.
7 Zij gaat (twice a week) zwemmen.
8 De trein vertrekt (at 18.47).

C

Write a short text in Dutch describing your daily routine using as many expressions of time as possible, e.g. IK STA ’S MORGENS OM ACHT UUR OP *etc.*

70 *Toch*

*Insert **toch** into the appropriate places in the sentences below and translate each one into English:*
1 Dat heeft u zelf gemaakt?
2 Hier kan hij niet slapen!
3 Hij verdient veel meer geld dan ik. – Ja, maar hij is de baas.
4 Waar kan hij zijn?
5 Zeg het!
6 Ik heb het erg druk maar wij ontmoeten elkaar een keer per week.
7 Ik weet dat hij vervelend is maar hij is mijn vriend.
8 Maar hij werkt niet meer?
9 Dat kun je niet doen!
10 Geef hem een kans!

71 UNDERSTAND: begrijpen or verstaan?

*Insert the correct forms of **begrijpen** or **verstaan** where appropriate:*
1 __ u de uitleg?
2 Kunt u wat luider spreken? Ik __ u slecht.
3 Ik __ niet hoe deze telefoon werkt.
4 Hij heeft zo'n sterk Haags accent. Ik __ hem helemaal niet.
5 Ik heb de sleutels op tafel laten liggen maar nu zijn ze weg. Ik __ het niet.
6 Wij __ niet waarom hij zo'n goede baan op wil geven.

72 USED TO: Dutch equivalents

Fill in the gaps below with the appropriate Dutch expression to render 'used to' and translate each sentence into English:
1 Het leven is niet meer wat het __ was.
2 Ik was __ veel dunner.
3 Wij gingen __ naar de opera.
4 Ik __ iedere morgen om zeven uur op __ staan. (*very formal*)
5 Hij was __ tandarts maar nu is hij gepensioneerd.

73 Verbs: summary of tenses[12]

A

Translate the following sentences into English:
1 Wij zullen niet klaar zijn.
2 Hij heeft nooit schaak gespeeld.
3 Het regende toen zij het huis verlieten.
4 Ik zal de brief geschreven hebben.
5 Ik zou hem niet herkend hebben.
6 Jij gelooft mij niet.
7 Zij waren te lang gebleven.
8 Ben je gisteravond uitgegaan?

B

1 *Put the following verbs into the appropriate form of (a) the present, (b) the simple past, (c) the future and (d) the conditional*:
1 ik WONEN   4 jij VINDEN
2 hij LEVEN   5 ik LEZEN
3 wij PRATEN   6 wij HOPEN

2 (i) *Put the following verbs into the appropriate form of (a) the perfect, (b) the pluperfect, (c) the future perfect and (d) the conditional perfect*:
1 ik DOEN   4 jij ZIJN
2 hij KOMEN   5 wij OPBELLEN
3 ik STUDEREN   6 hij ZICH
                                   VERGISSEN

(ii) *Put the following sentences into the tenses given in brackets*:
EXAMPLE: Jan werkt bij de bank. (simple past)
ANSWER: Jan **werkte** bij de bank.
 1 Ik wacht op jou. (simple past)
 2 Hij zegt niet veel. (perfect)
 3 Wij zijn op 27 februari verhuisd. (present)
 4 Zij praatten niet meer met elkaar. (present)
 5 Theo studeert Engels. (pluperfect)
 6 Zou u een cheque accepteren? (simple past)
 7 Ben jij langer gebleven? (present)

8 Ik stuur het op een floppydisk. (future)
9 Hij betaalt per creditcard. (conditional)
10 De toeristen wisselen meer geld. (conditional perfect)

74 Verbs derived from other words

1 *Derive verbs from the following nouns and translate your answers into English*:
1 boek   4 email
2 kop   5 station
3 school   6 detail

2 (i) ☞ *Exercises 32.2 for verb derivation with inseparable prefixes.*
(ii) ☞ *Exercises 64.2(iii) for verb derivation with separable prefixes.*

75 Verbs of position: *staan, liggen* and *zitten*

1 *Insert staan, liggen or zitten (present tense) into the gaps below where appropriate and translate each sentence into English*:
1 Waar zijn de papieren? – Ze __ op mijn bureau.
2 Wat __ er op de lijst?
3 Er __ een reep chocolade in jouw handtasje.
4 Er __ twee bomen in onze tuin.
5 De brieven __ op de grond.

2 *Insert staan, liggen or zitten into the gaps below where appropriate and translate each sentence into English. Take care to use the appropriate tense forms*:
1 Wat __ er in de boodschappentas? Hij was heel nat.
2 Enschede __ bij de Duitse grens.
3 Hoe wist jij van de moord? – Het __ in de krant.
4 Waar heeft de klerenkast __?
5 Ik heb mijn handschoenen in zijn auto laten __.

---

12 ☞ also the separate entries for each tense and *Irregular verbs.*

76 *Wel*

*Insert **wel** into the appropriate places in the sentences below and translate each one into English:*

1 Heb je de film niet gezien? – Ik heb de film gezien.
2 Houd jij niet meer van jouw man? – Ik houd van hem.
3 Willen jullie vanavond niet komen? – Ik niet maar mijn vrouw.
4 Hij heeft geld maar is niet zo rijk als zijn broer.
5 Ik had het gedacht!
6 Kom je vandaag? – Vandaag niet maar morgen.
7 Heb je de oefeningen al gedaan? – Ja, maar ik vond ze moeilijk.
8 Hij kan mij morgen niet bezoeken maar hij zal mij opbellen.

77 WHEN: Dutch equivalents

*Insert **wanneer**, **toen** or **als** into the gaps below where appropriate and translate each sentence into English:*

1 __ hij zijn koffie gedronken had, voelde hij zich beter.
2 __ kan ik dit laten repareren?
3 Ik kom je bezoeken, __ ik meer tijd heb.
4 Vroeger ging hij uit __ hij kon.
5 __ ik student was, had ik heel weinig geld.
6 __ hij 's avonds uitgaat, drinkt hij te veel.
7 Hij wil mij opbellen, __ hij het feestje georganiseerd heeft.
8 Ik zal het ophalen, __ ik terugkom.
9 Hij woonde hier, __ hij jonger was.
10 Wil jij naar Den Haag gaan? __?

78 Word order

A

Translate the following sentences into English and explain the order of the different elements:

1 Hij gaat vrijdag met zijn vriendin op vakantie.

2 Ik kan jou morgen op de markt ontmoeten.
3 Hij zal tegen half vier in Amsterdam aangekomen zijn.
4 Vandaag ga ik naar Groningen en morgen ga ik naar Zwolle.
5 Met hem wil ik niets meer te maken hebben.

B

1 *Insert the verbs in capitals into the appropriate place(s) in the following sentences:*
(i) EXAMPLE: Jan naar de bioscoop
GAAT
ANSWER: Jan **gaat** naar de bioscoop.
1 Ik met mijn vrienden. PRAAT
2 Wij een half uur op de bus. WACHTEN
3 Jij graag voetbal? SPEEL
4 Om twee uur ik een afspraak. HEB
5 Hij mij dinsdag. BELT OP
6 's Avonds hij gewoonlijk tv. KIJKT
7 Ik weet dat je heel laat naar bed. GAAT
8 Ik vraag me af, of hij het vóór woensdag. DOET
9 De vrouw die om de hoek. WOONT
10 Het meisje op wie mijn zoon verliefd. IS

(ii) EXAMPLE: Jan naar de bioscoop
IS GEGAAN
ANSWER: Jan **is** naar de bioscoop **gegaan**.
1 Ik een brief. HEB GESCHREVEN
2 Wij dinsdag om drie uur. ZIJN AANGEKOMEN
3 Jij de nieuwe film van Woody Allen? HEB GEZIEN
4 Gisteren mijn zoon heel laat. IS UITGEGAAN
5 Wij hem vanavond. ZULLEN OPBELLEN
6 Morgen het niet meer. ZAL REGENEN
7 Zij zijn gegaan voordat de taxi. WAS AANGEKOMEN
8 Ik ben ziek geworden omdat ik te laat buiten. BEN GEBLEVEN
9 Hij zegt dat hij de kamer. ZAL RESERVEREN
10 Dat is de auto die wij volgend jaar. ZULLEN KOPEN

(iii) *Rearrange the following phrases to form a correct Dutch sentence:*
1 zijn vriendin, iedere dag, ziet, hij.

2 vaak, gaat, met haar vriendinnen, zij, naar de stad.

3 je, ga, op vakantie, met Frederik, wanneer?

4 vind, ik, heel aardig, hem.

5 mijn man, overnachten, in Groningen, moet, vanwege zijn werk.

2 (i) *Go to Exercises* **17** *on conjunctions and do* **B1** *and* **B2**.

(ii) *Put the verbs in capitals into the simple past tense and change the word order if necessary*
EXAMPLE: Jan naar de bioscoop GAAN.
ANSWER: **Jan ging naar de bioscoop**.

1 Ik iedere morgen om acht uur OPSTAAN.

2 Toen ik om acht uur OPSTAAN, ik me niet goed VOELEN.

3 Toen ik het huis verlaten WILLEN, ik mijn sleutels niet vinden KUNNEN.

4 Hoewel hij op tijd AANKOMEN, ik nog niet klaar ZIJN en niet MEEGAAN.

5 Hoewel hij iedere dag heel hard werken MOETEN, hij nooit moe WORDEN.

6 Jij KENNEN het meisje dat tegenover mij WONEN?

7 Een week geleden ik mijn moeder bezoeken MOETEN die ziek ZIJN.

8 De student die lui ZIJN en zijn huiswerk nooit DOEN, steeds te laat KOMEN.

(iii) MODALS: *Put the following sentences into the perfect tense*
EXAMPLE: Jan wil naar de bioscoop gaan.
ANSWER: Jan **heeft** naar de bioscoop **willen gaan**.

1 Ik kan het nog niet organiseren.

2 Zij mogen niet langer blijven.

3 Zij moeten de rekeningen betalen.

4 Wij willen een kamer reserveren.

5 Mag hij een dag vrij nemen?

6 Kun jij het vóór maandagmorgen doen?

7 Ik hoop dat u de weg kan vinden.

8 Ik heb gehoord dat jij jouw auto laat repareren.

C

Write a short story in Dutch incorporating the following expressions of time, place and manner in the correct grammatical order. Try to use as many different word order patterns as you can, e.g. VORIG JAAR GING JAAP MET ZIJN VROUW OP VAKANTIE *etc.*

VANMORGEN = this morning
EEN UUR LATER = an hour later
OM HALF ZEVEN = at 6.30
VEEL TE LAAT = much too late
NAAR DE STAD = to town
ONDERWEG = on the way
IN EEN BAR = in a bar
NAAR HUIS = home
MET DE TRAM = by tram
HEEL MOE = very tired
DRONKEN = drunk
MET ZIJN VRIEND = with his friend

☺☺ **Dialogue**
Make sentences out of the following phrases and pay particular attention to word order :

Op de markt

Hanna: Hoeveel, tomaten, een kilo, kost?
Verkoper: Een kilo, vijf gulden, kost.
Hanna: Dan, ik, twee kilo, neem. Ik, tomatensoep, wil, maken. U, denkt, dat, is, twee kilo, genoeg?
Verkoper: Het, ervan, afhangt, hoeveel mensen, voor, kookt, u.
Hanna: Vier mensen, voor, kook, ik.
Verkoper: Dan, ik, eerder, drie kilo, nemen, zou.
Hanna: U, ook, kaas, heeft?
Verkoper: Het spijt me, mijn laatste stuk kaas, ik, al, verkocht, heb. Maar, weet, zeker, ik, dat, nog wat kaas, heeft, meneer van Dam. Hij, naast de bakker, staat.
Hanna: Bedankt. Ik, bij hem, even, kijken, zal. Hier, u, uw geld, heeft. Dag!
Verkoper: Dank u wel, mevrouw, en tot ziens!

79 *Zelf*: MYSELF, YOURSELF etc.

1 *Insert* **zelf** *into the appropriate places in the following sentences and translate each one into English:*

1 Hoe vind je het gebak? Ik heb het gemaakt.

2 Waarom moet ik jouw overhemd strijken? Doe het!

3 Hij zegt steeds dat alcohol slecht is maar hij drinkt vrij veel.

4 Zij bouwen een huis.

5 Ik moet Jantje met zijn huiswerk helpen maar ik begrijp het niet eens.

2 *Insert either* **zelf** *or reflexive pronouns where appropriate to translate the English forms in -***self** *below:*[13]

1 Hij scheert __ iedere morgen.

2 Hij moet de flat __ schoonmaken.

3 Ik vraag __ af, of het de moeite waard is.

4 Ik heb het __ erg druk.

5 Zij schamen __.

6 Zij organiseren de bruiloft __.

7 Wie doet het? Hij __.

8 Zij praat steeds over __.

1 He shaves himself every morning.

2 He has to clean the flat himself.

3 I ask myself whether it is worth the effort.

4 I am very busy myself.

5 They are ashamed of themselves.

6 They are organising the wedding themselves.

7 Who is doing it? He himself.

8 She is always talking about herself.

80 *Zou*

A

Translate the following sentences into English:

1 Ik zou hem niet meer dan honderd gulden geven.

2 Zou je niet vaker thuisblijven?

3 Ik zou hem deze boeken geven maar ik ben het helemaal vergeten.

4 Hij zou om zijn inkomsten gelogen hebben.

5 Zouden zij dat leuk vinden?

B

1 *Rewrite the following sentences, inserting* **zou(den)** *to render 'was/were going to' plus* **maar ik had/wij hadden etc. geen tijd** *and translate your answers into English:*

EXAMPLE: Ik bel je op.

ANSWER:

Ik **zou** je **opbellen maar ik had geen tijd**.

I was going to ring you but I didn't have time.

1 Ik doe boodschappen.

2 Wij gaan naar Amsterdam.

3 Mijn buurman repareert mijn auto.

2 *Rewrite the following sentences, inserting* **zou(den)** *to render 'to be alleged to' and translate your answers into English:*

EXAMPLE: Hij heeft een auto gestolen.

ANSWER:

Hij **zou** een auto **gestolen hebben**.

He is alleged to have stolen a car.

1 Haar man heeft een relatie met een andere vrouw gehad.

2 Zij zijn vorig jaar uit elkaar gegaan.

3 De jongen is heel gevaarlijk geweest.

---

13 ☞ also *Reflexive verbs* and related exercises.

Key to the exercises

1 1 Zij is zó jong, slechts drieëntwintig. 2 Ik hóóp dat ik kan komen. 3 Zij zijn geëvacueerd. 4 Jij kunt het zélf doen. 5 Ik heb géén idee. 6 Hij vindt mij wél aardig. 7 Wil je twee koekjes bij de koffie? – Nee, ik wil maar één koekje.

2 A1 (i) 1 Vowel dropped before single consonant + vowel -*e*. 2 No change because more than one consonant before -*e*. 3 Consonant doubled to keep vowel short. 4 No change because more than one consonant before -*e*. 5 As in 1 above but -*f* after long vowel becomes *v* before another vowel. 6 *f* does not become *v* because it follows a short vowel. Consonant doubled to keep vowel short. **(ii)** 1 -*e* before common gender noun. 2 No ending before indefinite neuter noun. 3 As in 1 above. 4 Neuter noun but definite ('my') so -*e* is added. **2** 1 Before indefinite neuter noun. 2 Adjective of foreign origin. 3 Adjective ending in -*en*. 4 Set phrase / proper name beginning with *het*. **B1** 1 gekke oude. 2 stout. 3 lege. 4 zwarte. 5 vroegere. 6 rode. 7 overwerkte. 8 vreselijke. **2** 1 betere. 2 kleiner. 3 gebroken. 4 wijze. 5 lila. 6 vurige. 7 dove. 8 lage. 9 ingewikkelde. 10 linkerbeen. ☺☺ alcoholvrij, witte, rode, vers, zwarte, afschuwelijk, sterk, sterke, warme, bruine, grote, klein, witte, zoete, grote, ronde, rechterkant, zelfgebakken, grotere, kleinere, koud, openstaande, mogelijk, onvriendelijke, slappe, harde, vervelend, lekker, vuil, duurste, slecht.

3 A 1 The story was endless. 2 She is very successful. 3 The film was very funny. 4 It was unimaginable. 5 He has fish-like eyes / eyes like a fish. **B1** 1 Amerikaans 'American'. 2 nevelig 'foggy'. 3 bereikbaar 'reachable / attainable'. 4 vaderlijk 'fatherly'. **2** 1 harig 'hairy'. 2 zonnig 'sunny'. 3 landelijk 'rural / country'. 4 Oostenrijks 'Austrian'.

5 herkenbaar 'recognisable', onherkenbaar 'unrecognisable'. 6 leesbaar 'readable / legible', onleesbaar 'unreadable / illegible'. 7 gevaarlijk 'dangerous', ongevaarlijk 'not dangerous'. 8 Groenig / groenachtig 'greenish'. 9 Utrechts 'of / from Utrecht'. 10 hartelijk 'hearty / warm', harteloos 'heartless', hartig 'spicy / strong', hartvormig 'heart-shaped'. 11 goddelijk 'divine', goddeloos 'godless'. 12 zwijgzaam 'quiet / taciturn'.

4 A1 1 The shy one. 2 The little ones. 3 The difficult thing. 4 Something better. **2** 1 Which boy do you mean? – The lazy one. 2 Do you know the deceased? 3 The annoying thing is that I don't have any money. 4 The best thing is that he is rich. 5 The house is nothing special. **B1** 1 Iets groters 'something bigger'. 2 Mijn nieuwe 'my new one'. 3 De zwarte 'the black one'. 4 Het laatste 'the last thing' or 'the latest thing'. **2** 1 die lange. 'Do / can you see that tall guy with the beard?' 2 het stomme. 'The silly / stupid thing is that I've forgotten my key.' 3 iets interessants. 'Tell me something interesting.' 4 iets warmers. 'Take something warmer with you.'

5 A 1 You are slow. – You eat slowly. 2 The song is good. – Geert sings well. 3 He is terrible. – He is terribly naughty. 4 It was an unbelievable situation. – It was an unbelievably difficult situation. **B** 1 snel. 2 slecht. 3 goed. 4 potentieel.

6 A 1 Who is going to the cinema? – We are all going / All of us are going. (*Allemaal* follows the verb.) 2 Everyone can do this exercise. (*Allen* refers to people.) 3 All applicants must arrive at eleven o'clock. (*Alle* precedes noun.) 4 All the best places / seats were occupied. (*Al* precedes articles, demonstrative pronouns, posessive pronouns etc.) 5 Anything / everything is possible. (*Alles* translates 'all'

meaning 'everything' / 'anything'.) **B** 1 alles.
2 al. 3 allemaal, *formal*: allen komen. 4 alle.
5 *formal*: allen, *less formal*: spreekt iedereen.
7 A 1 Apostrophe after vowels other than *e*.
2 No apostrophe after consonant other than *s*.
3 No apostrophe after *e*. 4 Apostrophe after *s*.
5 As in 2 above. 6 As in 1 above. 7 As in 3
above. 8 Apostrophe after abbreviations and
after vowels other than *e*. **B** 1 Erica's. 2 Jans.
3 Jos'. 4 BMW's. 5 meisjes.
8 A1 1 No *een* after *zijn* + profession. 2 *Een*
needed where adjective(s) present. 3 No *een*
after *zijn* + nationality. 4 *Een* present because
verb is not *zijn*, *worden* or *blijven*. **2** 1&2 Article
before abstract noun. 3 Article absent when
month specified, present when month not
specified. 4 Article absent with *spelen* +
musical instruments but present with meals.
5 Repetition of article in Dutch. **B1** 1 no
article. 2 een. 3 no article. 4 een. **2 (i)** 1 no
article. 2 no article. 3 no article. 4 no article.
(ii) 1 het. 2 no article. 3 de. 4 de. 5 no article.
6 het.
9 A1 1 I will keep waiting until he comes.
2 The children are still playing. 3 Are you
going to carry on living there? **2** 1 Ans spent
the whole day waiting for her friend. 2 Linda
and her friend carried on talking until two
o'clock in the morning. 3 I want to stay in bed
this morning. 4 Carry on working hard! /
Keep working hard! 5 During the
thunderstorm the child cried all the time.
B 1 Ik blijf hem opbellen. 2 Zij blijven mij
brieven schrijven. 3 Bens hond blijft blaffen.
2 1 Gisteren bleven de jongens de hele nacht
tv kijken. 2 Ik wil bij dit bedrijf blijven
werken. 3 Jan blijft zijn ex-vriendin bloemen
sturen hoewel zij het niet leuk vindt. 4 Blijf
maar lezen!
10 A 1 Who is going to the cinema? We are
both going / Both of us are going. (*Allebei*
follows the verb.) 2 My sons both study
chemistry / Both of my sons study chemistry
(*Allebei* follows the verb.) 3 Both (of them)
want to become teachers. (*Beiden* refers to
people.) 4 Both exercises were easy but they
were both too long. (*Beide* precedes nouns,
allebei follows verbs.) 5 Are you both stupid?

(*Allebei* follows verbs and pronouns.)
B 1 beide. 2 beiden. 3 allebei. 4 allebei.
5 beide *or* ik wil allebei.
11 1 Kom woensdag eens langs! 2 Linda heeft
een Duitse man. 3 Piet studeert Engels.
4 Kunt u deze brief in het Nederlands
vertalen? 5 's Morgens bezorgt Jan de krant
aan meneer Kramer. 6 Wanneer is jouw
verjaardag? Op twintig februari. 7 Ik praatte
met mevrouw Dijkstra op dinsdag 3 maart.
8 's Maandags ontmoeten de studenten
mevrouw Kok, hun lerares IJslands.
12 1 Z'n vrouw heeft 'm verlaten, hoor. 2 'K
had 't nooit gedacht. 3 Komt ie met Annika
d'r moeder? 4 Je hebt een heel aardig
dochtertje, hoor. 5 Neem maar een koekje!
6 – Zeg, heb je een asbak? – Ik moet even
kijken.
13 A 1 When Kees arrived he was very tired.
(Comma after verb sent to end.) 2 He is,
however, a very successful lawyer. (No
comma with *echter* 'however'.) 3 The students
who work hard will get the highest marks.
(Comma after verb sent to end.) 4 I am not
going unless Jan comes with us (too). (Comma
before clause which sends verb to end.)
5 Unemployment is very low at 15.3 per cent.
(Comma in Dutch while decimal point in
English.) **B** 1 Ik ga vanavond niet uit, omdat
ik geen geld heb. 2 Piet had altijd gedacht dat
zijn vader te streng was. 3 De film die deze
week in de bioscoop draait, is heel goed.
4 Saskia's man, die nu zo kaal als een
biljartbal is, heeft een andere vrouw. (2
commas because incidental information.)
5 Toen de katten de hond zagen, renden zij
weg.
14 A 1 Vowel dropped before single
consonant + vowel *-e*. 2 No change because
more than one consonant before *-e*.
3 Consonant doubled to keep vowel short.
4 As in 1 above but *f* after long vowel
becomes *v* before another vowel. **B1** 1 lager.
2 zwaarder. 3 dover. 4 witter. 5 viezer.
6 losser. 7 succesvoller. 8 puurder.
9 belangrijker. 10 geler. 11 oppervlakkiger.
12 helderder. **2** 1 beter. The book is better
than the film. 2 liever. Yes, but I do not like

reading. I prefer going to the cinema. 3 meer.
He eats more than me / than I do. 4 minder.
He has less money than her / than she has.
5 grotere, goedkoper, kleinere. The larger
scarf is much cheaper than the smaller one.
6 oudere, groter, nieuwere. The older house
is bigger than the newer one. 7 vroegere,
grappiger. I find his earlier films funnier.
8 intelligent. I am just as intelligent as you.
9 duurder. Wine is getting more and more
expensive. 10 rijker, gelukkiger. The richer I
become, the happier I am.

15 A 1 Linda is a housewife. 2 Jaap is a
veterinary surgeon. (*Dieren* is a plural form.
Vets deal with more than one animal.) 3 Jan
works in a flower shop. (*Bloemen* is a plural
form. The shop sells more than one flower.)
4 Anne is a shop assistant. 5 We are all
against child labour. (*Kind* has a special
compound form in -*er*.) 6 We have a new
governing party. (-*s* occurs after -*ing*.) 7 Fasten
your safety belt! (-*s* occurs after -*heid*.) **B1**
1 postkantoor 'post office'. 2 geldsom 'sum of
money'. 3 schooljongen 'schoolboy'.
4 klerenkast 'wardrobe'. 5 gezondheidszorg
'healthcare'. 6 kinderkamer 'nursery / child's
room'. **2** inktvlek 'ink stain', inktfles 'bottle of
ink', inktzwart 'as black as ink', wijnfles 'wine
bottle', wijnvlek 'wine stain', melkvlek 'milk
stain', melkfles 'milk bottle', zwartharig
'black-haired', zwartmaken 'to blacken'.

16 A 1 1 I would drink more beer. 2 The
wine would be too expensive. 3 The student
house / hall of residence would not have any
heating. 4 The child would not be so naughty.
2 1 I would not have written the letter. 2 We
would have stayed longer in The Hague. 3 I
would have expected more from you. 4 To
study in the Netherlands would have been a
good idea. **B1** 1 Frits zou bloemen aan zijn
vrouw geven. 2 De leraar zou heel boos
worden. 3 Marc en Ruud zouden voetbal
spelen. 4 De trein zou om vier uur vertrekken.
5 Zouden de studenten de les veel te moeilijk
vinden? **2 (i)** 1 Frits zou bloemen aan zijn
vrouw gegeven hebben / hebben gegeven.
2 De leraar zou heel boos geworden zijn / zijn
geworden. 3 Marc en Ruud zouden beter

voetbal gespeeld hebben / hebben gespeeld.
4 De trein zou om vier uur vertrokken zijn /
zijn vertrokken. 5 Zouden de studenten de les
veel te moeilijk gevonden hebben / hebben
gevonden? **2 (ii)** 1 Frits had bloemen aan zijn
vrouw gegeven. 2 De leraar was heel boos
geworden. 3 Marc en Ruud hadden voetbal
gespeeld. 4 De trein was om vier uur
vertrokken. 5 Hadden de studenten de les
veel te moeilijk gevonden?

17 A 1 Geert wants to bake a cake but he
hasn't any eggs. 2 When Frits was young he
always listened to ABBA. 3 Do you want to
come along or are you working tonight?
4 Piet asks Jaap whether Harald has a new
girlfriend. 5 Since I arrived the weather has
been very bad. 6 As far as I know he is still in
Utrecht. **B1** 1 Hij kwam aan maar het was te
laat. 2 Wij moeten hard werken want anders
krijgen wij lage cijfers. 3 Jullie moeten de
koffie klaar hebben, zodra zij vanavond
aankomen. 4 Ans was studente toen zij haar
eerste vriend ontmoette. 5 Piet is leraar en
zijn vrouw is tandarts. 6 Ik ga niet naar de
bruiloft, tenzij jij voor mij een nieuwe jurk
koopt. 7 Harald is heel dik, hoewel hij niet
veel eet. 8 Jij mag een biertje hebben, zolang
jij niet rijdt. **2** 1 Ik ben heel moe hoewel ik
gisteravond vroeg naar bed ging. 2 Zij moet
vandaag vroeger opstaan omdat zij haar
dochter naar school brengt. 3 Ik maak het
bad schoon terwijl jij de was doet. 4 Hij zag
haar in de bus zitten toen hij naar zijn werk
ging. 5 Wij moeten met de tram gaan omdat
mijn auto kapot is. 6 Er was een probleem
met de computer hoewel hij splinternieuw
was.

18 A 1 On Fridays Jan visits his father. 2 He
is coming on Tuesday, the nineteenth of May.
3 I will see you on Monday the twenty-first.
4 Annika is going to Amsterdam at the
beginning of August. **B** 1 Piet is op vrijdag
twaalf juli negentienhonderdachtenzestig (*or*
negentienachtenzestig) geboren. 2 Is jouw
verjaardag op de eerste? – Nee, op de tweede.
3 Kom je op zeven augustus of op één
oktober? 4 Dit jaar gaat zij op de dertigste op
vakantie. 5 Sinterklaas is op vijf december.

19 A 1 This wine is too dry. (*Deze* before common gender noun.) 2 How do you find / like this bread? (*Dit* before singular neuter noun.) 3 These tulips are prettier than those roses. (*Deze* and *die* before all plural nouns.) 4 Do you see that tree? (*Die* before common gender noun.) 5 That is not true. (*Dat* used independently before verb – i.e. it refers to no specific noun.) 6 These are my best friends. (*Dit* used independently before verb – the noun is mentioned later.) **B1** 1 die. 2 dat. 3 deze. 4 dit. 5 die. **2** 1 dit. 2 die. 3 deze, dat. 4 dit. 5 deze, die. 6 deze, die. 7 die. 8 dit, dat. 9 dit. 10 Hierop, daarop. **C** dit brood, deze tomaten, dit water, deze koffie; die kaas, die druiven, die koekjes, dat bier.

20 A 1 The kitten plays with the little mouse. 2 She has two little / younger brothers. 3 The girl speaks very softly. 4 He is a nice little boy. 5 He has a strange little car. **B1** 1 boekje. 2 peertje. 3 dekentje. 4 armpje. 5 sommetje. 6 slaapkamertje. 7 flesje. 8 tafeltje. 9 oorbelletje. 10 riempje. 11 harinkje. 12 pennetje. **2** 1 mannetjes. 2 vrouwtjes. 3 tomaatjes. 4 druifjes. 5 slaatje. 6 parapluutje. 7 zoontje. 8 glaasje. 9 jongetje. 10 zachtjes. 11 knusjes. 12 stiekempjes. **C** broekje, truitje, sokjes, schoentjes, jasjes, sjaaltjes, mutsje, laarsjes.

21 A 1 I have seen him there twice. (Place.) 2 Where is the chair? I am sitting on it. (Translates 'it' with preposition.) 3 They do not think about it any more. (Translates 'it' with preposition.) 4 There are five students in the class. (Introduces subject.) 5 In my class I have twenty. (Used with amount when noun is omitted.) **B1 (i)** 1 Ik wacht erop. 2 Wij weten er helemaal niets van. 3 Wat doe je ermee? 4 Zij praat er nog steeds over. 5 Ik heb er niet genoeg geld voor. 6 Denk eraan! **1 (ii)** 1 Ik heb er vijf meegebracht. 2 Zij hebben er geen. 3 Nee, hij heeft er niet veel. **1 (iii)** 1 Hij is er met zijn vriendin geweest. 2 Ik heb hem er gezien. 3 Ik ben er niet lang gebleven. 4 Jaap heeft zijn eerste vrouw er ontmoet. **2** 1 Er staat een oude roestige auto voor mijn deur. 2 Er spelen vier meisjes op het gras. 3 Was er gisteren iemand thuis?

4 Kijk! Er komt een bus. 5 Er wachten twee politieagenten voor het huis. 6 Wilt u een biertje? – Jawel, ik wil er twee, alstublieft! 7 Ben je ooit in Antwerpen geweest? – Ja, ik heb er zes jaar met een vriend gewoond. 8 Ik houd van Amsterdam. Er zijn veel grachten. – Ja, er zijn er ook veel in Utrecht. 9 Houd je van opera? – Nee, ik houd er helemaal niet van. 10 Dat vlees ziet er goed uit. – Ja, maar er zijn niet veel groenten bij.

22 A 1 Erica is a writer and her sister is a social worker. 2 Jaap's girlfriend is a communist. 3 Marieke's teacher is a Polish woman. 4 The Italian woman is a very good cook. 5 My mother is a policewoman. **B** 1 werkster. 2 kapster. 3 verkoopster. 4 specialiste. 5 hertogin. 6 keizerin. 7 Zweedse. 8 Turkse. 9 Nederlandse. 10 wolvin. 11 lerares. 12 dompteuse.

23 A1 1 I will be in Belgium tomorrow evening. 2 We will move before March. 3 The situation will become more difficult. 4 It will be very tiring. **2** 1 The travel agency will have arranged everything. 2 I will have met him. 3 They probably will have stayed until the weekend. 4 We will have left before / by half seven. **B1** 1 Piet en Geert zullen om acht uur aankomen. 2 Zal / zul jij bloemen aan je buurvrouw geven? 3 De trein zal vanavond vertrekken. 4 De kinderen zullen volgende week bij hun grootouders slapen. 5 Mijn buurman zal al zeventig zijn. **2 (i)** 1 Piet en Geert zullen om acht uur aangekomen zijn / zijn aangekomen. 2 Zal / zul jij bloemen aan je buurvrouw gegeven hebben / hebben gegeven? 3 De trein zal vanavond vertrokken zijn / zijn vertrokken. 4 De kinderen zullen volgende week bij hun grootouders geslapen hebben / hebben geslapen. 5 Mijn buurman zal al zeventig geweest zijn / zijn geweest. **(ii)** *Answers B1* 1, 3 and 4 can also be expressed using the present tense due to the occurrence of an expression of time within the sentence. By contrast, 2 would be ambiguous if the present tense was used (i.e. 'do you give flowers . . .?' or 'will you give flowers . . .?') As 5 expresses an assumption the future tense must be used here, otherwise it becomes a statement of fact (i.e. 'he is already seventy.')

24 A 1 I am not a tourist. I live here. 2 There is not one cinema in this town. 3 I am sorry, I do not have any change. 4 That is not a good photo. 5 These are not expensive shoes.
B 1 Ik heb geen idee. 2 Wil je geen biertje? 3 Zij is geen huisvrouw. 4 Het is geen wonder dat hij geen geld heeft. 5 Jaap en Wim zijn geen aardige jongens. 6 De student heeft dit jaar niet één boek gelezen.

25 A 1 Common. 2 Neuter. 3 Neuter. 4 Common. 5 Neuter. **B1** 1 de hond. 2 het hondje. 3 het leven . 4 de wijn. 5 het zwart. 6 het staal. 7 de man. 8 de vrouw. 9 het meisje. 10 het kind. 11 de bakker. 12 het gebak. 13 het begrip. 14 het woordenboek. 15 de vriendin. 16 de vertaling. 17 het verhaal. 18 het grappige. 19 de universiteit. 20 het feminisme. **2** 1 Woont hij in het noordoosten? – Nee, in het noordwesten. 2 Heb jij het nieuwe huis gezien? Nee, ik heb het niet gezien. 3 Hoe laat vertrekt de trein? – Hij vertrekt om twee uur. 4 Waar is de pen? – Heb jij hem gezien? 5 Hoe was de film? – Hij was heel goed. 6 Ken jij het meisje van de boekwinkel? – Nee, ik ken haar niet.

26 A 1 Jan really likes reading. 2 Frits prefers watching TV. 3 Doesn't he like going to the cinema? 4 My grandma likes listening to the radio best. 5 Do you like travelling or do you prefer to stay at home? **B** 1 Ik wou graag een taxi bestellen. 'I would like to order a taxi.' 2 Mijn man brengt u graag naar de luchthaven. 'My husband would be glad to take you to the airport.' 3 Waarom ga je niet graag naar school? 'Why don't you like going to school?' 4 Mijn baas werkt graag. 'My boss likes to work.' 5 Ik wou graag weten, hoe hij het doet. 'I would (really) like to know how he does it.'

27 A1 1 If my grandma drank one glass of wine she would get drunk. 2 If I went to Groningen I would take an umbrella with me. 3 If the students worked harder they would get better marks. 4 If we rang up this evening would you be at home? **2** 1 If uncle Jos had gone to Amsterdam he would have seen the tulips. 2 If the weather had been better I would have played tennis. 3 If the lesson had not been so late more students would have come. 4 If you had rung earlier we would have still been at home. **B1** 1 Als Piet 's morgens vroeger wakker werd, zou hij 's avonds moe zijn. 'If Piet woke up earlier in the mornings he would be tired in the evenings.' 2 Als Jaap meer tijd had, zou hij meer voetbal spelen. 'If Jaap had more time he would play more football.' 3 Als wij vroeger thuis kwamen, zouden wij naar de televisie kijken. 'If we came home earlier we would watch television.' 4 Als mevrouw Baayen geld aan haar zoon gaf, zou hij naar de bioscoop gaan. 'If Mrs Baayen gave her son money he would go to the cinema.' 5 Als de studenten dit boek lazen, zouden zij veel van de Nederlandse taal weten. 'If the students read this book they would know a lot about the Dutch language.' **2 (i)** 1 Als Piet 's morgens vroeger wakker geworden was, zou hij 's avonds moe geweest zijn. 'If Piet had woken up earlier in the mornings he would have been tired in the evenings.' 2 Als Jaap meer tijd gehad had, zou hij meer voetbal gespeeld hebben. 'If Jaap had had more time he would have played more football.' 3 Als wij vroeger thuis gekomen waren, zouden wij naar de televisie gekeken hebben. 'If we had come home earlier we would have watched television.' 4 Als mevrouw Baayen geld aan haar zoon gegeven had, zou hij naar de bioscoop gegaan zijn. 'If Mrs Baayen had given her son money he would have gone to the cinema.' 5 Als de studenten dit boek gelezen hadden, zouden zij veel van de Nederlandse taal geweten hebben. 'If the students had read this book they would have known a lot about the Dutch language.'
2 (ii) 1 Als Piet 's morgens vroeger wakker geworden was, was hij 's avonds moe geweest. 2 Als Jaap meer tijd gehad had, had hij meer voetbal gespeeld. 3 Als wij vroeger thuis gekomen waren, hadden wij naar de televisie gekeken. 4 Als mevrouw Baayen geld aan haar zoon gegeven had, was hij naar de bioscoop gegaan. 5 Als de studenten dit boek

gelezen hadden, hadden zij veel van de Nederlandse taal geweten.

28 A 1 Don't go out too often. 2 Don't be too late. 3 (Please) bring me a bottle of wine. 4 Let's celebrate / have a party! 5 NO PARKING. **B1** 1 laat. 2 slaap. 3 eet. 4 lees. 5 geef. **2** 1 bel . . . op. 2 kom morgenavond mee . . . 3 stuurt u. 4 loopt u. 5 wees. **C** Neem de bus . . . Stap . . . uit. Ga . . . rechtdoor. Steek . . . over. Sla . . . af. Wacht . . .

29 A 1 Everyone knows Jaap but no-one knows his wife. 2 Do you want to drink something / anything? No, nothing. 3 I've brought some fish (with me.) 4 Some languages are more difficult than others. 5 Mrs van Duin goes to Italy every year. 6 Her husband is so lazy. He doesn't want to do anything. **B** 1 wat. 2 sommige, andere. 3 sommigen, anderen. 4 iedere / elke. 5 iedereen. 6 iemand.

30 A 1 The policeman stood watching the burglar. (*te* used after verbs of position, e.g. *staan, zitten* etc.) 2 He saw him break into the house. (Bare infinitive after verbs of sensation, e.g. *zien, horen* etc.) 3 I work very hard to pay my rent. (*om . . . te* used in most cases.) 4 They sat in the car without talking to each other. (*te* after *zonder*.) 5 That is to be expected. (*te* + infinitive sometimes corresponds to English passive.) **B1 (i)** 1 Piet wil geld om naar de bioscoop te gaan. 2 Hij gaat boodschappen doen om zijn oma te helpen. 3 Ik heb meer bloem nodig om deze koekjes te bakken. 4 Heb je genoeg geld om die jurk te kopen? 5 Ik moet morgen heel vroeg naar mijn werk gaan om een fax vóór acht uur te sturen. **1 (ii)** 1 Geert zit zijn bier te drinken. 2 De hond staat naar de melkboer te blaffen. 3 De baby ligt de hele nacht te huilen. 4 De kinderen stonden naar het vliegtuig te kijken. 5 De kat lag te slapen. **2** 1 Jantje durft zijn leraar te beledigen. 2 Wie komt er tennissen? 3 Om zijn vrouw te ergeren, kwam Jaap laat thuis. 4 De kinderen gaan morgen zwemmen. 5 Hij weet heel goed vrouwen te verleiden. 6 Jij hoeft mij niet meer op te bellen. 7 Dat boek is makkelijk om te lezen. (*Also in spoken Dutch*: dat boek is

makkelijk te lezen.) 8 Ik probeer het morgenochtend te doen.

31 1 Ik zat de hele avond tv te kijken. 2 Zij hoorden de buren harde muziek spelen. 3 Hij ziet haar iedere morgen op de bus wachten. 4 Zij doet het zonder te denken. 5 Hij belt mij op in plaats van te schrijven. 6 Wie is de man die tegenover jou woont? 7 Wij wachtten de hele morgen en hoopten dat een bus zou komen. 8 Toen hij de trein uitstapte, zag hij haar op het perron wachten.

32 1 1(a) Hij vertelt het hele verhaal aan zijn vriend. (b) Hij heeft het hele verhaal aan zijn vriend verteld. 2(a) Ik herken hem niet meer. (b) Ik heb hem niet meer herkend. 3(a) De leraar herhaalt zijn vraag. (b) De leraar heeft zijn vraag herhaald. 4(a) Uw bezoek verrast ons. (b) Uw bezoek heeft ons verrast. 5(a) Jan bereikt de top. (b) Jan heeft de top bereikt. 6(a) Mijn broer ontwikkelt zijn eigen foto's. (b) Mijn broer heeft zijn eigen foto's ontwikkeld. **2** 1 bemannen 'to man' (e.g. a ship), ontmannen 'to castrate / emasculate', vermannen 'to take heart / be brave'. 2 bemoederen 'to mother'. 3 bekleden 'to clothe / dress', ontkleden 'to undress', verkleden 'to disguise', zich verkleden 'to change clothes'. 4 bespreken 'to discuss', zich verspreken 'to make a mistake in speaking'. 5 verharden 'to harden', ontharden 'to soften'. 6 heropenen 'to re-open'. 7 herlezen 'to revise', zich verlezen 'to make a mistake in reading / misread'. 8 bedekken 'to cover', ontdekken 'to discover', herontdekken 'to rediscover'.

33 A 1 I wrote to my friend but he did not read the letter. 2 They ate cheese and drank wine. 3 They brought him home. 4 The cup fell onto the ground. 5 I thought that I had understood it. **B1** 1 had – hadden – gehad. 2 was – waren – geweest (+ zijn). 3 wist – wisten – geweten. 4 dacht – dachten – gedacht. 5 zei – zeiden – gezegd. 6 zag – zagen – gezien. 7 kwam – kwamen – gekomen (+ zijn). 8 ging – gingen – gegaan (+ zijn). 9 deed – deden – gedaan. 10 zou – zouden – (*no past part.*). 11 vroeg – vroegen – gevraagd. 12 werd – werden – geworden

(+ zijn). **2** 1 bleef – bleven – gebleven (+ zijn).
2 keek – keken – gekeken. 3 verdween –
verdwenen – verdwenen (+ zijn). 4 sloot –
sloten – gesloten. 5 zocht – zochten – gezocht.
6.bezocht – bezochten – bezocht. 7 kocht –
kochten – gekocht. 8 hield – hielden –
gehouden. 9 sliep – sliepen – geslapen.
10 ving – vingen – gevangen. 11 at – aten –
gegeten. 12 nam – namen – genomen. 13 zat
– zaten – gezeten. 14 vond – vonden –
gevonden. 15 stond – stonden – gestaan.
16 koos – kozen – gekozen.
34 1 weet. 2 ken, weet. 3 ken. 4 weet. 5 weet.
6 ken. 7 kent.
35 A 1 Let me do it. 2 Mrs de Wit let her son
go to the party. 3 Let's go to Amsterdam
tomorrow. 4 You must not let your coffee go
cold. 5 I want to have my dress dry cleaned.
6 Jaap had his mother taken to the airport.
7 Piet had already had his computer repaired
once. **B** 1 Hij laat zijn auto naar een garage
brengen. 2 Wij laten ons huis iedere
donderdag schoonmaken. 3 Ik moet deze film
laten ontwikkelen. 4 Hij heeft een bos
bloemen aan zijn vrouw laten versturen.
5 Wij hebben een verjaardagsfeestje laten
organiseren.

36 A *Sample translation*

Amsterdam, 20 August 1996

Reisbureau AirWays
Postbus 918
1182 GP Amsterdam

Re: trip[1] to Calamar.

Dear Sir / Madam,

Last week I returned from a trip booked by
you to Calamar in Spain.[2] To my regret I
have to inform you that this did not at all live
up to the expectations raised by your folder.[3]

Firstly, the courier[4] was not present on my
arrival at the airport, as was promised in your
folder. As a result, I had to take a taxi to the

hotel myself which cost 100 guilders. On
checking into the Hotel Sol de Corazon it
appeared that there were no single rooms left
and, consequently,[5] I had to share a room
with somebody else from our group.[6] The
hotel management assured me that your
travel agency had not booked enough rooms.[7]
Finally, the information on excursions in your
folder was incorrect.[8] The courier only
organised an outing[9] to a monastery but the
promised excursion to Barcelona did not take
place because[10] the bus had not been booked
in time.

I would be very grateful if you would explain
to me why the folder contained false
information. In addition, I would very much
like to know the reason for the incorrect
number of reservations in the hotel. I feel that
some compensation for the cost of the taxi
and the cancelled excursion would be
appropriate.

I look forward to hearing from you soon.

Yours faithfully,

Paul van Haalen.

Paul van Haalen
Prinsengracht 23
1023 AC Amsterdam.

Alternative suggestions

1 holiday. 2 Last week I returned from a trip
to Calamar in Spain which was booked
through your agency. 3 I regret to inform you
that it did not at all live up to the expectations
raised by your folder. 4 tour guide.
5 therefore. 6 I had to share a room with one
of the other holidaymakers. 7 had not
reserved a sufficient number of rooms.
8 Finally, your folder also contained incorrect
information concerning excursions. 9 trip.
10 as.
37 1 woon. 2 leeft. 3 wonen. 4 leefde.
5 woonde. 6 leeft. 7 wonen. 8 leven.

38 A 1 That may/might be her boyfriend. 2 He may/might want to celebrate (it) with us. 3 They may/might have already sold it. 4 They may/might have moved house (by) now. 5 You may/might not be able to understand it. **B** 1 Misschien heb ik ongelijk. 2 Misschien is hij vandaag aangekomen / Hij kan vandaag aangekomen zijn. 3 Misschien is dat de melkboer / Dat kan de melkboer zijn / Dat zou de melkboer kunnen zijn. 4 Misschien heeft hij zijn vrouw verlaten / Hij kan zijn vrouw verlaten hebben. 5 Misschien heb jij het al gehoord / Jij kan het al gehoord hebben.

39 1 betekent. 2 bedoelt. 3 betekent. 4 bedoelt. 5 betekent. 6 bedoelt. 7 meent.

40 A 1 1 He wants to go out every evening / night. 2 We could not find the toilets. 3 May I ask you something? 4 They had to sell their house. **2** 1 Who has had to pay the bill? / Who had to pay the bill? 2 I had not wanted to disturb you. 3 We will not be allowed to visit him this evening. 4 They would not be able to leave on Tuesday. 5 A child could have done it better. 6 I should not have spent so much money. 7 You must have heard it. **B1 (i)** 1 Jan en Ans willen een kamer reserveren. 2 Mag je hier telefoneren? 3 De trein moet om acht uur aankomen. 4 Kunt u mij een brochure geven? 5 Waar kunnen de kinderen spelen? **(ii)** 1 Jan en Ans wilden / wouden een kamer reserveren. 2 Mocht je hier telefoneren? 3 De trein moest om acht uur aankomen. 4 Kon u mij een brochure geven? 5 Waar konden de kinderen spelen? **2(i)** 1(a) Jan en Ans zullen een kamer willen reserveren. (b) Jan en Ans hebben een kamer willen reserveren. 2(a) Zal / zul je hier mogen telefoneren? (b) Heb je hier mogen telefoneren? 3(a) De trein zal om acht uur moeten aankomen. (b) De trein heeft om acht uur moeten aankomen. 4(a) Zult / zal u mij een brochure kunnen geven? (b) Hebt / heeft u mij een brochure kunnen geven? 5(a) Waar zullen de kinderen kunnen spelen? (b) Waar hebben de kinderen kunnen spelen? **2(ii)** 1(a) Wij hadden vroeger naar bed kunnen gaan 'we could have gone to bed earlier'. (b) Wij hadden vroeger naar bed moeten gaan 'we should have gone to bed earlier'. 2(a) Jij had langer kunnen blijven 'you could have stayed longer'. (b) Jij had langer moeten blijven 'you should have stayed longer'. 3(a) Ik had de eerste trein om half acht kunnen nemen. 'I could have taken the first train at half past seven.' (b) Ik had de eerste trein om half acht moeten nemen. 'I should have taken the first train at half past seven.' 4(a) Zij hadden een goedkopere auto kunnen kopen. 'They could have bought a cheaper car.' (b) Zij hadden een goedkopere auto moeten kopen. 'They should have bought a cheaper car.' **2(iii)** 1 Ik kon het niet repareren. 2 Hij moest haar duizend gulden geven. 3 Ik wil morgen vertrekken. 4 Mijn zoon mag niet roken. 5 Moet je vroeg naar bed gaan? 6 Zul je vers brood kunnen kopen? 7 De studenten hebben de les niet kunnen begrijpen. 8 De jongen heeft niet naar school willen gaan.

41 A 1 He did not see the film this evening. (*Niet* at end of clause.) 2 I did not find the film especially exciting. (*Niet* precedes phrase with adjective.) 3 The train must not leave before ten o'clock in the morning. (*Niet* precedes phrase with preposition.) 4 I am not working today . (*Niet* at end of clause.) 5 I am working not today but tomorrow. (*Niet* placed before *vandaag* for emphasis.) **B1** 1 Ik rook niet. 2 Hij is niet dik. 3 Zij lezen niet veel. 4 Het staat niet in de kast. 5 Ik kom woensdag niet. 6 Hij wast de auto niet. 7 Zij hebben geen auto. **2 (i)** 1 Ging jij graag naar school? Ik niet. 2 Heb jij geen geld? Ik ook niet. 3 Hij heeft het nog niet gedaan. 4 Ik heb de man van Annika nooit aardig gevonden. 5 Hij heeft nooit een woord gezegd. **2 (ii)** 1 Jan heeft Jaap sinds vorige maand niet gezien. 2 Piet heeft twee jaar geleden niet bij zijn ouders gewoond. 3 Er zijn vandaag niet veel mensen in het café. 4 Dat is niet zijn nieuwe auto / Dat is zijn nieuwe auto niet. 5 Ik had de vleesgerechten niet kunnen aanbevelen. 6 De leraar kent dit jaar de nieuwe schoolkinderen en hun ouders niet zo goed. 7 Hij komt vanavond niet met zijn vrouw. 8 Roel gebruikt vandaag de computer niet die hij nu op zijn kantoor heeft /

Roel gebruikt vandaag de computer die hij nu op zijn kantoor heeft niet.
42 A1 (i) 1 Vowel dropped before single consonant + vowel *e*. 2 No change because more than one consonant before *e*.
3 Consonant doubled to keep vowel short.
4 No change because more than one consonant before *e*. 5 As in 1 above but *f* after a long vowel becomes *v* before another vowel.
6 *f* does not change to *v* because it follows a short vowel. Instead it is doubled to keep the preceding vowel short. 7 *s* becomes *z* after long vowel (in this case, diphthong). 8 *s* does not become *z* because it follows a short vowel. Instead it is doubled to keep the preceding vowel short. **1 (ii)** 1 Ends in -*en*. 2 Ends in -*er*. 3 Ends in -*aar* and refers to person. 4 Ends in -*el*. 5 Ends in a vowel. 6 Ends in a vowel other than *e* and therefore needs an apostrophe before *s*. **B1 (i)** 1 studenten. 2 studentes. 3 vogels. 4 muizen. 5 prijzen. 6 leugenaars. 7 brieven. 8 muren. 9 stenen. 10 meisjes. 11 leraressen. 12 bomen. 13 tuiniers. 14 bezems. 15 jassen. 16 vlaggen. **1 (ii)** 1 boek. 2 pen. 3 oog. 4 neus. 5 been. 6 ui. 7 neef. 8 fles. **2** 1 kinderen. 2 opa's. 3 films. 4 video's. 5 cd's. 6 dagen. 7 glazen. 8 raderen. 9 eieren. 10 steden. 11 gaten. 12 spelen. 13 wegen. 14 mogelijkheden. 15 leraren (*less common* leraars) . 16 zoons (*more formal* zonen.)
43 A 1 The teacher is experienced. – The teacher has a lot of experience. 2 Anne is always tired. – Anne suffers from tiredness. 3 The cupboard is too wide. – What is the exact width of the cupboard? 4 The police cannot prove it. – The police do not have any proof. 5 They giggle all the time. – He finds their stupid giggling annoying. **B** 1 de werkelijkheid 'reality'. 2 de waarheid 'truth'. 3 de hopeloosheid 'hopelessness'. 4 de aansluiting 'connection'. 5 de lezing 'lecture / reading', het lezen '(the act of) reading'. 6 het bereik 'reach'. 7 het verschil 'difference' 8 het gebrom 'buzzing'. 9 het gebons 'thumping'. 10 de dikte 'fatness / thickness'. 11 de wijdte 'width'. 12 de oppervlakkigheid 'superficiality'.
44 A 1 27. 2 151. 3 3088. 4 900.000.

5 4635. 6 31e. 7 1001e. 8 89e. 9 10e. 10 103e.
B 1 negenenvijftig. 2 tweehonderd-drieënzestig. 3 duizendhonderdtweeëndertig. 4 achthonderdzeven komma vijf. 5 vijfenzeventig (gulden) drieënnegentig. 6 de derde keer. 7 de vijfenveertigste student. 8 zijn honderdtweede verjaardag. 9 de helft van het huis / het halve huis. 10 vijf zesde van het bedrag.
45 A 1 I will show you the photos. 2 Give it to me. 3 I would like to tell you something about myself. 4 He is giving it to you, not to them. 5 I have lent it to my brother. **B** 1 Hij stuurt haar een kaartje / Hij stuurt een kaartje aan haar. 2 Ik heb de leraar mijn huiswerk gegeven / Ik heb mijn huiswerk aan de leraar gegeven. 3 Ik heb het (aan) hem gegeven. 4 Dat behoort aan mijn vriend. 5 Hij legde het probleem aan de student uit.
46 A 1 1 It is often said. 2 The burglar was arrested by the police. 3 The wedding has already been organised. 4 They had already been warned three times by their parents. **2** 1 Nothing was done. 2 There will be no more fighting. 3 I have been given these books. 4 She is often talked about. **B1** 1(a) Deze boeken worden door de studenten gelezen. (b) Deze boeken werden door de studenten gelezen. 2(a) Dit huis wordt door mijn vader gebouwd. (b) Dit huis werd door mijn vader gebouwd. 3(a) De essays worden door de docent bekritiseerd. (b) De essays werden door de docent bekritiseerd. 4(a) Het wordt (door iemand) gedaan. (b) Het werd (door iemand) gedaan. 5(a) De auto wordt door een goede monteur gerepareerd. (b) De auto werd door een goede monteur gerepareerd. 6(a) Deze koekjes worden (door iemand) voor ons gemaakt. (b) Deze koekjes werden (door iemand) voor ons gemaakt. **2 (i)** 1(a) Deze boeken zijn door de studenten gelezen. (b) Deze boeken waren door de studenten gelezen. 2(a) Dit huis is door mijn vader gebouwd. (b) Dit huis was door mijn vader gebouwd. 3(a) De essays zijn door de docent bekritiseerd. (b) De essays waren door de docent bekritiseerd. 4(a) Het is (door iemand) gedaan. (b) Het was (door iemand) gedaan.

5(a) De auto is door een goede monteur gerepareerd. (b) De auto was door een goede monteur gerepareerd. 6(a) Deze koekjes zijn (door iemand) voor ons gemaakt. (b) Deze koekjes waren (door iemand) voor ons gemaakt. **2 (ii)** 1 Het feest zal door hem georganiseerd worden / worden georganiseerd. 2 De jongens zullen door de leraar bestraft worden / worden bestraft. 3 Het boek zal door veel mensen gekocht worden / worden gekocht. 4 Het zou alleen door mij gedaan worden / worden gedaan. 5 De brieven zouden alleen door de advocaat gelezen worden / worden gelezen. **2 (iii)** 1 Men spreekt hier Engels. 2 In Enschede kan men Duits geld gebruiken / In Enschede kan je Duits geld gebruiken. 3 Iemand heeft mijn auto gestolen / Ze hebben mijn auto gestolen. **47 A1** 1, 2, 3 and 4 -*te* added to voiceless consonants *k, t, f* and *s* (contained in *'t kofschip*.) 5 and 6 -*de* added to remaining sounds (not contained in *'t kofschip*.) 7 -*de* added after *f* here because infinitive has *v* instead of *f*. 8 -*de* added to *s* here because infinitive has *z* instead of *s*. **2** 1 Past used in written narrative (i.e. when telling a story). 2 and 3 Past used after *toen* 'when'. 4 and 5 Past used with very common / frequently used verbs such as *zeggen* 'to say', *kunnen* 'to be able'. **B1** 1 ik werkte. 2 hij tankte. 3 het kostte. 4 wij voelden. 5 ik schreeuwde. 6 hij mompelde. 7 ik spelde. 8 jij speelde. 9 wij wasten. 10 u kookte. 11 jullie woonden. 12 wij leefden. **2** 1 ik heette. 2 wij haatten. 3 hij haastte zich. 4 wij brandden. 5 ik feliciteerde. 6 hij lette op. 7 jullie visten uit. 8 wij organiseerden. 9 wij verhuisden. 10 jullie verfden. 11 ik tekende. 12 hij hervatte. 13 jij knoopte aan. 14 ik leverde af. 15 hij lachte mee. 16 u bedoelde. ☺☺ ging, vond, stond ik te laat op, was, maakte, sliep, hoefde, had, dacht, sliep, huilde, maakte, kwam laat en ook heel moe bij het bedrijf aan, waren, legde uit, begrepen, leken, was, kon, vonden, stelde, kon, beantwoordde, glimlachte, vond, probeerde, leek, duurde, moest, maakte, hoorde, waren, voelde, kwam de secretaresse binnen, zei.

48 A 1, 2, and 3 -*t* added after voiceless consonants *k, f* and *s* (contained in *'t kofschip*.) 4 -*d* added to other sounds (not contained in *'t kofschip*.) 5 -*d* added to *f* because infinitive has *v* instead of *f*. 6 -*d* added to *s* because infinitive has *z* instead of *s*. 7 and 8 No *ge*- because verbs have inseparable prefixes (in these cases, *her*- and -*ont*). 7 Adds -*d* because after *l*. 8 Does not add extra -*t* because stem already ends in *t*. 9 Does not add extra -*d* because stem already ends in *d*. **2** 1 I went home. (Denotes movement from one place to another.) 2 My granddad died last year. (Change of condition / state.) 3 How you have grown! (Change of condition / state.) 4 Did you cycle to Liège? – Yes, we cycled for four hours. (*Zijn* for movement from one place to another, *hebben* when direction / destination not specified.) **B1 (i)** 1 Ik heb een jurk gemaakt. 2 Hoe heb je dat gespeld? 3 Hij heeft heel goed gitaar gespeeld. 4 Wij hebben in Amsterdam gewoond. 5 Zij hebben het feestje georganiseerd. 6 Zij hebben niet meer met elkaar gepraat. 7 Wat heeft / hebt u bedoeld? 8 Hij heeft de jongen gered. 9 Je hebt me verrast. 10 Heb je dat gehoord? **1 (ii)** 1 heeft. 2 zijn. 3 hebben. 4 is. 5 is. 6 zijn, hebben. **2** 1 Ik heb het gevreesd. 2 Wij hebben de slaapkamer geverfd. 3 Hij is iedere dag met de bus naar zijn werk gegaan. 4 De kinderen hebben in de les nooit opgelet. 5 Zij zijn om vier uur aangekomen. 6 Ik ben nooit ziek geweest. 7 De trein is al vertrokken. 8 Wij hebben haar in het café ontmoet. 9 Heb je geweten hoe haar man geheten heeft? – Ja, maar ik ben het vergeten. 10 Ben je naar Groningen gereden? – Ja, ik heb in mijn nieuwe auto gereden. ☺☺ heb gezien, ben geweest, hebt gelegen, heb rondgereisd, heb gemaakt, ben teruggekomen, heb bezocht, ben gegaan, heb overnacht / overnacht heb, ben uitgegaan, heb gegeten, heb kunnen betalen, heb gedaan, ben gevlogen, heb rondgelopen, heb ontmoet, heeft uitgenodigd, heeft gewoond, heeft rondgeleid, ben gebleven, ben gebleven, ben gestapt, hebben beloofd, hebt gehad, heb genoten.

49 A1 1 Can you (*polite*) help me? 2 She sees him every day. 3 He gives her flowers. 4 Are you ready? 5 Don't you (*informal plural*) live with them any more? 6 They were with us on holiday. 7 We are coming with you (*informal singular*.) 8 She is older than him (*literally **than he***) and I find her more friendly than him. **B** 1 Have you seen my earrings? (No stress needed.) 2 I can't find my earrings. Have <u>you</u> seen them? (Stress on *jij* because contrasts with *ik*.) 3 I haven't seen <u>them / those</u> but here are some others. (Stress on *die* because contrasts with *wat andere*.) 4 His parents? He said that he hated them. And what did <u>they</u> say? (Stress on *zij* because contrasts with *hij*.) 5 We are going to town. (No stress needed.) 6 You can stay at home but <u>we</u> are going to town. (Stress on *wij* because contrasts with *jullie*.) 7 He told me that he loved <u>me</u> and no other woman. (Stress on *mij* because contrasts with *geen andere vrouw*.) **B1 (i)** 1 hij. 2 zij. 3 ik. 4 zij. 5 jij. 6 ik, hem. 7 ik, haar. 8 hij, mij. 9 u. 10 wij, zij, ons. **1 (ii)** 1 jij, mij. 2 u, zij. 3 wij, hen (*colloquially* hun). 4 ik, hun. 5 zij, jou. **1 (iii)** Answers B1(i)[14] 1 -. 2 ze. 3 -. 4 ze. 5 – (je *not possible here*.) 6 -, -. 7 -, -. 8 – , me. 9 -. 10 we, ze, -. Answers B1 (ii) 1 je, me. 2 -, ze. 3 we, ze. 4 -, ze. 5 ze, je. **2 (i)** 1 je, jij. 2 je, jou. 3 je, mij. 4 jullie, wij. 5 jou, hem, haar. 6 u, me. 7 we, wij. 8 ze, zij, ze (*or* hen *or* hun). **2 (ii)** 1 hij. 2 het. 3 hem. 4 ze (*or* zij). 5 het. 6 hij. 7 het, hem. 8 er (*written together* erop). ☺☺ je, jou, je, jij, ik, we, we, ik, haar, ik, zij / ze, ze, we, haar, we, ik, hij, we, er, we, het, hem, hij, me, hij, ze, hij, hij.

50 A 1 I had telephoned my boss. 2 The performance / show had begun at half past seven. 3 We had ordered a taxi. 4 Our neighbour had already moved house three times. 5 We had already arrived. **B1 (i)** 1 Ik had een jurk gemaakt. 2 Hoe had je dat gespeld? 3 Hij had heel goed gitaar gespeeld. 4 Wij hadden in Amsterdam gewoond. 5 Zij hadden het feestje georganiseerd. 6 Zij hadden niet meer met elkaar gepraat. 7 Wat

had u bedoeld? 8 Hij had de jongen gered. 9 Jij had me verrast. 10 Had je dat gehoord? **1 (ii)** 1 had. 2 waren. 3 hadden. 4 was. 5 was. 6 waren, hadden. **2** 1 Ik had het gevreesd. 2 Wij hadden de slaapkamer geverfd. 3 Hij was iedere dag met de bus naar zijn werk gegaan. 4 De kinderen hadden in de les nooit opgelet. 5 Zij waren om vier uur aangekomen. 6 Ik was nooit ziek geweest. 7 De trein was al vertrokken. 8 Wij hadden haar in het café ontmoet. 9 Had je geweten hoe haar man geheten had? – Nee, ik was het vergeten. 10 Was je naar Groningen gereden? – Ja, ik had in mijn nieuwe auto gereden.

51 A 1 That is my husband's boss. 2 Here is our house. Hers is opposite. 3 Our room is big but Jaap's is even bigger. 4 My car is in the garage. Can / may I just take yours? **B1** 1 Meneer Zuidema's zoon / De zoon van meneer Zuidema. 2 Mevrouw de Wits bloemen / De bloemen van mevrouw de Wit. 3 De spitse tanden van Geerts hond / De spitse tanden van de hond van Geert. 4 Het geld van de oude man. 5 Het speelgoed van de kinderen. 6 Mijn nieuwe jas / De nieuwe jas van mij. 7 Jouw vrouw / Je vrouw / De vrouw van jou. 8 Frits' vrienden / De vrienden van Frits. **2 (i)** 1 mij. 2 jouwe. 3 jou. 4 hare. 5 mijne. **2 (ii)** 1 Nee, het is de mijne / hij is van mij. 2 Nee, het is het onze / het is van ons. 3 Nee, het zijn de hare / ze zijn van haar. 4 Ze zijn van jullie. 5 Het is niet het mijne. Het mijne is rood / Het is niet van mij. Dat van mij is rood. 6 Ja, de jouwe zijn groter dan de zijne / Ja, die van jou zijn groter dan die van hem.

52 A 1 Drink your coffee (up)! 2 She has problems with her boss. 3 He has invited his friends and family. 4 What do you do in your spare time? 5 Is that my book or your book? **B1** 1 mijn, haar. 2 hun. 3 onze, zijn. 4 ons. 5 uw. 6 jullie. 7 je. 8 uw, mijn. **2** 1 je. 2 jouw. 3 je. 4 jouw.

53 A 1 What are you doing at the weekend? 2 He was angry at me because I had asked for a cigarette. 3 At the party I talked to a lot of people about the European Union. 4 Do they know about the accident? 5 You can rely on

---

14 A dash is used to indicate that the pronoun has no unstressed equivalent in this context.

that doctor because he looks after his patients. 6 She is in love with her boss and wants to marry him. 7 Where is the newspaper? Are you sitting on it? 8 This pencil is blunt I cannot write with it. **B1** 1 op. The newspaper is lying on the ground. 2 op. I am waiting for you. 3 met. My son is playing with the boy next door. 4 met. My husband is talking to the neighbour / the man next door. 5 bij. Does he live with his parents? 6 bij. I work at C&A. 7 aan, op. Is she studying at university or is she still at school? 8 naar. They are going to America. **2** 1 om, bij. 2 met, met. 3 uit, vandaan. 4 (*no preposition*), voor. 5 over. 6 op, aan. 7 aan, naar. 8 met. ☺☺ op, op, naar, door, van, tot, met, om, over, op, van, sinds, met, aan, uit, van, volgens, aan, voor, ondanks, met, op, op.

54 A 1 My work is very tiring. 2 I have seen a flying saucer. 3 It is a very moving film. 4 He shook his head sighing. 5 He drove to work singing. **B** 1 spelend. 2 groeiend. 3 dromend. 4 slapend. 5 inkomend. 6 doende. 7 gaande. 8 uitgaand.

55 A 1 Vowel doubled to show that it is pronounced long after loss of vowel *e* after single consonant. 2 No change because more than one consonant after vowel. 3 Identical consonant dropped because at end of word. 4 Identical vowel dropped because at end of word. 5 As in 1 above but also *v* becomes *f* at the end of a word. 6 As in 1 above but *z* becomes *s* at the end of a word. **2** 1 Do you live in Amsterdam? 2 He gives her flowers every day. 3 He is arriving tomorrow / He arrives tomorrow / He will arrive tomorrow. 4 I have been working on this book for six months. 5 How long have you been married? **B1 (i)** 1 ik werk. 2 jij tankt. 3 het kost. 4 voel jij? 5 ik schreeuw. 6 hij mompelt. 7 ik spel. 8 jij speelt. 9 hij wast. 10 kook jij? 11 jullie wonen. 12 hij leeft. **1 (ii)** 1 Mijn vader droomt van een groot huis op het land. 2 De huurders geven hem honderd gulden per week. 3 Ga jij naar de stad? 4 Mijn man laat de kat uit. 5 Praten Theo en Annika met de buurman? 6 De studenten lezen de krant niet meer. **2 (i)** 1 ik heet. 2 wij haten. 3 hij haast

zich. 4 u zendt. 5 ik feliciteer. 6 jij let op. 7 hij vindt uit. 8 organiseer jij? 9 hij verhuist. 10 jij verft. 11 ik teken. 12 hij hervat. 13 jij knoopt aan. 14 ik lever af. 15 wij lachen mee. 16 u bedoelt. **2 (ii)** 1 Mijn broer komt om vier uur aan. 2 De kinderen zijn te moe. 3 Zullen meneer en mevrouw van Lenthe een kamer nodig hebben? 4 Mijn man heeft geen tijd. 5 Jij bent een goede vriend van Theo. ☺☺ gaat, kom, kan, bel ik je op, moet, is, heeft, ligt, hebben, haal ik ze op, kunnen, speelt, weet, spelen, weet, vraag, bel ik je op, doen, weet, ga, hoop, krijgen, hoeft, doe.

56 1 onderwijzer 'teacher' / 'instructor'. 2 schrijver 'writer'. 3 schoonmaker 'cleaner'. 4 fietser 'cyclist'. 5 voetballer 'footballer'. 6 visser 'fisher'. 7 leraar 'teacher'. 8 organisator 'organiser'. 9 examinator 'examiner'. 10 fluitist 'flautist'. 12 gitarist 'guitarist'. 13 tuinier 'gardener'.

57 A 1 I was watching TV when he came in. 2 What are you thinking about? 3 What are you doing this evening? – I am going to the cinema. 4 I am getting tired of all this work. 5 Breakfast is ready! – Yes, I'm coming! **B** 1 Hij is zijn auto aan het wassen / Hij is bezig zijn auto te wassen. 2 Zij zijn aan het verhuizen / Zij zijn bezig met verhuizen. 3 Ben jij nog aan het lezen? / Zit jij nog te lezen? / (*less common* Ben jij nog bezig met lezen?) 4 Zij stond op de bus te wachten. 5 Wacht even! Wij zijn nog aan het eten / Wij zijn nog bezig met eten / Wij zitten nog te eten.

58 A 1 Yes. {laaht} – {maaht}. 2 No. {kaahs} – {yas}. 3 Yes. {maiy} – {zaiy}. 4 No. {faiyn} – {beyn}. 5 No. {teen} – {steyn}. 6 Yes. {kouwt} – {chouw}. 7 No. {kouwt} – {auut}. 8 Yes. {mauus} – {hauus}. 9 No. {duurr} – {doon}. 10 No. {doo} – {durr}. 11 Yes. {zohn} – {bohm}. 12 No. {vaiyk} – {**ley**luhkh}[15]. **Phonetic transcription**: 1 [laːt] – [maːt]. 2 [kaːs] – [jɑs]. 3 [mɛɪ] – [zɛɪ]. 4 [fɛɪn] – [beːjn]. 5 [tiːn] – [steːjn]. 6 [kɑʊt] – [xɑʊ]. 7 [kɑʊt] – [œɛyt]. 8 [mœɛys] – [hœɛys]. 9 [dyːr] –

---

15 Stressed vowels are given in bold.

[du:n]. 10 [du:] – [dø:r]. 11 [zo:n] -[bo:m].
12 [vɛɪk] – ['le:ˠlək]. **B1 (i)** 1 {pit} – {dit}.
2 {hep} – {hebuh}. 3 {ouwt – **ou**wuh}.
4 {pek} – {pekh}. 5 {sok} – {skhok}.
6 {khaah} – {jaah}. 7 {shaahl} – {tshaah}.
8 {fol} – {vol}. 9 {rroht} – {dohrr}.
10 {rruhl**aah**tsee} – {kh**ey**vuh}. 11 {kap} –
{kaahp}. 12 {pen} – {peyn}. 13 {pot} –
{poht}. 14 {zin} – {zeen}. 15 {z**e**nduhrr} –
{p**i**tuhkh}. 16 {rrus} – {rrurs}. 17 {moorr}
– {muurr}. 18 {bl**aiy**vuh} – {bl**ey**vuh}.
19 {trrouw} – {trrauu}. 20 {drraahee} –
{khohee}. **Phonetic transcription**: 1 [pɪt]
– [dɪt]. 2 [hɛp] – ['hɛbə] 3 [aʊt] – ['aʊwə].
4 [pɛk] – [pɛx]. 5 [sɔk] – [sxɔk]. 6 [xɑ:] –
[jɑ:]. 7 [ʃɑ:l] – [tʃɑ:]. 8 [fɔɫ] – [vɔɫ]. 9 [ro:ʷt]
– [do:ʷr]¹⁶. 10 [rə'lɑ:tsi:] – ['xe:ˠvə].
11 [kɑp] – [kɑ:p]. 12 [pɛn] – [pe:ˠn]. 13 [pɔt] –
[po:ʷt]. 14 [zɪn] – [zi:n]. 15 ['zɛndər] –
['pɪtəx]. 16 [rʉs] – [rø:s]. 17 [mu:r] – [my:r].
18 ['blɛɪvə] – ['ble:ˠvə]. 19 [trauw] – [trœy].
20 [drɑ:ɪ] – [xo:ɪ]. **1 (ii)** 1 regenen.
2 knipogen. 3 herk*e*nnen. 4 *o*pgeven.
5 onderwijzer*e*s. 6 m*e*espelen.
7 verh*o*ngeren. 8 l*e*raar. 9 kokk*i*n.
10 *a*fstappen. 11 kruiden*ie*r. 12 organis*e*ren.
13 k*i*nderen. 14 diam*a*nt. 15 instit*uu*t.
16 l*o*pen. 17 h*a*rdlopen. 18 stud*e*ntentijd.
19 bew*e*ging. 20 muziekkritiek.
2 1 {**ee**duhruh dakh skhr**i**kuh duh
skh**oh**nmaahkuhrs fan duh kh**e**kuh
f**oh**khuhl}. 2 {rr**a**iyn**ee**rr rreyt rrohs in zaiyn
rr**oh**duh **ou**toh rront}. 3 {fand**aah**kh khaaht
duh man naahr duh stat}. 4 {yuh kuhnt
rr**uh**stuhkh met huhn zuhs in duh buhs
z**i**tuh}. 5 {duh klurr fan duh durr is
rrurzuh}. 6 {ruut d**uu**wduh duh d**uu**rruh
durr t**ey**khuh duh muurr}. 7 {haiy zaiy
t**ey**khuh maiy dat zaiy klaiyn laiykt}. 8 {in
duh tauun **a**khtuhr het hauus zit aiyn
mauus}. **Phonetic transcription**:
1 ['i:dərə dax 'sxrɪkə də 'sxo:ʷnmɑ:kərs fɑn
də 'xɛkə 'fo:ʷxəɫ]. 2 [rɛɪ'ni:r re:ˠt ro:ʷs ɪn
zɛɪn ro:ʷdə 'ɑʊto:ʷ rɔnt]¹⁶ 3 [fɑn'dɑ:x xɑ:t
də mɑn nɑ:r də stɑt]. 4 [jə kʉnt 'rʉstəx mɛt
hɑ:r zʉs ɪn də bʉs 'zɪtə]. 5 [də klø:r fɑn də

---

16 [r] may also be pronounced [ʁ] in all contexts.

dø:r ɪs 'rø:zə]. 6 [ry:t 'dy:wdə də 'dy:rə dø:r
'te:ˠxə də my:r]. 7 [hɛɪ zɛɪ 'te:ˠxə mɛɪ dɑt
zɛɪ klɛɪn lɛɪkt]. 8 [ɪn də tœyn 'ɑxtər het
hœys zɪt ɛɪn mœys].
59 A 1 doet. He always puts ketchup on his
chips. 2 stop / doe. I put the clothes in the
washing machine. 3 zet. She puts the cup on
the saucer. 4 doet. He puts milk in his coffee.
5 stopt / doet. He puts the letter in the
letterbox. **2** 1 leg. 'Put the papers on my desk,
please.' 2 gezet. 'I have put it on the list.'
3 kun je . . . leggen? 'Can you put the biscuits
on the plate?' 4 gestopt / gedaan. 'I have put
the ticket into my coat pocket.' 5 gelegd.
'Have you put the baby to bed?'
60 A 1 On which floor is the menswear
(department)? 2 Who is he talking to?
3 Whose is that money? 4 What does he
want? 5 What are you thinking about? 6 How
does that machine work? **B** 1 Welk boek heb
jij nodig en wanneer? 2 Geef mij de fles. –
Welke fles? 3 Welke van die auto's is van
hem? 4 Wie van jouw vrienden heeft
kinderen? 5 Waar is de melk? 6 Wat voor bier
heb jij thuis? 7 Waar gaat de film over?
8 Waar speel jij mee?
61 A 1 I am looking forward to this evening.
(No -*zelf* because reflexive verb and no stress.)
2 We asked ourselves whether it was worth
the effort. (As in 1 above.) 3 We know very
little about ourselves. (-*zelf* used because the
verb *weten* is not reflexive. -*zelf* forms are often
used after prepositions, e.g. *van*.) 4 She
washed the baby and then herself. (-*zelf* used
for emphasis because of contrast between *zij*
and *de baby*.) 5 You always think of yourself.
(As in 3 above. *Denken*, like *weten*, is not
reflexive but does take a preposition.) **B1** 1 Ik
kleed me uit. 2 Jij ergert je te veel. 3 Wij
vervelen ons. 4 Geert en Ruud herinneren
zich het verhaal niet zo goed. 5 Mijn zusje
had heimwee maar zij heeft zich snel
aangepast aan het land. **2** 1 je. 2 me. 3 zich.
4 je. 5 zich. 6 zich (*rarer* u). 7 ons. 8 je. 9 jezelf.
10 zichzelf.
62 A 1 I am meeting a friend who works with
me. (*Die* after common gender noun.) 2 I do
not want a child who cries all the time. (*Dat*

after singular neuter noun.) 3 This is the neighbour whose car I am repairing. (*Wie* used after preposition.) 4 That is Jan, who I play football with. (As in 3 above.) 5 This is the computer (that) I work with. (*Waar* used with preposition when referring to non-humans.) **B1 (i)** 1 Mijn vriend die Engels studeert. 2 De koffie die koud is. 3 Het huis dat leeg staat. 4 Het meisje dat tegenover mij woont. 5 De meisjes die met hun poppen spelen. **1 (ii)** 1 Het probleem waaraan mijn broer denkt. 2 Het programma waarnaar ik kijk. 3 De jaszak waarin de sleutels zitten. 4 De bal waarmee de jongen speelt. (*or* 1 Het probleem waar mijn broer aan denkt. 2 Het programma waar ik naar kijk. 3 De jaszak waar de sleutels in zitten. 4 De bal waar de jongen mee speelt.) **2 (i)** 1 De wijn die ik gedronken heb. 2 Het raam dat de jongens gebroken hebben. 3 Het meisje met wie hij naar school gaat. 4 (De) kleren, die ik vorige week gekocht heb. 5 De bakker van wie het brood heel goedkoop is. 6 De leraar voor wie mijn zoon bang is. 7 De klas waarin mijn dochter zit / De klas waar mijn dochter in zit. 8 De stoel waarop hij niet wil zitten / De stoel waar hij niet op wil zitten. **2 (ii)** 1 wat. I'll be back in a minute. I first have to make a phone call, which will not take long. 2 wat. He has passed his exams, which is very good for him. 3 wat. The butcher had nothing that I wanted.

63 A 1 dezelfde. 2 hetzelfde. 3 dezelfde. 4 dezelfde, dezelfde. 5 hetzelfde. 6 hetzelfde, dezelfde.

64 1 1 De trein komt om acht uur aan. 2 De muizen lopen van de kat weg. 3 Geert blijft liever thuis. 4 Ik geef het geld aan mijn vriend terug. 5 Wanneer levert hij de wasautomaat af? 6 Hij stelt zijn nieuwe vriendin aan zijn moeder voor. 7 Annika geeft haar baan op. 8 Jan laat de kat uit. **2 (i)** 1 De trein is om acht uur aangekomen. 2 De muizen zijn van de kat weggelopen. 3 Geert is liever thuisgebleven. 4 Ik heb het geld aan mijn vriend teruggegeven. 5 Wanneer heeft hij de wasautomaat afgeleverd? 6 Hij heeft zijn nieuwe vriendin aan zijn moeder voorgesteld.

7 Annika heeft haar baan opgegeven. 8 Jan heeft de kat uitgelaten. **2 (ii)** 1 Ik heb geen tijd om binnen te komen. 2 Ik heb geen tijd om 's avonds uit te gaan. 3 Ik heb geen tijd om met hem mee te spelen. 4 Ik heb geen tijd om het hele boek door te lezen. 5 Ik heb geen tijd om naar mijn kantoor terug te gaan.

2 (iii) 1 inademen 'breathe in / inhale', uitademen 'breathe out / exhale'. 2 inwerken 'to influence / affect', zich inwerken 'to work oneself in', uitwerken 'to work out / elaborate', meewerken 'to work with / co-operate', tegenwerken 'to work against / oppose, afwerken 'to finish off / get through', doorwerken 'work through / continue working', bijwerken 'to touch up / bring up to date', nawerken 'to produce after-effects', omwerken 'to remould / remodel / rewrite', opwerken 'to work up / touch up', overwerken 'to work overtime'. 3 nadenken 'to think about / reflect', doordenken 'to think through / consider', overdenken 'to think over / consider', uitdenken 'to think up / devise', meedenken 'to join in thinking', zich indenken 'to imagine'. 4 aanspreken 'to speak to / address', afspreken 'to agree upon / arrange', doorspreken 'to talk through / discuss / continue talking', meespreken 'to join in the conversation', naspreken 'repeat / echo', opspreken 'to speak out', tegenspreken 'to contradict', toespreken 'to speak to / address', uitspreken 'to pronounce / express', 'speak in favour of'.

65 A1 1 One vowel dropped before single consonant + vowel *e*. 2 No change because more than one consonant before *e*. 3 Consonant doubled to keep preceding vowel short. 4 No change because more than one consonant before *e*. 5 As in 1 above, but *f* after a long vowel changes to *v* before another vowel. 6 *f* has not changed to *v* because it follows a short vowel. *f* is doubled to keep the preceding vowel short. **2** 1 *s* after a long vowel (or, in this case, a diphthong) becomes *z* before another vowel. 2 *s* does not become *z* because it follows a short vowel. *s* is doubled to keep the preceding vowel short. 3 Consonant doubled to keep preceding

vowel short. 4 Consonant not doubled
because the preceding vowel is unstressed.
Spelling changes apply to stressed vowels
only. **B1 (i)** 1 smakken. 2 smaken.
3 woorden. 4 neuzen. 5 temperaturen.
6 koppen. 7 soepen. 8 uien. 9 graven.
10 neven. 11 rijen. 12 bazen. 13 dassen.
14 vellen. 15 middelen. 16 sterren. **1 (ii)**
1 hoger. 2 ouder. 3 lager. 4 bozer. 5 losser.
6 braver. 7 laffer. 8 wijzer. **2 (i)** 1 been.
2 beeld. 3 tomaat. 4 druif. 5 sok. 6 doos.
7 muis. 8 oog. **2 (ii)** 1 ik koop. 2 ik haat. 3 ik
haast me. 4 ik geloof . 5 ik speel. 6 ik spel. 7 ik
vrees. 8 ik was.
66 1 zo'n. 'I have never seen such a big man.'
2 zulke. 'I have never heard such music.'
3 zulke. 'He never talks about such things.'
4 zo'n. 'I would (really) like such a hat.'
5 zulke. 'She does not want anything to do
with such people.' 6 zo'n. 'It is such a nice
day.' 7 zulke. 'I am not interested in such
stories.' 8 zulk. 'He finds such food too hot /
spicy.'
67 A 1 He has the biggest car but I have the
fastest. 2 These strawberries are good but
those are the best of all. 3 She was the most
cynical (one) in the group. 4 Kees drinks the
most. 5 When was he (the) happiest? **B1**
1 hoogst. 2 zwaarst. 3 viest. 4 best. 5 witst.
6 wijst (*or* meest wijs). 7 succesvolst. 8 meest
praktisch. 9 belangrijkst. 10 echtst.
11 oppervlakkigst. 12 meest tragisch.
2 (i) 1 spannendste. 2 fijnste. 3 braafste.
4 hardst / hardste. **2 (ii)** 1 de luiste. 2 het
lekkerste. 3 het goedkoopste. 4 de aardigste.
5 het minst. 6 het beste.
68 1 dan. 'He is going to France and then to
Spain.' 2 toen. 'I had no money then / at that
time.' 3 toen. 'Then I saw him lying on the
ground.' 4 dan. 'If that happens what will you
do then?' 5 toen. 'What did he do then?'
6 toen. 'I had not liked him then / at that
time.' 7 toen. 'He took her by the hand. –
And then?' 8 dan. 'Ring me up first and then
I will pick you up.' 9 dan. 'We will meet in
town first and then go to the café together.'
10 toen. 'They waited five minutes and then
the bus came.'

69 A 1 It is ten to twelve. 2 Is he coming at
half past three or half past four? 3 He will be
arriving in two hours' (time.) 4 The train has
already left. It is five past ten. 5 What time is
it? – It is twenty-five to eleven. 6 I will wait
until twenty past eleven. **B1** 1 zeven uur.
2 half acht. 3 kwart voor een. 4 kwart over
zes. 5 tien over half elf. 6 tien voor acht. 7 vijf
voor half negen. 8 vijf over half tien. **2** 1 om
acht uur precies. 2 om een uur of negen.
3 tegen half drie 's morgens. 4 tien minuten
geleden. 5 op het hele uur, op het halve uur.
6 over een kwartier. 7 twee keer per week.
8 om achttien (uur) zevenenveertig.
70 1 Dat heeft u toch zelf gemaakt? 'You
made that yourself, didn't you?' 2 Hier kan
hij toch niet slapen! 'But he can't sleep here!'
3 Hij verdient (toch) veel meer geld dan ik. –
Ja, maar hij is toch de baas. 'He earns much
more money than I do (doesn't he?). – Yes,
but he is the boss after all.' 4 Waar kan hij
toch zijn? 'Wherever can he be?' 5 Zeg het
toch! 'Go on, say it!' 6 Ik heb het erg druk
maar wij ontmoeten elkaar toch een keer per
week. 'I am very busy but we still meet each
other once a week (nevertheless).' 7 Ik weet
dat hij vervelend is maar hij is toch mijn
vriend. 'I know that he's annoying but he is
my friend, after all' (*or* ik weet toch dat hij
vervelend is maar hij is mijn vriend 'I *know*
(i.e. you don't have to tell me) that he's
annoying but he's my friend.') 8 Maar hij
werkt toch niet meer? 'But he doesn't work
any more, does he?' 9 Dat kun je toch niet
doen! 'But you can't do that!' 10 Geef hem
toch een kans! 'Go on, give him a chance!'
71 1 begrijpt. 2 versta. 3 begrijp. 4 versta.
5 begrijp. 6 begrijpen.
72 1 vroeger. Life is not what it used to be.
2 vroeger. I used to be a lot thinner. 3 vroeger
(vaak) / gewoonlijk. We (often) used to go to
the opera. 4 placht . . . te. I used to get up
every morning at seven o'clock. 5 vroeger. He
used to be a dentist but now he's retired.
73 A 1 We will not be ready. 2 He has never
played chess. 3 It was raining when they left
the house. 4 I will have written the letter. 5 I
would not have recognised him. 6 You do not

believe me. 7 They had stayed too long. 8 Did you go out last night? **B1 (a)** 1 ik woon. 2 hij leeft. 3 wij praten. 4 jij vindt. 5 ik lees. 6 wij hopen. **(b)** 1 ik woonde. 2 hij leefde. 3 wij praatten. 4 jij vond. 5 ik las. 6 wij hoopten. **(c)** 1 ik zal wonen. 2 hij zal leven. 3 wij zullen praten. 4 jij zult / zal vinden. 5 ik zal lezen. 6 wij zullen hopen. **(d)** 1 ik zou wonen. 2 hij zou leven. 3 wij zouden praten. 4 jij zou vinden. 5 ik zou lezen. 6 wij zouden hopen. **2(i) (a)** 1 ik heb gedaan. 2 hij is gekomen. 3 ik heb gestudeerd. 4 jij bent geweest. 5 wij hebben opgebeld. 6 hij heeft zich vergist. **(b)** 1 ik had gedaan. 2 hij was gekomen. 3 ik had gestudeerd. 4 jij was geweest. 5 wij hadden opgebeld. 6 hij had zich vergist. **(c)** 1 ik zal gedaan hebben / hebben gedaan. 2 hij zal gekomen zijn / zijn gekomen. 3 ik zal gestudeerd hebben / hebben gestudeerd. 4 jij zult / zal geweest zijn / zijn geweest. 5 wij zullen opgebeld hebben / hebben opgebeld. 6 hij zal zich vergist hebben / hebben vergist. **(d)** 1 ik zou gedaan hebben / hebben gedaan. 2 hij zou gekomen zijn / zijn gekomen. 3 ik zou gestudeerd hebben / hebben gestudeerd. 4 jij zou geweest zijn / zijn geweest. 5 wij zouden opgebeld hebben / hebben opgebeld. 6 hij zou zich vergist hebben / hebben vergist. (Contracted forms: 1 ik had gedaan. 2 hij was gekomen. 3 ik had gestudeerd. 4 jij was geweest. 5 wij hadden opgebeld. 6 hij had zich vergist.) **2 (ii)** 1 Ik wachtte op jou. 2 Hij heeft niet veel gezegd. 3 Wij verhuizen op 27 februari. 4. Zij praten niet meer met elkaar. 5 Theo had Engels gestudeerd. 6 Accepteerde u een cheque? 7. Blijf jij langer? 8 Ik zal het op een floppydisk sturen. 9 Hij zou per creditcard betalen. 10 De toeristen zouden meer geld gewisseld hebben / hebben gewisseld. (*or* De toeristen hadden meer geld gewisseld.)
74 1 1 boeken 'to book'. 2 koppen 'to head' (e.g. in football.) 3 scholen 'to school / train'. 4 emailen 'to email'. 5 stationeren 'to station / place'. 6 detaileren 'to detail / specify'. **2 (i)** ☞ *32.2* above. **2 (ii)** ☞ *64.2 (iii)* above.
75 1 1 liggen. 'Where are the papers? – They are (lying) on my desk.' 2 staat. 'What is on

the list?' 3 zit. 'There's a bar of chocolate in your handbag.' 4 staan. 'There are two trees in our garden.' 5 liggen. 'The letters are (lying) on the ground.' **2** 1 zat. 'What was in the shopping bag? It was very wet.' 2 ligt. 'Enschede is near the German border.' 3 stond. 'How did you know about the murder? – It was in the newspaper.' 4 gestaan. 'Where was the wardrobe?' / 'Where did the wardrobe stand?' 5 liggen. 'I have left my gloves (lying) in his car.'
76 A 1 Heb je de film niet gezien? – Ik heb de film wel gezien. 'Didn't you see the film? – I did see the film.' 2 Houd jij niet meer van jouw man? – Ik houd wel van hem. 'Don't you love your husband any more? – I do love him.' 3 Willen jullie vanavond niet komen? – Ik niet maar mijn vrouw wel. 'Don't you want to come tonight? – I don't but my wife does.' 4 Hij heeft wel geld maar is niet zo rijk als zijn broer. 'He does have money but is not as rich as his brother.' 5 Ik had het wel gedacht! 'I thought as much!' 6 Kom je vandaag? – Vandaag niet maar morgen wel. 'Are you coming today? – Not today but tomorrow.' 7 Heb je de oefeningen al gedaan? – Ja, maar ik vond ze wel moeilijk. 'Have you done the exercises already? – Yes, but I did find them difficult.' 8 Hij kan mij morgen niet bezoeken maar hij zal mij wel opbellen. 'He cannot visit me tomorrow but he will ring me up (though).'
77 1 toen. 'When he had drunk his coffee he felt better.' 2 wanneer. 'When can I get this repaired?' 3 wanneer / als. 'I'll come and visit you when I have more time.' 4 wanneer. 'He used to go out whenever he could.' 5 toen. 'When I was a student I had very little money'. 6 wanneer / als. 'Whenever he goes out in the evenings he drinks too much.' 7 wanneer / als. 'He wants to ring me up when he has organised the party.' 8 wanneer / als. 'I will pick it up when I come back.' 9 toen. 'He lived here when he was younger.' 10 wanneer? 'Do you want to go to The Hague? When?'
78 A 1 He is going on holiday with his girlfriend on Friday. (Subject – Verb. Time –

Manner – Place in Dutch.) 2 I can meet you tomorrow at the market. (Subject – Verb – Object. Time – Place. Infinitive at end in Dutch.) 3 He will have arrived in Amsterdam at around half past three. (Subject – Verb. Time – Place. Participle and infinitive at end in Dutch.) 4 Today I am going to Groningen and tomorrow I am going to Zwolle. (Expressions of time placed at the beginning. Finite verb must be SECOND idea in Dutch. Therefore subject *ik* must follow verb.) 5 I do not want anything more to do with <u>him</u>. (*Met hem* placed at beginning for emphasis. Verb SECOND. Subject *ik* follows verb. Infinitive at end.) **B1 (i)** 1 Ik praat met mijn vrienden. 2 Wij wachten een half uur op de bus. 3 Speel jij graag voetbal? 4 Om twee uur heb ik een afspraak. 5 Hij belt mij dinsdag op. 6 's Avonds kijkt hij gewoonlijk tv. 7 Ik weet dat je heel laat naar bed gaat. 8 Ik vraag me af, of hij het vóór woensdag doet. 9 De vrouw die om de hoek woont. 10 Het meisje op wie mijn zoon verliefd is. **1 (ii)** 1 Ik heb een brief geschreven. 2 Wij zijn dinsdag om drie uur aangekomen. 3 Heb jij de nieuwe film van Woody Allen gezien? 4 Gisteren is mijn zoon heel laat uitgegaan. 5 Wij zullen hem vanavond opbellen. 6 Morgen zal het niet meer regenen. 7 Zij zijn gegaan voordat de taxi aangekomen was / was aangekomen. 8 Ik ben ziek geworden omdat ik te laat buiten gebleven ben / ben gebleven. 9 Hij zegt dat hij de kamer reserveren zal / zal reserveren. 10 Dat is de auto die wij volgend jaar kopen zullen / zullen kopen. **1 (iii)** 1 Hij ziet zijn vriendin iedere dag. 2 Zij gaat vaak met haar vriendinnen naar de stad. 3 Wanneer ga je met Frederik op vakantie? 4 Ik vind hem heel aardig. 5 Mijn man moet vanwege zijn werk in Groningen overnachten. **2 (i)** ☞ *17B* above. **2 (ii)** 1 Ik stond iedere morgen om acht uur op. 2 Toen ik om acht uur opstond, voelde ik me niet goed. 3 Toen ik het huis wilde verlaten / verlaten wilde, kon ik mijn sleutels niet vinden. 4 Hoewel hij op tijd aankwam, was ik nog niet klaar en ging niet mee. 5 Hoewel hij iedere dag heel hard moest werken / werken moest, werd hij nooit moe.

6 Kende jij het meisje dat tegenover mij woonde?' 7 Een week geleden moest ik mijn moeder bezoeken die ziek was. 8 De student die lui was en zijn huiswerk nooit deed, kwam steeds te laat. **2 (iii)** 1 Ik heb het nog niet kunnen organiseren. 2 Zij hebben niet langer mogen blijven. 3 Zij hebben de rekeningen moeten betalen. 4 Wij hebben een kamer willen reserveren. 5 Heeft hij een dag vrij mogen nemen? 6 Heb jij het vóór maandagmorgen kunnen doen? 7 Ik hoop dat u de weg heeft kunnen vinden. (Ik hoop dat u de weg hebt kunnen vinden.) 8 Ik heb gehoord dat jij jouw auto hebt laten repareren. ☺☺ Hoeveel kost een kilo tomaten? Een kilo kost vijf gulden. Dan neem ik twee kilo. Ik wil tomatensoep maken. Denkt u dat twee kilo genoeg is? Het hangt ervan af, voor hoeveel mensen u kookt. Ik kook voor vier mensen. Dan zou ik eerder drie kilo nemen. Heeft u ook kaas? Het spijt me, ik heb mijn laastse stuk kaas al verkocht. Maar ik weet zeker dat meneer van Dam nog wat kaas heeft. Hij staat naast de bakker. Bedankt. Ik zal even bij hem kijken. Hier heeft u uw geld. Dag! Dank u wel, mevrouw, en tot ziens!

79 1 1 Hoe vind je het gebak? Ik heb het zelf gemaakt. 'How do you find / do you like the cake? I made it myself.' 2 Waarom moet ik jouw overhemd strijken? Doe het zelf! 'Why do I have to iron your shirt? Do it yourself!' 3 Hij zegt steeds dat alcohol slecht is maar hij drinkt zelf vrij veel. 'He is always saying that alcohol is bad but he drinks quite a lot himself.' 4 Zij bouwen zelf een huis. 'They are building a house themselves.' 5 Ik moet Jantje met zijn huiswerk helpen maar ik begrijp het zelf niet eens. 'I have to help Jantje with his homework but I don't even understand it myself.' **2** 1 Hij scheert zich iedere morgen. 2 Hij moet de flat zelf schoonmaken. 3 Ik vraag me af, of het de moeite waard is. 4 Ik heb het zelf erg druk. 5 Zij schamen zich. 6 Zij organiseren de bruiloft zelf. 7 Wie doet het? Hij zelf. 8 Zij praat steeds over zichzelf.

80 A 1 I would not give him more than a

hundred guilders. 2 Shouldn't you be staying at home more often? 3 I was going to / was meant to / was supposed to give him these books but I completely forgot. 4 He is said / alleged to have lied about his income. 5 I wonder if they would like that? **B1** 1 Ik zou boodschappen doen maar ik had geen tijd. 'I was going to do the shopping but I didn't have time.' 2 Wij zouden naar Amsterdam gaan maar wij hadden geen tijd. 'We were going to go to Amsterdam but we didn't have time.' 3 Mijn buurman zou mijn auto repareren maar hij had geen tijd. 'My neighbour was going to repair my car but he didn't have time.' **2** 1 Haar man zou een relatie met een andere vrouw gehad hebben / hebben gehad. 'Her husband is alleged to have had a relationship with another woman.' 2 Zij zouden vorig jaar uit elkaar gegaan zijn / zijn gegaan. 'They are said / alleged to have split up last year.' 3 De jongen zou heel gevaarlijk geweest zijn / zijn geweest. 'The boy is said / alleged to have been very dangerous.'

Appendix: Common irregular verbs

bakken	bakte	bakten	gebakken	bake
barsten	barstte	barstten	gebarsten	burst
bedriegen	bedroog	bedrogen	bedrogen	deceive
beginnen	begon	begonnen	begonnen[z]	begin
bevelen	beval	bevalen	bevolen	command
bidden	bad	baden	gebeden	pray
bieden	bood	boden	geboden	offer
bijten	beet	beten	gebeten	bite
binden	bond	bonden	gebonden	bind
blazen	blies	bliezen	geblazen	blow
blijken	bleek	bleken	gebleken[z]	appear
blijven	bleef	bleven	gebleven[z]	stay
braden	braadde	braadden	gebraden	roast
breken	brak	braken	gebroken	break
brengen	bracht	brachten	gebracht	bring
brouwen	brouwde	brouwden	gebrouwen	brew
buigen	boog	bogen	gebogen	bend
denken	dacht	dachten	gedacht	think
doen	deed	deden	gedaan	do
dragen	droeg	droegen	gedragen	carry, wear
drijven	dreef	dreven	gedreven[h/z]	float, drive, propel
dringen	drong	drongen	gedrongen[h/z]	push (forward)
drinken	dronk	dronken	gedronken	drink
druipen	droop	dropen	gedropen	drip
duiken	dook	doken	gedoken[h/z]	dive
dwingen	dwong	dwongen	gedwongen	force
eten	at	aten	gegeten	eat
fluiten	floot	floten	gefloten	whistle
gaan	ging	gingen	gegaan[z]	go
gelden	gold	golden	gegolden	be valid
genieten	genoot	genoten	genoten	enjoy
geven	gaf	gaven	gegeven	give
gieten	goot	goten	gegoten	pour
glijden	gleed	gleden	gegleden[h/z]	slide, glide
graven	groef	groeven	gegraven	dig
grijpen	greep	grepen	gegrepen	grasp, seize
hangen	hing	hingen	gehangen	hang
hebben	had	hadden	gehad	have

---

[z] = verbs taking *zijn* in the (plu)perfect.
[h/z] = verbs taking *hebben* or *zijn*.

heffen	*hief*	*hieven*	*geheven*	lift
helpen	*hielp*	*hielpen*	*geholpen*	help
heten	*heette*	*heetten*	*geheten*	be called
houden	*hield*	*hielden*	*gehouden*	hold
jagen	*joeg*	*joegen*	*gejaagd*	chase
	jaagde	*jaagden*	*gejaagd*	hunt
kiezen	*koos*	*kozen*	*gekozen*	choose
kijken	*keek*	*keken*	*gekeken*	look
klinken	*klonk*	*klonken*	*geklonken*	sound
komen	*kwam*	*kwamen*	*gekomen*[z]	come
kopen	*kocht*	*kochten*	*gekocht*	buy
krijgen	*kreeg*	*kregen*	*gekregen*	receive, get
krimpen	*kromp*	*krompen*	*gekrompen*	shrink
kruipen	*kroop*	*kropen*	*gekropen*[h/z]	creep, crawl
kunnen	*kon*	*konden*	*gekund*	be able
lachen	*lachte*	*lachten*	*gelachen*	laugh
laden	*laadde*	*laadden*	*geladen*	load
laten	*liet*	*lieten*	*gelaten*	let
lezen	*las*	*lazen*	*gelezen*	read
liegen	*loog*	*logen*	*gelogen*	tell lies
liggen	*lag*	*lagen*	*gelegen*	lie
lijden	*leed*	*leden*	*geleden*	suffer
lijken	*leek*	*leken*	*geleken*	seem, resemble
lopen	*liep*	*liepen*	*gelopen*[h/z]	walk
malen	*maalde*	*maalden*	*gemalen*	grind
meten	*mat*	*maten*	*gemeten*	measure
moeten	*moest*	*moesten*	*gemoeten*	must, have to
mogen	*mocht*	*mochten*	*gemogen*	be allowed
nemen	*nam*	*namen*	*genomen*	take
plegen	*placht*	*plachten*	————	be used to (*very formal*)
prijzen	*prees*	*prezen*	*geprezen*	praise
raden	*raadde*	*raadden*	*geraden*	guess
rijden	*reed*	*reden*	*gereden*[h/z]	ride, drive
rijzen	*rees*	*rezen*	*gerezen*[z]	rise
roepen	*riep*	*riepen*	*geroepen*	shout, call
ruiken	*rook*	*roken*	*geroken*	smell
scheiden	*scheidde*	*scheidden*	*gescheiden*	separate
schelden	*schold*	*scholden*	*gescholden*	abuse, revile
schenken	*schonk*	*schonken*	*geschonken*	pour (a drink)
scheren	*schoor*	*schoren*	*geschoren*	shave, shear
schieten	*schoot*	*schoten*	*geschoten*	shoot
schijnen	*scheen*	*schenen*	*geschenen*	shine, seem
schrijven	*schreef*	*schreven*	*geschreven*	write
schrikken	*schrok*	*schrokken*	*geschrokken*[z]	be frightened
schuiven	*schoof*	*schoven*	*geschoven*[h/z]	shove, push
slaan	*sloeg*	*sloegen*	*geslagen*	hit
slapen	*sliep*	*sliepen*	*geslapen*	sleep
sluipen	*sloop*	*slopen*	*geslopen*	sneak, skulk

sluiten	*sloot*	*sloten*	*gesloten*	shut
smelten	*smolt*	*smolten*	*gesmolten*[h/z]	melt
snijden	*sneed*	*sneden*	*gesneden*	cut
snuiven	*snoof*	*snoven*	*gesnoven*	sniff
spannen	*spande*	*spanden*	*gespannen*	stretch
spijten	*speet*	*speten*	*gespeten*	be sorry
spinnen	*spon*	*sponnen*	*gesponnen*	spin
splijten	*spleet*	*spleten*	*gespleten*	split
spreken	*sprak*	*spraken*	*gesproken*	speak
springen	*sprong*	*sprongen*	*gesprongen*[h/z]	jump
spruiten	*sproot*	*sproten*	*gesproten*[z]	sprout
spugen	*spoog*	*spogen*	*gespogen*	spit
	(spuugde)	*(spuugden)*	*(gespuugd)*	
spuiten	*spoot*	*spoten*	*gespoten*	spout, squirt
staan	*stond*	*stonden*	*gestaan*	stand
steken	*stak*	*staken*	*gestoken*	stab
stelen	*stal*	*stolen*	*gestolen*	steal
sterven	*stierf*	*stierven*	*gestorven*[z]	die
stijgen	*steeg*	*stegen*	*gestegen*[z]	rise, climb
stinken	*stonk*	*stonken*	*gestonken*	stink
stoten	*stootte*	*stootten*	*gestoten*	push
treden	*trad*	*traden*	*getreden*[z]	step, tread
treffen	*trof*	*troffen*	*getroffen*	hit
trekken	*trok*	*trokken*	*getrokken*	pull
vallen	*viel*	*vielen*	*gevallen*[z]	fall
vangen	*ving*	*vingen*	*gevangen*	catch
varen	*voer*	*voeren*	*gevaren*[h/z]	sail
vechten	*vocht*	*vochten*	*gevochten*	fight
verbieden	*verbood*	*verboden*	*verboden*	forbid
verdwijnen	*verdween*	*verdwenen*	*verdwenen*[z]	disappear
vergeten	*vergat*	*vergaten*	*vergeten*[z]	forget
verliezen	*verloor*	*verloren*	*verloren*	lose
vermijden	*vermeed*	*vermeden*	*vermeden*	avoid
vinden	*vond*	*vonden*	*gevonden*	find
vliegen	*vloog*	*vlogen*	*gevlogen*[h/z]	fly
vouwen	*vouwde*	*vouwden*	*gevouwen*	fold
vragen	*vroeg*	*vroegen*	*gevraagd*	ask
vreten	*vrat*	*vraten*	*gevreten*	eat (of animals)
vriezen	*vroor*	*vroren*	*gevroren*	freeze
wassen	*waste*	*wasten*	*gewassen*	wash
wegen	*woog*	*wogen*	*gewogen*	weigh
werpen	*wierp*	*wierpen*	*geworpen*	throw
weten	*wist*	*wisten*	*geweten*	know
weven	*weefde*	*weefden*	*geweven*	weave
wijzen	*wees*	*wezen*	*gewezen*	point out
willen	*wilde*	*wilden*	*gewild*	want to
	wou	*wouden*		
winden	*wond*	*wonden*	*gewonden*	wind

winnen	*won*	*wonnen*	*gewonnen*	win
worden	*werd*	*werden*	*geworden*[z]	become
wringen	*wrong*	*wrongen*	*gewrongen*	wring
zeggen	*zei*	*zeiden*	*gezegd*	say
zenden	*zond*	*zonden*	*gezonden*	send, broadcast
zien	*zag*	*zagen*	*gezien*	see
zijn	*was*	*waren*	*geweest*[z]	be
zingen	*zong*	*zongen*	*gezongen*	sing
zinken	*zonk*	*zonken*	*gezonken*[z]	sink
zitten	*zat*	*zaten*	*gezeten*	sit
zoeken	*zocht*	*zochten*	*gezocht*	look for
zouten	*zoutte*	*zoutten*	*gezouten*	salt
zuigen	*zoog*	*zogen*	*gezogen*	suck
zullen	*zou*	*zouden*	———	will
zwellen	*zwol*	*zwollen*	*gezwollen*[z]	swell
zwemmen	*zwom*	*zwommen*	*gezwommen*[h/z]	swim
zweren	*zwoer*	*zwoeren*	*gezworen*	swear (an oath)
zwijgen	*zweeg*	*zwegen*	*gezwegen*	be silent

Index[1]

---

1 Where more than one section reference is given for
  a particular topic, the numbers in bold print
  indicate the section in which the topic is dealt with
  in the most detail.